The New International Monetary System

The New International Monetary System brings together twelve original contributions by leading scholars and practitioners to a conference convened in May 2008 on the occasion of the retirement of Alexander Swoboda. The contributions are arranged in three main parts. Part I deals with the international financial architecture, Part II examines the ever-controversial role of exchange rate regimes and Part III takes stock of the conduct of monetary policy and the challenges posed by the inflation-targeting strategy. The chapters provide considered assessments of virtually all the hotly debated issues that concern monetary policies seen from an international perspective.

Edited by and with an introduction from Charles Wyplosz, the collection includes contributions from some of the key international figures in the field of monetary policy, central banking and exchange rate regimes to discuss contemporary international monetary issues. Contributors include Michael Bordo, Barry Eichengreen, Ronald McKinnon and Charles Goodhart. The volume also contains a tribute from Paul Volcker.

This book will be relevant to postgraduate students and researchers interested in the international monetary system, monetary policy, central banks and exchange rates. It will also be of interest to professionals in central banks, governments and international institutions.

Charles Wyplosz is Professor of International Economics at the Graduate Institute in Geneva where he is Director of the International Centre for Money and Banking Studies. Currently a member of the Group of Independent Economic Advisors to the President of the European Commission, of the Panel of Experts of the European Parliament's Economic and Monetary Affairs Committee and of the "Bellagio Group." Charles Wyplosz is an occasional consultant to the European Commission, the IMF, the World Bank, the United Nations, the Asian Development Bank and the Inter-American Development Bank.

Routledge international studies in money and banking

1 **Private Banking in Europe**
Lynn Bicker

2 **Bank Deregulation and Monetary Order**
George Selgin

3 **Money in Islam**
A study in Islamic political economy
Masudul Alam Choudhury

4 **The Future of European Financial Centres**
Kirsten Bindemann

5 **Payment Systems in Global Perspective**
Maxwell J Fry, Isaak Kilato, Sandra Roger, Krzysztof Senderowicz, David Sheppard, Francisco Solis and John Trundle

6 **What is Money?**
John Smithin

7 **Finance**
A characteristics approach
Edited by David Blake

8 **Organisational Change and Retail Finance**
An ethnographic perspective
Richard Harper, Dave Randall and Mark Rouncefield

9 **The History of the Bundesbank**
Lessons for the European Central Bank
Jakob de Haan

10 **The Euro**
A challenge and opportunity for financial markets
Published on behalf of *Société Universitaire Européenne de Recherches Financières (SUERF)*
Edited by Michael Artis, Axel Weber and Elizabeth Hennessy

11 **Central Banking in Eastern Europe**
Edited by Nigel Healey and Barry Harrison

12 **Money, Credit and Prices Stability**
Paul Dalziel

13 Monetary Policy, Capital Flows and Exchange Rates
Essays in memory of Maxwell Fry
Edited by William Allen and David Dickinson

14 Adapting to Financial Globalisation
Published on behalf of Société Universitaire Européenne de Recherches Financières (SUERF)
Edited by Morten Balling, Eduard H. Hochreiter and Elizabeth Hennessy

15 Monetary Macroeconomics
A new approach
Alvaro Cencini

16 Monetary Stability in Europe
Stefan Collignon

17 Technology and Finance
Challenges for financial markets, business strategies and policy makers
Published on behalf of *Société Universitaire Européenne de Recherches Financières (SUERF)*
Edited by Morten Balling, Frank Lierman and Andrew Mullineux

18 Monetary Unions
Theory, history, public choice
Edited by Forrest H. Capie and Geoffrey E. Wood

19 HRM and Occupational Health and Safety
Carol Boyd

20 Central Banking Systems Compared
The ECB, the pre-Euro Bundesbank and the Federal Reserve System
Emmanuel Apel

21 A History of Monetary Unions
John Chown

22 Dollarization
Lessons from Europe and the Americas
Edited by Louis-Philippe Rochon and Mario Seccareccia

23 Islamic Economics and Finance: A Glossary, 2nd Edition
Muhammad Akram Khan

24 Financial Market Risk
Measurement and analysis
Cornelis A. Los

25 Financial Geography
A Banker's view
Risto Laulajainen

26 Money Doctors
The experience of international financial advising 1850–2000
Edited by Marc Flandreau

27 Exchange Rate Dynamics
A new open economy macroeconomics perspective
Edited by Jean-Oliver Hairault and Thepthida Sopraseuth

28 Fixing Financial Crises in the 21st Century
Edited by Andrew G. Haldane

29 Monetary Policy and Unemployment
The U.S., Euro-area and Japan
Edited by Willi Semmler

30 Exchange Rates, Capital Flows and Policy
Edited by Peter Sinclair, Rebecca Driver and Christoph Thoenissen

31 Great Architects of International Finance
The Bretton Woods era
Anthony M. Endres

32 The Means to Prosperity
Fiscal policy reconsidered
Edited by Per Gunnar Berglund and Matias Vernengo

33 Competition and Profitability in European Financial Services
Strategic, systemic and policy issues
Edited by Morten Balling, Frank Lierman and Andy Mullineux

34 Tax Systems and Tax Reforms in South and East Asia
Edited by Luigi Bernardi, Angela Fraschini and Parthasarathi Shome

35 Institutional Change in the Payments System and Monetary Policy
Edited by Stefan W. Schmitz and Geoffrey E. Wood

36 The Lender of Last Resort
Edited by F.H. Capie and G.E. Wood

37 The Structure of Financial Regulation
Edited by David G. Mayes and Geoffrey E. Wood

38 Monetary Policy in Central Europe
Miroslav Beblavý

39 Money and Payments in Theory and Practice
Sergio Rossi

40 Open Market Operations and Financial Markets
Edited by David G. Mayes and Jan Toporowski

41 Banking in Central and Eastern Europe 1980–2006:
A comprehensive analysis of banking sector transformation in the former Soviet Union, Czechoslovakia, East Germany, Yugoslavia, Belarus, Bulgaria, Croatia, the Czech Republic, Hungary, Kazakhstan, Poland, Romania, the Russian Federation, Serbia and Montenegro, Slovakia, Ukraine and Uzbekistan
Stephan Barisitz

42 Debt, Risk and Liquidity in Futures Markets
Edited by Barry A. Goss

43 The Future of Payment Systems
Edited by Stephen Millard, Andrew G. Haldane and Victoria Saporta

44 Credit and Collateral
Vania Sena

45 **Tax Systems and Tax Reforms in Latin America**
Edited by Luigi Bernardi, Alberto Barreix, Anna Marenzi and Paola Profeta

46 **The Dynamics of Organizational Collapse**
The case of Barings Bank
Helga Drummond

47 **International Financial Co-operation**
Political economics of compliance with the 1988 Basel Accord
Bryce Quillin

48 **Bank Performance**
A Theoretical and empirical framework for the analysis of profitability, competition and efficiency
Jacob Bikker and Jaap W.B. Bos

49 **Monetary Growth Theory**
Money, interest, prices, capital, knowledge and economic structure over time and space
Wei-Bin Zhang

50 **Money, Uncertainty and Time**
Giuseppe Fontana

51 **Central Banking, Asset Prices and Financial Fragility**
Éric Tymoigne

52 **Financial Markets and the Macroeconomy**
Willi Semmler, Peter Flaschel, Carl Chiarella and Reiner Franke

53 **Inflation Theory in Economics**
Welfare, velocity, growth and business cycles
Max Gillman

54 **Monetary Policy Over Fifty Years**
Heinz Herrman (Deutsche Bundesbank)

55 **Designing Central Banks**
David Mayes and Geoffrey Wood

56 **Inflation Expectations**
Peter J.N. Sinclair

57 **The New International Monetary System**
Essays in honor of Alexander Swoboda
Edited by Charles Wyplosz

The New International Monetary System

Essays in honor of Alexander Swoboda

Edited by Charles Wyplosz

Routledge
Taylor & Francis Group
LONDON AND NEW YORK

First published 2010
by Routledge
2 Park Square, Milton Park, Abingdon, Oxon OX14 4RN

Simultaneously published in the USA and Canada
by Routledge
270 Madison Ave, New York, NY 10016

Routledge is an imprint of the Taylor & Francis Group, an informa business

Typeset in Times by Wearset Ltd, Boldon, Tyne and Wear
Printed and bound in Great Britain by TJI Digital, Padstow, Cornwall

British Library Cataloguing in Publication Data
A catalogue record for this book is available from the British Library

Library of Congress Cataloging in Publication Data
The new international monetary system: essays in honour of Alexander Swoboda/edited by Charles Wyplosz.
p. cm.
Includes bibliographical references and index.
1. International Monetary Fund–Congresses. 2. International finance–Congresses. 3. Foreign exchange rates–Congresses. 4. International liquidity–Congresses. I. Swoboda, Alexander K. II. Wyplosz, Charles.
HG3881.5.I58N49 2010
332.4′5–dc22 2009033179

ISBN10: 0-415-56052-7 (hbk)
ISBN10: 0-203-85839-5 (ebk)

ISBN13: 978-0-415-56052-8 (hbk)
ISBN13: 978-0-203-85839-4 (ebk)

Contents

Contributors

Editor

Charles Wyplosz, The Graduate Institute, Geneva, Switzerland, and CEPR.

Contributors

Michael Bordo, Rutgers University, U.S.A. and NBER.

Barry Eichengreen, University of California, Berkeley, U.S.A.

Hans Genberg, Graduate Institute of International Studies and Hong Kong Monetary Authority.

Stefan Gerlach, Institute for Monetary and Financial Stability, Frankfurt University, Germany, CEPR and CFS.

Charles A.E. Goodhart, Financial Markets Group, London School of Economics, UK.

Atish R. Ghosh, Research Department, IMF.

Harold James, Princeton University, U.S.A. and European University Institute.

Olivier Jeanne, Johns Hopkins University, U.S.A. and IMF.

Ulrich Kohli, Swiss National Bank, Switzerland.

Ronald McKinnon, Stanford University, U.S.A.

Yung Chul Park, Seoul University, Korea.

Michael K. Salemi, University of North Carolina at Chapel Hill, U.S.A.

Gunther Schnabl, Leipzig University, Germany.

Marco E. Terrones, Research Department, IMF.

Cédric Tille, Graduate Institute of International and Development Studies and CEPR.

Paul Volcker, former chairman of the Federal Reserve Board.

Jeromin Zettelmeyer, Research Department, IMF.

Introduction

Charles Wyplosz

This volume brings together twelve contributions to a conference convened in May 2008 on the occasion of the retirement of Alexander Swoboda. The themes covered reflect Alexander's own research interests pursued over four decades. It is a testimony to his vision that these themes remain burning issues today. As several contributions highlight, some of his results have well sustained the passage of time. But the papers collected here all look forward as they provide considered assessments by some of the best researchers of virtually all the hotly debated issues that concern monetary policies see from an international perspective.

The contributions were specially commissioned from people who (1) have been associated with Alexander Swoboda, and (2) have made important contributions to the policy-relevant literature. They were asked to reflect on the state of the art and to provide their best judgment of where the respective debates may be leading us to. The chapters are arranged in three main parts. Part I deals with the international financial architecture (Chapters 1 and 2). Part II examines the ever-controversial role of exchange rate regimes (Chapters 3 to 7). Part III takes stock of the conduct of monetary policy and the challenges posed by the inflation-targeting strategy (Chapters 8 and 11). The book concludes with a personal appreciation by Paul Volcker, whose tenure at the head of the Fed was marked by the shift to the interest rate instrument.

How has the IMF changed?

Observers like to note that the IMF has reinvented itself several times since its creation in the immediate postwar period. Given how the world has changed since then, this is not particularly surprising. More interesting is how it has changed. The past twenty years have proven to be very challenging for the IMF. During the 1980s, the Reagan–Thatcher–Kohl years, it has spearheaded what is commonly called "globalization" and is more accurately defined as financial liberalization. The IMF has tirelessly encouraged member countries to let a thousand flowers bloom on their domestic financial markets and to link them up with the existing financial centers. Many countries obliged, often grudgingly, only to be confronted with new challenges called banking crises, speculative attacks on their currencies or sudden stops of capital inflows. The IMF soon found itself in the position of Sorcerer's Apprentice with more crises to deal with than it could cope with. It also found itself reasoning in terms of current account crises while financial flows were rushing through the capital account. Obviously, the IMF had to reinvent itself to deal with the world that it had contributed to create, but it took quite some time to do so. Meanwhile, it unleashed a steady flow of criticism.

In Chapter 1, Michael Bordo and Harold James recall these events. They offer a synthetic survey of two decades of debates about the International Monetary Fund (IMF). They present a host of past proposals, some of which have been followed, others ignored or rejected. They focus on the challenge posed by the global imbalances and large reserve accumulation, especially in Asia, and they advance their own proposal: delegating to the IMF the management of a significant part of world foreign exchange reserves. In their view this would assure adequate returns to owners, provide the IMF with resources to stabilize countries and the world economy, and give it authority to identify exchange rate misalignments. Whether this is politically feasible remains to be seen.

The IMF met its most daunting challenge with the East Asian crisis that started in 1997. The crisis hit the flying dragons, those countries the IMF had identified as successful examples of the benefits of commercial and financial opening. All of a sudden, the best graduates of the Washington Consensus school of thought found themselves in desperate situations, and the IMF had failed to foresee the troubles. Worse, the conditions imposed were often misguided and many of them had to be subsequently reversed. Even worse, the conditions were more intrusive than ever; they were perceived as national humiliations, leaving a blot in the region that has not healed yet. The main lesson that East Asian countries drew from their traumatic encounter with financial globalization was that they would never again call the IMF to the rescue. The main conclusion was that they would try to develop a collective line of defense against financial instability.

In Chapter 2, Yung Chul Park and I look at the IMF from a regional perspective. We note that, since the mid-1970s Europe has taken over a number of IMF functions. Reserves were pooled, exchange rate arrangements were agreed upon and mutual support was established as part of the European Monetary System. Then, the process that resulted in the creation of the euro included mutual surveillance. We describe how, largely as a reaction to IMF interventions during the 1997 crisis, the East Asian countries attempt to follow a similar, but not identical path. They have started to pool reserves for mutual insurance but, lacking a regional surveillance mechanism, they continue to rely on the IMF for significant support. They also fear political disapproval after the rejection in 1998 by the US of the idea of establishing an Asian Monetary Fund. Inasmuch as other regions may follow in the steps of Europe and East Asia, the issue is whether the IMF should encourage regional integration projects of various forms. Our response is positive but, obviously, it is not universally shared.

Exchange rate regimes: old debate, new answers

Chapters 3 to 7 deal with the role of the exchange rate and the choice of a regime. All authors remind us that this is an old debate and all try to seek new responses from recent theoretical and empirical advances. Indeed, it is quite amazing to note how the same issues keep coming back, sometimes but not always with different answers, and often with no firm answer at all.

In Chapter 3 Hans Genberg recalls the debate on global inflation that he and Swoboda contributed to start in the 1970s. They then argued convincingly that under the fixed exchange rate system adopted in Bretton Woods, with the exception of the US, the center-currency country, individual countries had little control over their inflation rates. Genberg asks whether this result still holds now that many of the largest countries let their exchange rates float. It is indeed striking that inflation went up nearly universally in the 1980s, declined in the 1990s and reached low levels in the 2000s, with a global peak in 2007 and generalized concern about disinflation during the crisis. Is it a common driving factor, or a fashion that authorities adopt?

Genberg's answer is that monetary policy has limited effectiveness in open economies, a conclusion that applies to exchange rates. This leads him to take a look at the global imbalances that are often seen as the result of exchange rate misalignments. Like other contributors to this volume, Genberg disagrees with the dominant view that deep exchange rate changes will be needed to solve the imbalance problem because he does not see exchange rate misalignments as the root cause of global imbalances.

The choice of an exchange rate regime is another issue that will not go away, for many reasons. The first is that the exchange rate is an extraordinary versatile variable: it can affect trade competitiveness and real incomes, it determines asset returns and the cost of international borrowing and guesses about its evolution trigger capital flows that can, at times, be overwhelming. Knowledge about these effects has progressed over the years, but their sheer complexity implies that we are a long way from a consensus. The second reason follows from the first. Debates about what the exchange does translate into debates about what we would like to do with it. Third, it is pretty clear that any exchange rate regime has pros and cons. Balancing advantages and disadvantages is bound to be controversial. Fourth, answers to many of these questions change as the world itself changes.

A particular example of this last observation is the financial globalization process. Following the end of the Bretton Woods system, many countries concluded that the best exchange rate regime was the intermediate one, which combined flexibility with some commitment by the authorities. This was logical: facing many tradeoffs, the optimal choice would surely be interior. Swoboda is among those who argued early on that financial integration would in fact support the corner solutions. This came to be known as the bipolar view. It is examined in two chapters.

In Chapter 4, Olivier Jeanne offers a theoretical exploration of the bipolar view. One original aspect of this work is that Jeanne explicitly takes into account financial stability, as he allows for the possibility of a credit crisis of the kind that occurred in 2007 to 2008. One might think that the need to intervene as a lender in last resort makes it desirable for a central bank to adopt an intermediate regime, one that combines discipline and flexibility. In fact, Jeanne's elegant model tends to support the bipolar view, in particular the advantage of flexible inflation targeting and exchange rate flexibility. Very intuitively, the risk of financial crisis puts flexibility at a premium while inflation targeting also brings in credibility. Importantly, Jeanne also finds that international cooperation – in the form of mutual insurance – is desirable even when all countries adopt flexible exchange rate regimes.

In Chapter 5, Barry Eichengreen also looks at the bipolar view, this time from and empirical angle as he revisits the evidence about exchange rate regimes over the past two decades. He finds growing support for the bipolar view as he notes that capital mobility has pushed the developed countries into either the floating or the rigidly fixed exchange rate, the latter being reflected in the creation of a monetary union in Europe that now includes sixteen countries. Using the past as a guide to the future, Eichengreen predicts that continuing economic development and financial integration will lead an increasing number of countries to travel the same route.

It is all very fine to ask what regimes are adopted and for what reasons, but does this choice make a difference? A large literature has looked at the effects on growth and inflation. In Chapter 6, Atish Ghosh, Marco E. Terrones, and Jeromin Zettelmeyer examine another potential impact of exchange rate regimes as they ask what difference the regime makes empirically to the behavior of current accounts. They remind us of the Friedman prediction – during the Bretton Woods years – that exchange rate flexibility automatically corrects current account imbalances. By and large, this has become the conventional wisdom. Looking at a vast set of experiments, Ghosh, Terrones, and Zettelmeyer reach a more nuanced conclusion. They look at both the size and the persistence of current account imbalances, distinguishing between developed, emerging and developing countries. In a nutshell, they find that exchange rate flexibility tends to limit the size of imbalances but does not systematically allow for a faster elimination of these imbalances. Their interpretation emphasizes the distinction between large imbalances, which are rare when the exchange is flexible, and small imbalances, which are more persistent when the exchange rate is fixed.

The same question is explored in Chapter 7 by Ronald McKinnon and Gunther Schnabl, this time focusing on the emblematic case of China. To a surprising degree, perhaps, McKinnon and Schnabl's conclusions are well in line with those reached by Genberg and by Ghosh, Terrones, and Zettelmeyer. They express considerable doubts on the role of the exchange rate in causing the imbalance between the US and Chinese current accounts. This leads them to support the fixed exchange rate regime of the renminbi, and to advocate cooperation to reduce *domestic* saving imbalances in both countries.

Central banking: a revolution under way?

The remaining chapters are devoted to the evolution of monetary policy. Before the global financial crisis, many central banks had adopted, explicitly or implicitly, the flexible inflation-targeting strategy. The long period of fast growth and low inflation that lasted from 2002 to 2007 was seen as the outcome of this highly successful strategy. Central banks and academic economists largely agreed on the broad characteristics of the strategy. Disagreements concerned issues seen to be of secondary importance, like the communication strategy or whether central banks should deal with asset price bubbles. Central bankers were of the view that their mission was to establish and maintain price stability, possibly paying attention to the output gap and employment as they refined their policy moves, but they were nearly unanimous that they did not have any instrument to deal with asset price movements.

The authors of the four contributions were asked whether the monetary policy strategy was a "revolution," whether we had reached a stage where the correct formula had been identified and only needed refinements. Interestingly, all authors struck a skeptical tone.

The conference took place halfway between the initial freezing of interbank markets in August 2007 and the dramatic collapse of Lehman Brothers in September 2008. By then it was clear that banks were in deep trouble because housing price bubbles had been ignored, but most central banks felt that the situation would be no worse than in 2001, in the aftermath of the bursting of the high-tech bubble. With hindsight we know that this was not to be the case and some of these concerns appear in all the chapters.

Part III starts with Chapter 8 where Stefan Gerlach and Cédric Tille offer a thoughtful evaluation of the implications of the New Keynesian approach for monetary policy in open economies. This approach, which has been widely adopted by central banks in their modeling – through the adoption of the DSGE methodology – and empirical works – and the emphasis on VAR methods – provides some backing for the views expressed in several other contributions concerning the limited role of exchange rates as policy instruments. Reviewing the particular experience of Hong Kong, which operates a currency board arrangement, they suggest caution regarding the use of the exchange rate as an anchor, noting that successes (Hong Kong, for instance) should not lead us to overlook failures (Argentina, for example).

In Chapter 9, Charles Goodhart rejects the "price-stability only" view of central banking as he considers that central banks must keep a close watch on asset price bubbles. He argues that there exists a tension between the two unavoidable objectives of central banks: price stability and financial stability. He does not say how bubbles can be dealt with, preferring instead to focus on ways to reduce financial market instability. The detailed discussion of financial market regulation that he offers is now being taken on board as regulators mull over their post-crisis responses. Perhaps as important is Goodhart's implicit suggestion that bank regulation and supervision may be seen as a second instrument that could allow the monetary authorities to deal with their two objectives. This view leads him to favor giving central banks the task of bank regulation and supervision.

Ulrich Kohli is quite skeptical about the revolutionary nature of the new monetary policy wisdom. In Chapter 10 he expresses the view that inflation targeting is a particular case of the generalized post-money aggregate targeting strategy. He discusses a number of issues that continue to preoccupy central banks, quite irrespective of the particular strategy adopted: the publication of forecasts, the risk of financial bubbles, the tolerance towards temporary deviations of inflation and the link with the exchange rate. The final chapter, by Michael Salemi, discusses the methods used to reveal central bank preferences. Reviewing the literature, he focuses on the case of Switzerland and reports how, over time, the Swiss National Bank has navigated through different policy instruments and priorities.

The last contribution is an appreciation of Alexander Swoboda's work by Paul Volcker, President of the Fed, who will remain known for having adopted the interest rate as the policy instrument and then erased inflation in the US. Volcker uses this occasion to discuss the relationship between central bankers and monetary economists, with hints that the latter are not necessarily fit to become the former.

The conference brought an amazing array of luminaries, many of whom have played a crucial role either in conducting monetary policies or in shaping monetary theory. All past coauthors of Alexander Swoboda were present with the sole exceptions of those who had passed away: Bill Branson, Rudi Dornbusch and Harry Johnson.

The conference was made possible through the generosity of the Graduate Institute – the successor of HEI, which Alexander directed for eight years – and its director, Philippe Burrin, and of the International Center of Monetary and Banking Studies, which Alexander founded and directed for three decades. I also want to thank the "Groupement des Banquiers Privés Genevois," the Association of Foreign Banks in Switzerland and its Vice-Chairman, Maurice Monbaron, and the Swiss National Bank for having created three scholarships on the occasion.

Part I

How has the IMF changed?

1 The past and future of IMF reform

A proposal

Michael Bordo and Harold James

Introduction

After over sixty years of existence, in the course of which there have been numerous ups and downs, there is probably today less conflict about the role and importance of the IMF than in previous eras. This is largely because the IMF has been almost completely sidelined from many of the major governance issues of the international financial system. Is there any need for an institution such as the IMF? This chapter argues that there may be a case for reviving some part of the original vision of the 1944 Bretton Woods conference; and in particular that the IMF may play a central and useful role as a manager of reserves.

The original mandate of the Fund, as laid down in the Bretton Woods Articles of Agreement, was very general: to promote international monetary cooperation, facilitate the growth of world trade, promote exchange rate stability, and to help to create a multilateral system of payments. In order to achieve these objectives, the Fund was supposed to provide short-term balance of payments support to countries in need of additional reserves. The best way of thinking about the IMF's functions during the early period, the so-called Bretton Woods system (1945–1973), is not so much as an institution, but rather as the embodiment of a system of rules as laid out in the Articles of Agreement. But in the early 1970s the core of the rule-based system, the requirement on member countries to adopt a par value, disappeared.

The IMF's evolution since the 1970s has reflected both the demand for its services in the light of new and perceived market failures and its willingness to provide those services. There has been a fundamental change of environment: the breakdown of the par value system, and the new mobility of capital, and financial deregulation. Capital flows have taken a role that no one expected at the time the IMF was created. The international political system has changed too: there are many new countries, with quite new problems, and the Soviet bloc collapsed both economically and politically.

The IMF developed in response to these external challenges. There was an expansion of the scope of policies considered as part of the surveillance exercise. The number and length of duration of stabilization packages increased, but these were successful in only a few cases. In the 1990s, in responses to crises in a globalized capital market, the IMF engaged in liquidity crisis management. A response to the new politics of the 1990s involved an expansion into non-macroeconomic policy areas, such as criticisms of military spending, corruption, and non-democratic practices. After the Asian crises in 1997 and since, the IMF also discussed areas such as corporate governance and accounting practices that traditionally lay outside its purview.

The situation at the millennium

Eight years ago we summarized the outcome of the post-1973 order as follows (Bordo and James 2000). IMF surveillance produces highly useful general reports (World Economic Outlook, Capital Markets); but Article IV consultations have a questionable use in that they frequently lack bite when the country concerned is not engaged in an IMF program. In particular, they seem largely irrelevant for most of the advanced industrial countries. A perceived over-extension of the IMF into new areas of policy concern involves unpopular interventions into national sovereignty. The poorer clients of the IMF often become trapped in a welfare dependency. The management of liquidity crises has contributed to moral hazard and at the same time has not stopped crises spreading.

In 2000 we argued that markets are powerful mechanisms for discipline, but that they can be usefully supplemented by IMF policies and advice. In general, the historical record suggests that the IMF should operate as a traffic policeman as much as a fireman: anticipating and preventing disasters rather than dealing with their painful aftermath. Such a mission would involve:

- A commitment to improve the reliability and timeliness of statistics.
- Independence from politics (since the political instrumentalization of the IMF conflicts with and harms its core mission, which is aimed at macroeconomic stability).
- Transparency of operations.
- The establishment of as many rules as possible which are contingent and incentive-compatible. This would enhance transparency. Pre-qualification for crisis lending is desirable, and may become a powerful instrument to achieve better national policies. However, there will then still remain the possibility of crises with potentially damaging systemic effects arising in non pre-qualified countries. A further problem is that a country might cease to pre-qualify, and that such a development would set off an investor panic and thus frustrate the whole pre-qualification strategy (Cordella and Levy Yeyati 2006; Kenen 2007). In these cases (in order to avoid moral hazard as far as possible) there may be a case for creative ambiguity, in which the IMF would need some room for discretion, and may not be able fully to announce likely policy responses in advance.
- The willingness to link lending to policy conditionality. Such conditionality, in the past an essential part of the IMF's mode of operations, has been severely criticized by the Meltzer Commission in 2000, and it has been too

complicated and remains potentially politicized. But at present it still remains the principal lever through which the IMF can effect improvement of members' policies. Its complete abolition would only make sense if the IMF was restricted to strictly rule-based pre-qualified crisis assistance; but such a situation is unlikely in the immediate future.

In general, it was clear that the IMF is best equipped to handle a more limited range of tasks that lie closer to its historical mission. Such a realization implies a retreat to its core area of expertise and responsibility. Such a core includes data standards, liquidity management, and surveillance (the provision of information that markets cannot provide). Longer term concessional lending to very poor LDCs does not fit well into this core, and might be handled better by the World Bank.

Such proposals were consistent with the IMF's mandate. To go further than this could not have been achieved at the insistence of one country alone, even of the most powerful economy in the world. Rather it would have required a new and constructive Bretton Woods conference, which is truly unlikely in the conditions of the early twenty-first century.

The post-millennial debate

Since 2000, the debate has shifted considerably. Many of the issues that generated ferocious controversy in the early years of the new millennium have slid into historical oblivion.

1 There is no longer much debate as to whether the IMF should take on an analogous function to a bankruptcy court in domestic law and be able to supervise an orderly reduction of claims while a borrowing country restructures its financial obligations. Such proposals, originally set out by Jeffrey Sachs (1989) and others, were taken up in a modified form by the IMF's Deputy Managing Director, Anne Krueger as the Sovereign Debt Reduction Mechanism (SDRM) (Krueger 2001). They were widely opposed, by banks but also by the U.S. administration.
2 The alternative discussion of collective action clauses in bond contracts, as championed in academic discussions by Peter Kenen (2001) and Barry Eichengreen (2003), and as taken up by the U.S. administration, fared better, but has not really been tested in a large-scale emerging market crisis.
3 The debates about whether IMF conditionality was excessive have also faded, owing to the dramatic reduction in the volume of IMF lending.
4 Joseph Stiglitz (2002) and others accused the IMF of being run to bail out the financial system and in particular the big banks. The Fund had been captured in his view by Wall Street. But in 2007 and 2008, as investment banks in advanced industrial countries began to demand new forms of bailout, it was clear that the Fund was not suited to such an operation, and that national fiscal authorities in the big industrial countries would be the last stop of the financial system.

5 In 2003 and 2004 it was often argued that the IMF was inadequately funded to manage big emerging market crises of the future. The coincidence of crises in Argentina, Turkey and Brazil had led to an overstretching of the Fund's financial resources. Commentators saw the likelihood of future crises in some big emerging markets, such as India or China, and concluded that the Fund would be unable to manage, but the growth of emerging market country reserves has made the prospect of such a crisis decreasingly likely. Most countries self-insure against crises, with the result that reforms such as the Contingent Financing Facility became a practical irrelevance.

In general, then, the decline of the IMF's lending activities led to a decline in controversies about the Fund. From the post-millennial perspective, we can clearly see some long-term trends in IMF lending: relative to world exports, drawings on the Fund increased, reaching a high point in the 1980s Latin American debt crisis. Since then there has been a decline, interrupted by a surge of lending in the wake of the 1997 to 1998 Asia (and Russia and Brazil) crises, but since 2003 the outstanding drawings have been repaid, and there has been virtually no new lending (Figure 1.1). Such low levels of lending had been seen

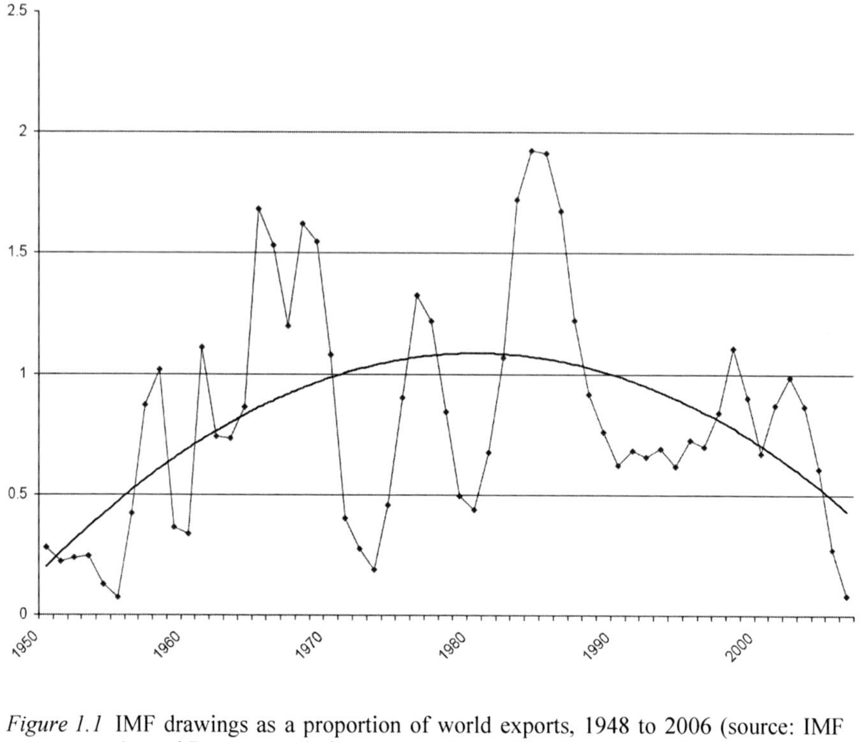

Figure 1.1 IMF drawings as a proportion of world exports, 1948 to 2006 (source: IMF Annual Reports; trade from International Financial Statistics).

before, in the mid-1950s and the early 1970s, but a rather dramatic trend now seems unmistakable.

Decreased lending has also led to a debate about the funding of IMF operations, since the day-to-day activities have largely been paid for through charges applied to borrowers. Following precedents from the 1970s (when there had also been a sharp decline in Fund lending and income), the IMF's Executive Board in April 2008 set out a new income model including an endowment funded by IMF gold sales.

The question then arises of whether the IMF can again be relevant. There are issues relating to the IMF's performance and role that are still alive, as well as a new type of problem. At the end of the 1990s, concern with governance issues was not usually presented as a central part of critiques of the IMF. In 1999 De Gregorio, Eichengreen, Ito, and Wyplosz called for a structure that resembled more of an independent central bank, but this demand was generally regarded as politically infeasible and also undesirable, in that it would remove any element of accountability (while central banks are subject to national legislation). In the course of the 2000s, criticism mounted in two influential critiques from the Bank of England and the Bank of Canada (Dodge 2006; King 2006; see also Santor 2006).

Two parallel problems are crucial for the governance debate: first, the issue of the degree of control of the staff and management by the Executive Board that represents the member states; and second, the outdated basis on which shares and votes are determined, and which has been only slowly modified in the light of persistent critique of the over-representation of Europeans and the under-representation of Asian emerging market economies. This chapter will propose a solution that would both make the IMF more representative and more flexible, through the addition of a separate and parallel voting system based on reserve assets deposited at the Fund. The Fund's ownership would thus reflect the international distribution of reserves.

There may on some occasions be a conflict of interest between a staff that sees itself as dedicated to furthering global public goods, and an Executive Board that is dominated by the political agendas of member states, especially the more powerful states with the larger quotas. The Managing Director is poised between the staff and the Executive Board. Critiques of the Fund have pointed out how a Managing Director might feel under pressure to satisfy the large shareholders who appointed him. The First Deputy Managing Director is by convention a U.S. appointee and on occasions appears to follow the general lines set by the U.S. administration. But on some prominent issues, most recently over the question of the IMF's involvement in debt reduction, the U.S. administration shot down initiatives that came from the staff and the FDMD.

One of the most persistent problems of the IMF in the past decade has arisen from the belief of rapidly growing Asian members that they are relatively neglected. In 1997 there was even a short-lived discussion of the idea of establishing a separate Asian Monetary Fund, which was aborted by the United States. Since then, Asian countries have cooperated in establishing an Asian bond market; and some also discuss the prospect of closer currency cooperation in a manner analogous to Europe's slow evolution of monetary union. The IMF by contrast has always insisted that its task is a global one, and that regional institutions are less well equipped to handle global questions of confidence and liquidity.

At the moment, the U.S. has 16.79 percent of the votes in the IMF which, because a majority of 85 percent is required for many crucial decisions, can constitute a veto on Fund policy. The European Union has 32.09 percent of the votes (and members of the Euro currency zone 22.57 percent), so that if either the EU or the Eurozone were a single member, it would be the largest member. By contrast, China has 3.68 percent of the votes, Saudi Arabia 3.18 percent, Russia 2.70 percent, India 1.89 percent, and Brazil 1.39 percent. The politics of recalculating quotas has meant that the process of rebalancing the Fund is excruciatingly slow. It took very long negotiations for China to be awarded a "special" quota increase when it reabsorbed Hong Kong, even though it was already abundantly clear that China was a systemically important country. In spring 2008, the Board of Governors agreed to a process of modest but continuing reform, which would eventually result in the U.S. vote being reduced slightly to 16.73 percent, while increasing that of China (3.81 percent) and India (2.34 percent) but reducing that of the Russian Federation (2.39 percent).

At the same time as the old issues are fading from debate, the IMF has become very vulnerable because its financing model depends largely on revenue generated by its lending activity, which is also fading fast. In consequence, questions about the IMF's viability and role are being asked with much greater urgency.

Three major issues have developed instead as focuses of international debate: the design of the exchange rate regime and the appropriateness of exchange rates; the question of reserve management; as well as the management of financial globalization. The first two (but not the third) of these topics had been major elements of the initial Bretton Woods vision, but none has been at all central to the recent focus of the IMF.

Exchange rates

With the re-emergence of large U.S. deficits corresponding to surpluses in emerging Asia and in the oil producers, a discussion emerged as to whether Asian economies were artificially holding down their exchange rates in order to achieve rapid export-led growth, and to absorb large quantities of discontented rural labor. The so-called Bretton Woods II thesis (Dooley *et al.* 2003) saw China and other Asian states behaving in a fashion analogous to Germany and Japan in the 1960s, which had also had export-led growth and big surpluses, and had been highly resistant to proposals for parity changes. Concern about currency manipulation emerged in a political form as a potent source of new trade protectionism, as when Senator Charles Schumer proposed to subject Chinese goods to a special tariff as a compensation for the exchange rate manipulation.

In the global imbalances debate, it was always unclear where the adjustment should take place. Some commentators, notably Cheung Chinn and Fuji, have produced arguments that would support the Chinese position, namely that in the light of a number of institutional factors, including the large extent of non-performing loans, public sector corruption and inefficiency, the renminbi is actually not overvalued. However, no one in China is likely to make explicit their support for this interpretation, and no one in the U.S. is likely to believe such an argument given the size of the bilateral trade deficit. Since a large part of the problem lies in the U.S. current account deficit, it is equally plausible to argue that the correction should lie in U.S. adjustment. Such adjustment, which has been taking place since 2005, is however likely to depress world economic growth.

In a few isolated historic cases, the IMF had taken up exchange rate issues and in "special" consultations issued rulings against Korea and Sweden for exchange rate dumping. Some other Scandinavian countries had complained about the extent of the Swedish devaluation of October 1982; and in 1987 the United States criticized the large current account surplus of Korea which it attributed to the undervaluation of the Korean won. But in the 1980s, while the IMF was prepared to deal with Korea, the Fund shrank from involvement in the much more highly politicized question of the Japanese exchange rate. Clearly, in the 2000s, there is no mechanism that would simply require China to adopt a new exchange rate policy at the demand of importing or competing countries. The issue of the Chinese exchange rate does appear in Article IV consultations, where the topic is dealt with in a sane and largely unpolitical way. The advice given may have convinced Chinese officials to embark on a limited move to more exchange rate flexibility since 2005, but the IMF has no greater standing in these Article IV reports than the coherence of its intellectual case. In this sense, the Fund is no more powerful than some of the eminent academic economists such as Ronald McKinnon, Robert Mundell, and Jeffrey Frankel, who have offered (contradictory) opinions on the appropriate course of Chinese currency policy.

A more promising vehicle is the multilateral surveillance mechanism agreed by the International Monetary and Financial Committee in April 2007 as a way of addressing the global imbalances issue. Kenen (2007) went much further and proposed that the IMF staff should be given greater latitude to publish specific country recommendations without the endorsement of either the Fund Executive Board or of the International Monetary and Financial Committee. Such a development would clearly be an important step in the establishment of a more autonomous or apolitical Fund.

There are some indications that the new approach may be effective. China has certainly responded to the debate about its exchange rate policy, although it is unclear how much if any of the new flexibility is the result specifically of a need to deal with the new Fund mechanism, and how much it has simply followed from general developments and in particular from the rapid depreciation of the dollar (and the fact that the dollar has depreciated less against the rinminbi than against other currencies such as the euro). In the course of the initial negotiations,

China agreed to a statement that: "The exchange rate formation mechanism will be improved in a gradual and controllable manner. Exchange rate flexibility will gradually increase, with attention paid to the value of a basket of currencies. Efforts will be made to cultivate the foreign exchange market and deepen reform of foreign exchange administration. Restrictions will be further relaxed on holding and use of foreign exchange by enterprises and individuals." In the course of March and April 2008, it appeared that the Chinese authorities were prepared to see much greater flexibility in the dollar–renminbi rate.

As to the United States, adjustment is taking place but not as a consequence of any policy initiative generated through discussions with the IMF or through Fund surveillance. Since 2005 a surprisingly orderly depreciation of the dollar has taken place, latterly speeded up by the loose U.S. monetary policy response to the sub-prime crisis and to fears of U.S. financial instability and possible recession. The U.S. adjustment might well be interpreted as a testimony to the ability of markets to self-correct.

But there is a difficulty in the way of the market-based view. Large emerging markets have acquired such high levels of reserves that any changes in their reserve holdings may dramatically affect market expectations. In this sense exchange rate issues have become ever more closely bound up with the controversial topic of reserve management.

Reserve management

One way of understanding the interwar situation, to which Bretton Woods was the policy response, is of a world in which reserves were highly unstable owing to the substitution of a gold dollar standard for a pure gold standard. The Fund as a kind of credit cooperative (in an analogy popularized by Peter Kenen) was a solution to the reserve problem. Its lending facilities could be a substitute for absent reserves.

The world of the early twenty-first century is also characterized by instability and worries about reserve positions. On the face of it, the new development of very substantial international reserves is a signal that something was wrong in the international economy long before the present outbreak of credit market panic. John Maynard Keynes and the other makers of the 1944 Bretton Woods conferences had seen central bank management of reserves as a significant part of the instability of the pre-1939 system, and proposed to replace reserves by collective assets or quotas held at the new institution, the International Monetary Fund. Today's greatly increased reserves held by single countries may be understood either as a misallocation of assets, or alternately as the use by financially underdeveloped economies of the U.S, as a global financial intermediator (analogous to the banking role of the U.S. described by Despres *et al.* (1966)). In this view, emerging market savings are successively recycled through their central banks, then the U.S. bill market, U.S. banks, U.S. corporations back to emerging markets. Such complex financial intermediation is costly and potentially destabilizing.

The rapid growth of reserves of emerging markets since the turn of the millennium – one of the major policy developments of our time – presents a puzzle. Between 2002 and 2006 they have more than doubled in terms of SDRs, the IMF's international unit of account, and almost tripled in dollar terms. Reserves are supposed to facilitate international transactions, in that they help countries deal with unanticipated declines in export revenues, or increases in import prices, or sudden withdrawals of foreign credits. Since there are continuously local shocks, and ups and downs in the international economy, the size of reserves should also be expected to fluctuate (as the length of a cab rank grows and falls as new taxis arrive and lined-up taxis are hired).

In the global economy of the past decade, world reserves did not really fluctuate but instead moved in a mostly linear direction. Industrial countries needed reserves less, while poorer and emerging countries wanted them more. The United States never had or needed very extensive foreign exchange reserves (in April 2008 the level stood at just $75 bn, while China had $1760 bn and India $313 bn; by contrast the European Central Bank held $63 bn and the Eurosystem as a whole $542 bn). In particular, the bad consequences of not having reserves in a crisis had appeared in 1997 to 1998 in the Asia crisis. The crisis was a cruel reminder of the vulnerability of very dynamic economies with big capital imports and inadequate foreign reserves. China, and other Asian economies, then tried to ensure that they would not be vulnerable again. The costs of the crisis were so great that countries (especially poorer countries) were powerfully motivated to build additional reserves. But then they went on and on accumulating. In the 1960s, the distinguished international economist Fritz Machlup formulated a different view of reserves, which he called the theory of "Mrs. Machlup's wardrobe." Mrs. Machlup apparently always liked to buy new dresses while resisting giving away old ones: so the stock of dresses went on increasing. Since the millennium, the reserves of Japan, Taiwan, Korea, and Malaysia have all more than doubled, while that of China more than quintupled. Are the reserves really needed and when is the optimal point reached? One Korean central bank official said: "There is no limit to the amount of reserves that are needed" (Cheung and Qian 2007). Asian reserves now look more like Imelda Marcos's shoe collection than Mrs. Machlup's wardrobe.

Because reserves are held mostly in short dated and very low-risk securities (traditionally Treasury bills issued by a few industrial countries), the world pile-up of assets has driven down short-term interest rates, and prompted a global expansion of liquidity that then helped to power asset price bubbles, especially in the housing markets of countries with current account deficits and higher interest rates, especially the United States, Australia, or the United Kingdom.

The rapid accumulation of reserves follows from high savings rates, both in the private and the public sector, in oil-producing and emerging Asian economies. While overall savings in non-industrialized countries have fallen, the countries classified by the IMF as "developing Asia" have seen big increases in savings: from 32.9 percent in the 1990s to 42.2 percent in 2006. Especially quickly growing but politically unstable and insecure countries experienced dramatic rises in savings rates, as citizens felt unsure about their future and were unable to rely on state support mechanisms. The private choices are a response to the unavailability of insurance for old age and sickness, and the rapidly increasing cost of education: individuals need to save so much because they are dependent on their own resources. The paradigmatic case again is that of China, where consumption rates have actually fallen as incomes rose: by 2005, Chinese households consumed less than 40 percent of GDP, and Chinese households moved to very high savings rates (of around 30 percent). With simultaneous high saving by the government and by enterprises, the outcome is a large amount of capital in search of security. But the savings surge and the accompanying positive current account balance is not just a Chinese peculiarity, but may be found in most Asian, South Asian and Gulf States economies. For the Middle East, the savings rate rose from 24.2 percent in the 1990s to 40.4 percent in 2006. In the latter case, the surge in oil prices has been responsible for the growth in savings, but in Asia it reflects the combination of stronger growth and increased precautionary saving (IMF, *World Economic Outlook*, April 2007, Table 43). Reserve growth represents one way, though not a particularly cost-effective one, of investing the savings generated in more apparently secure (and foreign) economic and political settings.

The surprising savings behavior is not just the outcome of private decisions. Public policy has played a central role. The emerging market states have chosen to build up large levels of reserves, in part to avoid an appreciation of their currencies that would make their highly dynamic export sector less competitive.

But the countries that are building up these enormous reserves are setting themselves a new kind of trap that relates to their composition, in terms both of choice of currency and of the class of securities chosen. The accumulations are so large that even the announcement of a small shift in assets, for instance, a declaration that there may be a shift to more euros and fewer dollars, is enough to move markets and to cause disruptions and panics. In the past, reserve regimes in which there was a choice of assets brought an inherent instability. For instance, in the interwar period the world had a choice of the dollar, the pound and gold and reserve currencies, and was deeply destabilized by the sudden loss of confidence in the pound in 1931. In the run-up to the financial crisis, private speculators, but also other central banks, rapidly tried to convert pounds into dollars or gold. After the pound was decoupled from gold, speculation turned against the dollar, until Franklin Roosevelt followed Britain and left the gold standard. This feature of the old order reserve system was exactly why Keynes and his Bretton Woods colleagues were suspicious of the prewar order, and felt that it led to the possibility of devastating speculative attacks on central banks, who could only defend their currencies and their reserves by taking measures that would be highly damaging to the domestic economy.

There are also problems relating to the management of the domestic economy. Reserves are often sterilized to prevent an impact on the domestic money supply and inflation. But there is a limit to such sterilization, as governments cannot issue debt indefinitely without crowding out private sector investment. In consequence, the outcome of rapid reserve accumulation is often inflationary, as it was in Germany and Japan in the 1960s; and as it appears to be in China's recent past (Sohmen 1964; Yongding 2007; Humpage and Schenk 2008).

In recent times, a number of solutions have been put forward to the threat to stability posed by the big buildup of reserve assets. The most obvious is to follow the path of central banks in the rich industrial countries and look for a broader range of reserve assets. Why should central banks only hold low-yielding Treasury bills? Why should they in effect subsidize the U.S. government by holding its debt liabilities? The emerging Asian economies have indeed gradually looked to longer term assets in place of short Treasury bills, and have also moved to buy other government agency securities, and even some corporate bonds. Asian governments are also tempted to look to equities as a way of obtaining higher yields, but by doing this they expose themselves to more volatility.

In practice, the attempts by the new surplus countries to look for alternative reserve assets have been highly problematic. Most of the attention has been fixed on China's more than one trillion dollars in reserves, and its nervous search for ways of maintaining the value of those assets. Diversification from U.S. Treasury bills by investing some $3 bn in the Blackstone private equity fund this summer was swiftly followed by an embarrassing collapse in value.

The search for alternative institutions of asset management

When assets are managed in an alternative way, through sovereign wealth funds (SWFs), there are even greater difficulties. On the receiving end, industrial countries' governments are increasingly anxious that SWFs be used strategically, rather than simply following the logic of the market. They may be used as a way of gaining control of key sectors of the economy, especially since the credit crunch has made the world's largest banks look for new injections of capital. In November 2007, Abu Dhabi recapitalized Citigroup with $7.5 bn, and in December the Government of Singapore Investment Corporation took a CHF 19.4 bn ($17.2 bn) stake in the Swiss bank UBS. The more activist Singapore institution, Temasek, has acquired stakes in Standard Chartered, Barclays, Bank of China, and the China Construction Bank. Since the second quarter of 2007, SWFs have put at least $46 bn into financial companies in developing countries (*Financial Times* 2007). Other investments have attracted substantial attention, such as the failed attempt of Dubai Ports World to buy the British company P & O which managed six major U.S. ports; or the blocked bid in 2005 of the China National Offshore Oil Company for the Californian oil company Unocal. Even the highly successful model for the sovereign wealth funds, Singapore's Temasek, which for a long time went largely unnoticed, is now attracting an attention which from the point of view of its owners and managers is highly undesirable and has announced that it intends to avoid stakes at "iconic" companies. It is possible to imagine a voluntary code of good management by SWFs, in which they apply a self-denying resolution not to purchase commanding shares in key industries, but even that will not be enough to calm the nerves of the old industrial countries.

Norway has adopted such a code, but few recipient countries are likely to see Norwegian investment as a threat. The IMF has recently tried to formulate a new role in creating a code of conduct, but the debates are highly contentious.

Even without the politics, the simple size of the SWFs makes them a major actor in financial markets. With a capital of at least $2.5 trillion, they are larger than the world total of hedge funds, and are large enough to move global markets. They have in part funded the major expansion of global stock markets over the past five years. The total world stock market capitalization was only $20.4 trillion in September 2002, but is currently $63 trillion (October 2007) (World Federation of Exchanges 2007). In effect, the flow of savings from emerging markets has driven the global equities boom that followed the collapse of the dot.com bubble (Bernanke 2005).

The capital markets are no longer effectively an arena in which outcomes result from the interplay of millions of independent guesses, decisions, or strategies. Instead the central banks of emerging markets and new sovereign wealth funds provide so much of the market that they might dominate it. When entities of such a size make decisions, they are bound to act in a strategic way. All the parties begin to suspect political manipulation.

Both the problems of the owners of the new assets and the targets of ownership can be resolved, and the political venom inherent in the accumulation of strategic ownership interests neutralized, through the operation of institutions that have a commitment to and an interest in an overarching general good. They should not be in a position where they may be suspected of a particular strategic manipulation.

The IMF as an independent asset manager

What kind of institution is committed to the overall good? It was such an aspiration that drove the establishment of the IMF immediately after the Second World War. In the past, IMF surveillance of individual countries had teeth because the IMF also had financial power, and because countries taking its advice were borrowing from the Fund or might need to borrow in the future (James 1995). Unlike the OECD, it could put its money where its mouth was. At its most effective moments, the IMF had a powerful leverage over countries whose behavior was vital to the health of the international monetary system.

The IMF originally supervised the rules of the par value system under the Bretton Woods order, which disintegrated in 1971. It was initially envisaged as a sort of rotating credit cooperative, which would support member countries in need of resources to deal with short-term balance of payments problems. It was also intended to have some leverage over perennial surplus countries through the "scarce currency clause," though this provision of the original agreement was never acted on. In the first instance in the 1950s, such action would have required taking measures that penalized the U.S.

The effectiveness of multilateral surveillance as it developed in the 1960s within the context of the G-10 and OECD's Working Party Three was linked to the IMF's presence as a really major financial intermediary as its lending expanded (see Figure 1.1). The major problem at this time involved the chronic strain and frequent eruption of crises in Britain's balance of payments, while the U.S. regarded Britain's role as a reserve center as a central part of the international order and as an outer perimeter defense of the dollar. At this time the IMF went well beyond its own quota-based resources, and its financial power was enhanced by a new ability to raise additional resources through the General Arrangements to Borrow (concluded in 1961). Its ability to give powerful advice to the systemically important countries, such as the United Kingdom, was enhanced by the dependence of those countries on IMF resources. It was the financial power of the IMF that gave it real analytical bite and real powers of persuasion.

In the years following the collapse of Bretton Woods, the IMF reinvented itself as a principal vehicle for the management of the surpluses of the time. It borrowed from the new surplus countries, especially Iran, the Gulf States, and Saudi Arabia, who in this way in part managed their new assets through the intermediation of the IMF. As a consequence, it was able to lend (through the newly introduced Oil Facilities) to those countries which suffered shocks as a result of the increase in petroleum prices.

In principle, any very large financial actor can have a similarly stabilizing role through its ability to take positions against speculative attacks. In the more distant past, market expectations were stabilized during panics by the counter-cyclical behavior of very large private institutions. The multinational house of Rothschild made the first half of the nineteenth century more stable, not only by lending in crises, but also by combining its assistance with a policy conditionality intended to ensure that the credits were more likely to be repaid. Niall Ferguson's survey of the Rothschild history (1998) makes clear how much this central role allowed the expansion of financial activity, and hence also of economic and industrial activity. In the great waves of panic of 1893 to 1896 and 1907, U.S. financial markets were calmed by J.P. Morgan (Strouse 1999). At the time of the Great Depression in the 1930s, there was no house of equivalent power: Morgans failed to calm the U.S. market in 1929; and when the Swedish financier Ivar Kreuger tried to stabilize European markets in 1932, his financial empire collapsed. In 2007, there are some signs that Goldman Sachs feels a duty to lean against the wind in order to stabilize markets. It presents itself, like the Rothschilds or Morgans of the past, as having both a more cautious approach to risk as well as the massive financial firepower that enables it to act as a stabilizing force.

It is therefore quite conceivable that emerging market economies could simply turn to some large private sector Western financial institutions to manage their assets. They might hope that there would be a large benevolent and foresighted private sector player that might serve as an international lender of last resort, and stave off panics. But the problems raised by the delegation of the control of emerging market government assets remain quite intractable.

There is an unpleasant choice implied by tying a powerful emerging market country to a large private sector actor in a different country. If the emerging market governments take a major equity stake, as in the case of Citigroup or UBS, they may be accused of trying to exercise some form of political strategy involving taking control of some commanding heights of the industrial economies and then holding those traditional powers to ransom. If, on the other hand, they do not attempt to assert any control over the governance of the financial institutions they are buying, they will have lost control and may be more vulnerable to loss. Moreover, the benevolent hegemonic private sector actor is usually treated with considerable suspicion. In the domestic market and political context of the U.S. one century ago, rivals and critics turned on J.P. Morgan after the rescue of 1907. The ensuing public debate led to Morgan's embarrassment before the Pujo Committee, and to an early death; and also led to the establishment of a public stabilizing institution, the Federal Reserve System. An analogous debate after the Second World War applied on the global rather than the national level, and led to the idea that an international institution was a crucial part of the world's financial architecture.

The IMF could again become a very powerful financial stabilizer if it managed a significant part of the reserve assets of the new surplus countries. It would be in a powerful position to take bets against speculators. The stabilizing action would ultimately benefit both the world economy and the interests of the owners of the reserve assets, who have (simply by the fact of the accumulation of the surpluses) a similar interest in world economic and financial stability. At the same time, the management of reserve assets by an internationally controlled asset manager would remove suspicions and doubts about the use of assets for strategic political purposes.

In the course of developing new functions, it would be important to distinguish between routine day-to-day transactions and crisis management (in the same way as central banks and national regulators do in their management of domestic affairs). The large stock of assets under the routine management of the IMF would in the first place represent a major *masse de maneuver* that would frighten off speculative attacks or irrational panics. The Fund would be in a situation to intervene pre-emptively, possibly but not necessarily at the request of the target of the speculative attack; so that the speculation would become impossibly costly. The enhanced asset base of the IMF would also give it the possibility of switching into crisis mode without long discussions and formal negotiations. There could be very quick responses; and, as the shifting of assets by asset managers, they would also be noiseless. One of the problems of IMF functions in the past – whether it was in trying to define "scarce currencies" in the immediate postwar period, or asking whether there was a sufficient world supply of liquidity – was that these determinations had to be made in such a formalized way that there could in practice never be an agreement on the issue. Operating as an asset manager, the IMF would be able to affect currency exchange rates without requiring authorization through a formal decision.

The IMF in this new role could directly provide crisis-stricken countries with very large amounts of support: a sort of revival of its traditional role. It is also conceivable that it might intervene directly in currency markets, in cases where its management was satisfied that the crisis was entirely or predominantly speculative in origin and did not correspond to fundamental problems. This would be a decision not directly controlled by governments or by the Executive Board, but at the same time informed by the process of multilateral surveillance. Ultimately, the management would bear the responsibility for mistakes and would be accountable to the board and the governments which own the IMF.

Asset managers are conventionally held to performance benchmarks and other comparative criteria. In evaluating the IMF's performance as an asset manager, and in particular of its crisis response functions, it would be inappropriate to take short-term benchmarks, since such a criterion would require the IMF to "follow the herd" in a panic and liquidate assets in a crisis-stricken country, thus intensifying the crisis. But a multi-year framework would offer an appropriate basis for performance evaluation, since crisis countries supported by the IMF would be expected to undertake reform, and to bounce back from the speculative attack.

The management of financial globalization

As part of the response to the new problems and threats posed by liberalized global capital markets, the IMF established a Capital Markets Division in 1999, which has produced high-quality semi-academic reports on major developments. These reports gave warnings about the potential for destabilization from financial innovation, and saw hedge funds as a source of potential threat.

In responding to the 2007 to 2008 financial crisis, the IMF's new Managing Director, Dominique Strauss-Kahn, has complained that the IMF has been effectively sidelined. In particular, the U.S. never signed on to the joint IMF–World Bank initiative of 1999 (Financial Sector Assessment Program) designed to alert countries to financial vulnerabilities. Strauss-Kahn was quoted as saying, "What is interesting is that … the United States had refused to have an FSAP. We can't be responsible for lack of supervision … owing to the fact that our main instrument to make that kind of supervision was not used in the country" (*Financial Times* 2008). The FSAP mechanism was largely intended, as might be deduced from the date of inception, to deal with ways of examining the financial sectors of emerging market economies, which had been one of the central problems in the 1997 to 1998 Asia crisis. Strauss-Kahn's comment sounds like a rather regrettable instance of international institutions trying to build legitimacy by sounding a cheap anti-American note.

But the IMF is completely right to think that it is largely on the sidelines as far as financial stability issues are concerned. It never evolved in the direction of the "large IMF" outlined by one of the authors in 1996 (James 1996, pp. 618–619), and instead remained resolutely a "small IMF." The major institutional involvement of the Financial Stability Forum is with the Bank for International Settlements (BIS). Given that the major task is to formulate monetary policy as well as regulatory responses to financial developments, it is appropriate that financial stability issues should be handled by an institution that is owned by central banks, rather than by governments (as is the Fund). Indeed the strikingly rapid growth of capital markets was in general a development that had not been predicted at Bretton Woods, and had not been desired by the makers of Bretton Woods, who wanted to move away from the interwar world of central bank-based international cooperation. At that time they had seen central banks as insufficiently committed to mandates to achieve macro-economic stabilization and growth.

Reform of IMF governance

For some time there has existed a substantial consensus, even from fundamentally sympathetic critics, that IMF governance is outdated and in need of reform (for sober assessments see Van Houtven 2002; Woods 2005; Kenen 2007). The rise in reserves in many Asian countries was a deliberate response to the 1997 Asia crisis, in which there was substantial disillusionment with the IMF. A precondition of the IMF acting as a global reserve manager would be a governance reform in which the new surplus countries were able to exercise substantive influence through the IMF. They would need to feel absolutely secure that they were not being the subject of some politically motivated manipulation. In particular, if the IMF were to be in a position of an asset manager who could shift assets from one market to another, it would need to be at a longer distance from U.S. influence and attempts at control: otherwise it would be seen as a device for propping up the dollar for political rather than economic reasons.

In the past, the IMF has frequently run into precisely this sort of difficulty. In the early 1970s, the IMF's Managing Director Pierre-Paul Schweitzer was thought to be pressing for a devaluation of the dollar, and the U.S. insisted on removing him. In later high-profile country cases involving countries such as Egypt or Russia or even Argentina where the U.S. saw a strong security interest, the U.S. pressed against the advice of technical experts from the IMF (see Blustein 2001, 2005).

Above all, while reports of the IMF on aspects of U.S. economic and financial management were often crucial, the IMF has no real leverage over the U.S. Unlike in the case of Great Britain in the 1960s and 1970s, it is unable firmly to press American governments for policy reform or fiscal adjustment. But part of the theory of the usefulness of international institutions involves the ability of a commitment via an externalized and depoliticized process to act as a lever for policy reform that brings long-term collective benefits, even though there are short-term political costs associated with adjustment. Reference to the external pressure – as in the relation of member countries to the European Union – can be a very effective way of overriding the shorter run political opposition in order to bring about the needed economic adjustment.

In a revised approach, votes would be allocated or "bought" to a large extent through the assets held at the IMF. The proportion of votes determined in this way might be as high as 50 percent in a new Reserve College, while the rest would be allocated in the traditional way in the existing Membership College. There is an analogy to this double determination of voting power in the U.S. Constitution, according to which all states have an equal share of Senate votes, but very different numbers of seats in the House of Representatives, where their differing population is reflected. As in the U.S. Congress, a concurrence of both houses or Colleges would be required.

Reserve positions in the IMF would be established, as they are now, by deposits in convertible currency of another member country. The voting in the Reserve College would follow the reserve positions held in the IMF. Voting might only be possible with some time delay (as is often the practice with votes in the stock of private corporations), so as to make sudden reserve deposits (and withdrawals) with the object of obtaining some particular political objective (such as the selection of the IMF's Managing Director) an unappealing option.

Traditionally, the counting of votes has not been very important in shaping particular Fund policy, as the institution and the Board largely operates on the basis of consensus. The eventuality of a vote taking place nevertheless helps to shape the way in which consensus is arrived at, and the extent to which diverging interests are respected and heard. Requiring majorities (with specially qualified votes as in the current voting system of the Fund's Board of Governors) in both houses or Colleges may appear to make likely the possibility of stalemates arising; at the same time it may be argued that such a threat of stalemate would create additional incentives for cooperation and consensus-building.

How would such a system look? It is obviously hard to estimate in advance what share of reserves member countries would actually choose to invest through the new mechanism. Moreover, reserves fluctuate, and every country's share of world reserves is likely to move quite considerably. The following examples thus provide only an extreme outlier of the maximum effect that would be produced by the investment of global reserves *at current levels*, and in that sense is deliberately unrealistic. In the unlikely event that every member country decided to put all its existing reserves into the new Fund mechanism and not to find additional reserves, the weight of voting in the Reserve College would allocate 25 percent to China, 14 percent to Japan, 9 percent to the European Central Bank and the Eurosystem, 4 percent to India, and only 1 percent to the U.S. Under such an arrangement, of course, the U.S. and especially Congress might not see much attraction to this development – unless it saw a likely need for large-scale coordinated action to prop up some major part of the world's financial system.

The large allocation in this hypothetical calculation would of course not be necessary for the system to work, or even desirable: the figures are only presented to give some sense of the upper bound possibilities. It might also be conceivable that the U.S. would want to make supplementary reserve deposits to bring up its voting share. But overwhelmingly, the Reserve College would be likely to be, in current circumstances, an institution which gives a powerful voice to emerging market economies. In a longer term view, their share might be expected to decline again, as some of the current reasons for high reserves fade (fear of financial crisis; financial underdevelopment; and a perception that an undervalued exchange rate creates growth, employment, and political stability in the export sector).

Making a substantial part of Fund voting a reflection of the reserve positions held in the IMF would allow very quick adjustments to new international realities.

It would make the IMF more of a market institution, in much the same way as the changing ownership of joint-stock companies can shift quickly and noiselessly. There would be no need for constant and cumbersome processes of quota renegotiation and revision. A revision of the voting system that meant an automatic reflection of reserve assets held in the Fund would at a stroke eliminate political complications and make the IMF appear much more like a market-oriented organization: in short, the type of credit cooperative that Keynes and the other makers of the postwar monetary settlement envisaged at the 1944 Bretton Woods conference.

Conclusions

In the 1970s the IMF's engagement with large industrial countries came to an end, and in the 1980s and 1990s it became principally an institution engaged in emerging market economies (as well as in very poor countries). The problem with the new mission is that by the 2000s, the emerging markets also graduated in that they have long-term debt markets in their own currencies and are hence less vulnerable to financial shocks. As a result they may look as if they no longer need the IMF (although it is quite possible to imagine new emerging crises arising that might require the more traditional fire-fighting functions of the Fund). As a consequence, all that is left of the original mission of the Fund is the poor country issue (where the micro-economic nature of many of the problems makes the World Bank look like a more suitable agency); and surveillance. But surveillance without the association of financial power that characterized the IMF's modus operandi in the 1960s and 1970s is likely to be rather toothless. The involvement of the IMF in reserve management would provide a powerful set of new financial teeth.

In order to reorient the focus of the IMF in this manner, some simple principles would need to be followed.

First, the IMF's new function as an asset manager would need to be handled separately from the much smaller traditional quota resources used to provide the classical balance of payments assistance through the so-called "General Department" of the Fund. Some portion of the new assets could perhaps be invested adventurously in long-term infrastructure projects for poorer economies, not simply as a public good but in the expectation of long-term returns. The management of assets could be subject to specific guidelines as to which assets might be inappropriate for investment by the IMF. But the fundamental aim of the new Asset Department would be to generate satisfactory and stable returns that would make the reserve assets financially more rewarding (and actually less risky) than under the current system as it is emerging with the problematic growth of SWFs. The Asset Department would thus be subject – like other asset managers – to a clear financial measure of its performance.

Second, but only in exceptional circumstances of a generalized threat to global financial stability, the IMF's new resources would be used to stake out positions to defeat speculative attacks in situations where the fundamental position might be judged to be sound. Like a traditional lender of last resort in a domestic context, it would then lend against collateral at a normal, non-crisis valuation. But, as in its traditional mission, it might also impose policy conditionality in the case of crisis lending to governments.

Third, the new operations would be separated from the existing regular assessment of country policy (the so-called Article IV consultation process or surveillance). Otherwise there would be the suspicion that judgments are influenced by the financial stance of the IMF. This is of course a problem that private sector institutions also face, and which they deal with by establishing "Chinese walls" between research and investment banking activities.

Fourth, in order to carry out this completely new task, the IMF would need to regain the trust of its members. This would require a reform of IMF governance, and in particular of the highly contentious issue of the voting arrangements.

Addendum

This chapter was prepared on the eve of the outbreak of the credit and financial crisis in August 2007. The crisis highlighted some of the problems with SWF investments. Financial distress also brought the IMF back into the center of international policy discussions, but in its traditional firefighting role. The expansion of IMF resources at the April 2009 G-20 meeting in London was an effective way of stopping contagion in emerging markets after problems in highly indebted east and central European economies. But the G-20 summit left untouched the basic governance problems of the IMF, with only a small move in the direction of increased emerging market representation. Indeed many commentators suggested that the enhanced role of the G-20 might sideline the policy advice functions of the IMF. If the IMF is to be able to address such global questions as the appropriate adjustment to international imbalances, it would require a radically different governance structure, not just a slight modification. In this respect, these suggestions, made before the crisis, may still have some relevance.

December 1, 2009

References

Bernanke, Ben, 2005. "The Global Saving Glut and the U.S. Current Account Deficit." Speech to the Virginia Association of Economics in Richmond on March 10, 2005: www.federalreserve.gov/boarddocs/speeches/2005/200503102/default.htm.

Blustein, Paul, 2001. *The Chastening: Inside the Crisis that Rocked the Global Financial System and Humbled the IMF*, New York: Public Affairs.

Blustein, Paul, 2005. *And the Money Kept Rolling in (and out): Wall Street, the IMF, and the Bankrupting of Argentina*, New York: Public Affairs.

Bordo, Michael and Harold James, 2000. "The International Monetary Fund: Its Role in Historical Perspective," U.S. Congressional International Financial Institution Advisory Commission.

Cheung, Yin-Wong and Xing Wang Qian, 2007. "Hoarding of International Reserves: Mrs. Machlup's Wardrobe and the Jones," CESifo WP 2065, July.

Cordella, Tito and Eduardo Levy Yeyati, 2006. "A (New) Country Insurance Facility," *International Finance* 9, 1–36.

de Gregorio, Jose, Barry Eichengreen, Takatoshi Ito, and Charles Wyplosz, 1999. *An Independent and Accountable IMF*, International Center for Monetary and Banking Studies.

Despres, Emile, Charles P. Kindleberger, and Walter S. Salant, 1966. "The Dollar and World Liquidity: A Minority View," *The Economist*, February 11.

Dodge, David, 2006. "The Evolving International Monetary Order and the Need for an Evolving IMF." Speech to the Woodrow Wilson School of Public and International Affairs, March 30.

Dooley, Michael P., David Folkerts-Landau, and Peter Garber, 2003. "An Essay on the Revived Bretton Woods System," NBER WP 9971.

Eichengreen, Barry, 2003. "Restructuring Sovereign Debt," *Journal of Economic Perspectives* 17, 4

Eichengreen, Barry J. and Mody, Ashoka, 2004. "Do Collective Action Clauses Raise Borrowing Costs?," *Economic Journal* 114(495), 247–264.

Ferguson, Niall, 1998. *The House of Rothschild: Money's Prophets 1798–1848*, New York: Viking.

Financial Times, 2007. "$46 bn. Invested in Western Institutions," December 12, p. 16.

Financial Times, 2008. "IMF Rejects Criticism over Foreseeing Global Turmoil," April 11: www.ft.com/cms/s/0/35236db8–075f-11dd-b41e-0000779fd2ac.html.

Humpage, Owen F. and Michael Shenk, 2008. "Chinese Inflation and the Renminbi:" www.clevelandfed.org/research/trends/2008/0208/01intmar.cfm.

James, Harold, 1995. "The Historical Development of the Principle of Surveillance," *IMF Staff Papers* 42(4), 762–791.

James, Harold, 1996. *International Monetary Cooperation Since Bretton Woods*, New York: Oxford University Press.

Kenen, Peter B., 1986. *Adjustment and the International Monetary Fund*, Washington DC: Brookings.

Kenen, Peter B., 2001. *The International Financial Architecture: What's New? What's Missing?* Washington DC: Institute for International Economics

Kenen, Peter B., 2007. *Reform of the International Monetary Fund*, CSR 29, Council on Foreign Relations.

King, Mervyn, 2006. "Reform of the International Monetary Fund." Speech to Indian Council for Research on International Economic Relations, New Delhi, February 20.

Krueger, Anne O., 2001. "International Financial Architecture for 2002: A New Approach to Sovereign Debt Restructuring." Address at the National Economists' Club Annual Members' Dinner, American Enterprise Institute, Washington DC, November 26: www.imf.org/external/np/speeches/2001/112601.htm.

Sachs, Jeffrey, 1989. "Efficient Debt Reduction," in Ishrat Husain and Ishac Diwan (eds), *Dealing with the Debt Crisis*, Washington DC: A World Bank Symposium.

Santor, Eric, 2006. "Governance and the IMF: Does the Fund Follow Corporate Best Practice?," Bank of Canada WP 2006–2032.

Sohmen, Egon, 1964. *International Monetary Problems and the Foreign Exchanges*, Special Papers in International Economics, Princeton, NJ: International Finance Session.

Stiglitz, Joseph E., 2002. *Globalization and its Discontents*, New York: W.W. Norton.

Strouse, Jean, 1999. *Morgan: American Financier*, New York: Random House.

Van Houtven, Leo, 2002. *Governance of the IMF: Decision-making, Institutional Oversight, Transparency and Accountability*, IMF Pamphlet Series No. 53.

Woods, Ngaire, 2005. "Making the IMF and the World Bank More Accountable," in Ariel Buira (ed.), *Reforming the IMF and the World Bank*, London: Anthem Press.

World Federation of Exchanges, 2007. *Annual Report*.

Yu Yongding, 2007. "Global Imbalances and China," *Australia Economic Review*, March.

2 The future of the IMF and of regional cooperation in East Asia[1]

Yung Chul Park and Charles Wyplosz

1 Introduction

The U.S. sub-prime crisis that broke out in August 2007 has since developed into a full-scale global financial crisis. Despite a series of measures taken by the United States and European countries, investors are in a state of panic and financial markets display an extreme degree of volatility all over the world.

Having experienced a major financial crisis in 1997 to 1998, most East Asian countries are expected to be better prepared for managing the fallout from the current crisis. Perhaps partly for this reason, East Asia has so far suffered less compared to other regions. But with the crisis deepening, the region will not be immune to what appears to be the most serious recession since the 1929 depression. Already some of the East Asian economies are sliding into recession and are afflicted by severe financial market instability. However, since the crisis has originated in the U.S. and economic fundamentals of most East Asian economies are relatively stronger than those of other emerging economies in different regions, there is a widespread view that the economic deterioration in East Asia could be arrested and hence its effects could be milder. This outcome would depend on whether the member states of ASEAN+3 could cooperate more closely to coordinate expansionary macro-economic policy and provide mutual liquidity support by activating the bilateral swap arrangements (BSAs) under the Chiang Mai Initiative (CMI), a system of currency swaps among members that was established as the region's response to the 1997 to 1998 Asian crisis as a means of warding off or better managing future crises.[2]

The system of bilateral currency swaps has undergone many structural changes since its inception. Current efforts aim at developing a self-managed reserve pooling arrangement (SRPA), which is due to replace the existing swap system in 2009. This, however, requires that the members agree on operational details including surveillance. To the disappointment of many in the region, leaders of ASEAN+3 have so far been unable to agree on the structure, operational details, and management of the SRPA. Because of this disagreement, the completion of the SRPA is likely to take longer than expected.

The unfolding global crisis has exposed many structural defects of the existing international financial system. Understandably, a chorus of voices is now calling for the creation of a new international financial architecture. Although the structural defects have yet to be clearly identified, it is almost certain that further reforms of the International Monetary Fund (IMF) will occupy center stage of the debate on a new international financial architecture.

Our purpose is to analyze the role of a regional financial arrangement such as the BSAs or the SRPA in East Asia in the context of the expected global financial reform. Can a regional arrangement be a building block for a new international financial architecture by complementing the lending and surveillance operations of a new IMF that may emerge after the completion of the reform? Section 2 discusses the role of the IMF in the management of the 1997 to 1998 Asian crisis. It argues that the IMF then failed to be efficient, restoring stability at minimum cost, and that this mismanagement is in part responsible for its loss of credibility in East Asia. Sections 3 and 4 are devoted to an examination of policies and regional cooperative measures – including the regional movement that led to the creation of the Chiang Mai Initiative – taken by East Asia's crisis-hit countries in their efforts to prevent future crises. Section 5 discusses prospects for future regional financial cooperation within the framework of the SRPA and whether reserve pooling at the regional level can be an important component of a new international financial architecture. Concluding remarks are in a final section.

2 IMF and management of the 1997 to 1998 East Asia's capital account crisis

Advance warning

A number of recent studies (Park 2007; Park and Wyplosz 2008; Takagi 2008) show that the IMF erred in several ways in its management of the 1997 to 1998 Asian crisis. One was the failure to identify *ex ante* the structural vulnerabilities of the crisis-affected countries that had made them susceptible to a financial crisis – weaknesses of both the financial and corporate sectors and macroeconomic policies that prevented speedy adjustment to external shocks. Instead of warning about their vulnerability, the IMF was giving misleading information on the prospects of the economies that were about to be swept over by a crisis. For instance, the Staff Report of the 1997 Article IV consultation with Indonesia, which was released in June of the same year, stated that contagion of the Thai crisis would be limited, that Indonesia's economic fundamentals were sound, and that the prospects for maintaining development momentum were promising (Takagi 2008). The 1997 Article IV consultation for Korea, which took place a month before the country was engulfed in a crisis, was very sanguine about Korea's future economic prospects as it concluded that the country was well prepared to deal with further external pressure.[3]

Capital account crisis

In retrospect, it is clear that the IMF did not fully comprehend the nature and depth of the crisis, which originated in the capital account rather than in the current account. This failure led to the imposition of policy adjustments inappropriate to a capital account crisis, such as fiscal tightening and high interest rate policy. A review of management of the 1997 to 1998 Asian crisis by the Independent Evaluation Office of the IMF (2003) makes clear that it was a capital account crisis and as such required a management and resolution strategy different from the traditional IMF recipe for crises originating from current account deterioration. In the run-up to the crisis, a large increase in capital inflows into some East Asian countries set off an asset market boom and a precipitous increase in the current account deficit, thereby making these countries susceptible to speculative attacks and sudden stops. The perception of vulnerability of these countries triggered a sharp and major capital outflow, which was further aggravated by the panic and herding of foreign investors. Once the dollar peg had become indefensible, the value of the currencies plummeted. Many banks and corporations with balance sheet mismatches could not service their foreign currency-denominated debts and eventually became insolvent. A sharp contraction in the level of output then followed.

Structural reforms

In addition to fiscal and monetary tightening, the crisis resolution strategy of the IMF required the crisis-hit countries to undertake a wide range of institutional reforms in the corporate, financial, and public sectors with the aim of strengthening the structural foundation of the economy and thereby restoring the confidence of international lenders. Even before the crisis, cynics would often express doubt by saying that nothing short of a major shock could force East Asian economies to accept reforms that were badly needed and overdue. It was not surprising, therefore, that the IMF rescue programs for the crisis countries mandated structural reforms along the lines of the Washington Consensus. More surprising was the lack of concern about the appropriateness of some measures and reform capacity. Implementing deep reforms in the midst of a crisis is a questionable objective. As a result, many of these reforms were ignored, put on the backburner, or, at best, resulted in cosmetic changes. The view that structural problems were the root cause of the crisis has not been borne out by subsequent events.

With the stated aim to restore foreign investors' confidence, the Fund requested that the three East Asian crisis countries undertake structural reforms that were overwhelming in terms of their number, scope, and detail of structural policy conditions. As recounted by Goldstein (2003), "the number of structural policy conditions included in these programs with the three Asian crisis economies is very large: many more than you can count using all your fingers and toes." At the peak, Indonesia faced 140 conditions, South Korea 94, and Thailand 73.

Particularly striking is the case of Indonesia. The Fund program included a surprising number of nontraditional areas of conditionality:

> There were, *inter alia*, a measure dealing with reforestation programs; the phasing-out of local content programs for motor vehicles; discontinuation of support for a particular aircraft project and of special privileges granted to the National Car; abolition of the compulsory 2 percent after-tax contribution to charity foundations; appointment of high-level advisors for monetary policy; development of rules for the Jakarta Clearing House; the end of restrictive marketing arrangements for cement, paper, and plywood; the elimination of the Clove Marketing Board; the termination of requirements on credit scheme to assist small businesses, and the raising of stumpage fees.
>
> (Goldstein 2003)

Goldstein speculates that these reform measures were included "for anti-corruption reasons, to facilitate monitoring of commitments, and (for some commitments) to reflect the structural policy agendas of either other IFIs (the World Bank and the Asian Development Bank) or certain creditor countries" (p. 401).[4]

To make matters worse, there has been a widespread perception that the imposition was dictated by the IMF's major shareholders (Blustein 2001) and that the IMF took the crisis and its position as a lender as an opportunity to push through many of the reforms that the crisis-hit countries had refused to implement earlier. Such an attempt, which may have been justifiable, was viewed as opportunistic, earned the resentment of the general public, and more importantly, may have overburdened the reform capacity of the crisis-affected country to increase the cost of crisis resolution and delay recovery.

The regional dimension

When a crisis originates in the capital account, policy coordination, or at least policy dialogue and review among neighboring countries, is essential in preventing contagion. In the absence of a constant exchange of information and policy dialogue among close economic partners, individual countries often find it difficult to assess the causes of major changes in capital flows and exchange rates and hence they fail to coordinate their policies. At the time of the 1997 crisis, the IMF did not have the institutional capacity to monitor developments in regional financial markets, which is crucial for policy coordination at the regional level. It still does not have such capacity. Moreover, to the extent that it cannot serve as a lender of last resort, the IMF cannot serve notice to the international financial markets that it is ready to supply whatever amount of liquidity it takes to thwart an impending speculative attack.

To manage a capital account crisis, instead of tightening monetary and fiscal policy as the IMF required, an effective strategy would have focused on quelling speculation by supplying a large amount of short-term financing to replenish foreign exchange reserves. But there were neither regional nor global lenders of last resort. With limited financial resources, the IMF could not resolve the East Asian crisis by itself; in the end, it had to enlist the financial support of the G-7 and other countries.

At the time of the crisis, the ASEAN+3 countries jointly held about US$700 billion in foreign reserves. The total amount of financing committed by the IMF, other international financial institutions, and a number of donor countries to restore financial stability in Indonesia, Korea, and Thailand amounted to US$111.7 billion. If the countries belonging to the ASEAN+3 group had established a cooperative mechanism into which they could have pooled their reserves and immediately supplied liquidity to stave off speculative attacks, they could have nipped the Thai crisis in the bud and minimized contagion by making available a small fraction of their total reserves. In view of the large loss of output and employment that followed, such a cooperative arrangement was indeed desirable.

Lessons from the crisis

Should, then, the IMF be criticized and bear responsibility for the mismanagement of the crisis? The answer is no. The IMF should not be criticized for its failure to develop a comprehensive framework *ex post facto*. After all, the IMF did not have the luxury of spending many months designing a coherent program. It could not give due consideration to possible conflicts between different reform objectives, as the crisis was deepening every day–threatening the total collapse of the various reform measures that were presumed to help restore market confidence, reduce the likelihood of a recurrence, and improve the long-term economic performance of these countries. From the outset, the IMF reform programs for the crisis countries did not have a well-defined road map to guide the formulation and implementation of stabilization policies, financial and corporate restructuring, or institutional reforms, except for the general policy prescription of the Washington Consensus (Lane *et al.* 1999). Truth is that the economic profession could not agree on how to deal with a capital account crisis in emerging economies, even when it saw one.

What confounded the East Asian policymakers and public in general was that "the IMF has remained defensive and refused to engage in frank and constructive dialogue with stakeholders in Asia instead of explaining the errors it committed with openness and humility" (Takagi 2008). This failure deprived the IMF of the opportunity to regain its credibility in East Asia. As the situation today shows, a financial crisis can break out in any economy whether it is developed or underdeveloped, because bubbles, excesses, and calamities are inherent to financial development, which East Asia has accepted as its model. The U.S. 2002 enactment of the Sarbanes–Oxley Act to reform public company accounting and investor protection demonstrated that governance problems related to auditing disclosure and non-transparency of internal control were not unique to East Asian corporations. In retrospect, it is clear that the IMF did not have a viable framework for corporate reform.

Nevertheless, the IMF continues to argue that financial and corporate-sector frailties were at the root of the crisis and that the crisis-hit countries have made a great deal of progress in improving the efficiency and safety of their financial systems (Burton 2007). This has created an environment in which East Asia's emerging economies do not seek, and often ignore, the IMF's policy advice and even its economic analyses.

3 Monetary and financial integration in East Asia

East Asia's responses to the 1997 crisis

The 1997 Asian financial crisis marked a watershed in the region's recent economic history. It signaled the end of the East Asian economic miracle and opened up a long and painful period of economic reform and restructuring. As part of their efforts to build resilience to external shocks, most of the East Asian countries including the crisis-hit ones have voluntarily or under external pressure increased the flexibility of their foreign exchange rate system and the pace and scope of domestic financial and corporate reform. In order to draw a secure line of defense against speculative attacks, they have also amassed large amounts of reserves. In theory, floating rates and capital account liberalization are supposed to minimize holdings of reserves.

In contrast to theory, however, the East Asian countries have increased their accumulation of reserves since the 1997 crisis. Part of the reason, of course, is that they have not let their currencies float freely and have resisted a significant appreciation vis-à-vis the depreciating US dollar. Another part of the reason is the widely held belief that large reserve stocks provide insurance against currency crises. Except for Malaysia, all other crisis countries have deregulated their capital account transactions to a considerable degree since 1998. This liberalization has increased, not reduced, Asian demand for reserves. The emerging market countries have not witnessed any marked improvement in their access to international capital markets. Crucially, they perceive that capital flows remain unstable and unpredictable.

There is also the argument that East Asia is using the financial services of the U.S. to channel its savings, and will continue to do so for many years (Dooley *et al.* 2003), much as Europe did in the 1950s and 1960s, as then argued by Kindleberger (1965). These various reasons explain the heated controversy over whether reserve accumulation has been excessive in some countries. On the other hand, the widely held belief that large amounts of reserves provide a solid guarantee against speculative attacks may one day be revealed to be mistaken.

Before the onset of capital account liberalization in the 1990s, as far as the adequacy of reserves was concerned, developing economies were generally preoccupied with the management of their current accounts. A popular rule of thumb was to hold an amount of reserves equivalent to three to four months of imports. With considerably increased capital mobility, this rule has become inadequate. For instance, since the last crisis, Korea has accumulated a large volume

Table 2.1 Foreign exchange reserves as a percentage of GDP

	2000	*2008*
China	13.8	39.8
Hong Kong	63.6	70.4
Indonesia	17.1	11.5
Korea	18.7	27.0
Malaysia	29.2	58.2
Philippines	17.1	18.9
Singapore	79.9	91.8
Taiwan	33.2	68.7
Thailand	26.0	37.9

Source: International Financial Statistics, IMF.

Note
GDP for 2008 (IMF estimates).

of foreign reserves (US$260 billion as of the end of 2007) equivalent to 25.5 percent of its GDP (Table 2.1). At the same time, its capital account transactions have increased tenfold in gross terms.

This has led to another rule of thumb, sometimes referred to as the Greenspan–Guidotti–Fischer (GGF) rule, which prescribes holding reserves equal to a country's short-term foreign currency liabilities. The intuition is simple: in an emergency, the rule would enable a central bank to buy back all the liabilities that investors could liquidate. This intuition can be deceptive, even though there is no doubt that very large reserves stocks discourage speculative activity. Determined markets can virtually overwhelm any stock. Speculators chiefly operate by taking short positions in a currency that they perceive as weak. If expectations are unsure, they will not act when facing a central bank that holds sufficient reserves to sustain a speculative attack, because the outcome could be costly for them. If, however, the market sentiment builds up and expectations are firm, speculators can hold short positions of any size. In effect, a speculative attack is a run on the reserves of the central bank; the larger the reserves, the bigger the run.[5] The main advantage of very large stocks of reserves is that they are likely to raise the level of conviction required for markets to dare to trigger a speculative attack. Yet, once an attack is under way, this protection is lost.

Regional cooperation

The 1997 financial turmoil has also served as a catalyst for a movement for building a region-wide defense system against future crises as well as for financial market and monetary integration in East Asia. This movement has culminated in the institutionalization of the two regional initiatives: the Chiang Mai Initiative (CMI) and Asian Bond Market Development Initiative (ABMI).

In 1997, the leaders of ASEAN invited China, Japan, and Korea to join an effort to build a regional mechanism for economic cooperation in East Asia. The outcome was the creation of the grouping known as ASEAN+3 committed to a wide range of areas for regional cooperation. Meeting in May 2000 in Chiang Mai, Thailand, the finance ministers agreed to set up a system of bilateral currency swap arrangements (BSAs) among the original eight members of ASEAN+3.[6,7] In addition to the annual ASEAN+3 summit, the eight countries participating in the CMI have also institutionalized regular meetings of finance ministers (ASEAN+3 Finance Ministers' Meeting, dubbed AFMM+3) and deputy ministers (ASEAN+3 Finance and Central Bank Deputies' Meeting, AFDM+3) for policy dialogue and coordination and concerted efforts at financial reform in the region.

The CMI rests on three pillars: liquidity assistance, monitoring and surveillance, and exchange rate and other policy cooperation. It is anticipated that cooperation will evolve over time, much as has been the case in Europe. The initial mutual credit arrangement in the form of bilateral swaps has been restructured into foreign reserve pooling without any commitment to exchange rate coordination.

The currency swap arrangements

The CMI consists of two regional financial arrangements: a network of bilateral swaps and repurchase agreements among the original eight members of ASEAN+3 and an expanded ASEAN swap arrangement (ASA) created by the original five ASEAN countries in 1977. In May 2000, the ASA was expanded to include the five new ASEAN members and the total amount of the facility was raised from the initial amount of US$200 million to US$1 billion.[8]

- *Structure:* The bilateral swap arrangements (BSAs) provide for liquidity assistance in the form of swaps of U.S. dollars for the domestic currencies of the participating countries.[9] A member country can automatically draw up to 10 percent (now 20 percent) of the contracted amount; beyond that, assistance is conditional upon IMF surveillance, including macro-economic and structural adjustment programs. Participating countries are able to draw from their respective BSAs for a period of ninety days. The first drawing may be renewed seven times. The interest rate applicable to the drawing is the LIBOR (London interbank offered rate) plus a premium of 150 basis points for the first drawing and the first renewal. Thereafter, the premium rises by an additional 50 basis points for every two renewals, but it is not to exceed 300 basis points.

  The BSAs include one-way and two-way swaps. China's and Japan's initial contracts with the five Southeast Asian countries were one-way BSAs from which only the ASEAN five can draw. The amount of liquidity available from the CMI has been progressively raised to US$84 billion.
- *Surveillance:* Most participating countries agree that, in principle, the BSA network needs to be supported by an independent monitoring and surveillance system. At this stage, however, they do not seem to be prepared to establish such a system, relying instead on the IMF beyond the first 20

> percent disbursement. There is no provision for the resolution of defaults on repayments. With the increase in the size of the BSAs and of the automatic drawing limit, a consensus has now emerged that CMI needs its own surveillance mechanism.
>
> As currently structured, the CMI is a small regional source of financial assistance but bilateral swaps are not guaranteed to be activated in times of crisis. Some of the swap-providing countries could exercise their right to opt out. Any country wishing to obtain short-term liquidity must negotiate activation with all swap-providing countries individually. If many members refused to provide swaps or if different swap providers demanded different terms and conditions, then the CMI could cease to be an efficient liquidity support system.

These deficiencies do not mean that the CMI is irrelevant. It evolved into a regional forum for policy dialogue and even coordination for regional financial stability. Most CMI members have amassed large amounts of foreign exchange reserves. At the end of 2007, the seven CMI members excluding Japan held more than $2.5 trillion in reserves.

The ASEAN+3 countries have turned their attention to policy dialogue and coordination. This has led to the institutionalization of a peer review mechanism known as "Economic Review and Policy Dialogue" (ERPD). ERPD assesses regularly the overall economic outlook of the region and serves as a forum for policy dialogues among members. ASEAN+3 members have also established an early-warning system for crisis management and formal and informal communication channels within the framework of the CMI on significant market changes such as a large appreciation or depreciation of any regional currency caused by speculative capital inflows or outflows.

Regional cooperation may open other formal and informal channels of liquidity support, in addition to the BSAs among the ASEAN+3 countries. For example, in 2005 when Indonesia and the Philippines showed signs of financial strain that was deemed contagious, ASEAN+3 policymakers considered short-term public sector loans a first line of defense before activating the BSAs. In 2007, when Vietnam was suffering from a gaping current account deficit, both China and Japan reportedly offered short-term U.S. dollar loans, although Vietnam does not participate in the BSAs. In the end, in all three cases, these loans were not needed. In 2008, China and Japan also offered loans to Korea.

The self-managed reserve pooling arrangement (SRPA)

In 2006, the BSA bilateral contracts were converted into a single contract informally known as a common fund or a self-managed reserve pooling arrangement (SRPA). The ASEAN+3 finance ministers "agreed in principle that a self-managed reserve pooling arrangement governed by a single contractual agreement is an appropriate form of multi-lateralization" of the existing swap system (ASEAN+3 2007).

The conditions and covenants of borrowing from the pool will be those of the BSAs, including the 20 percent IMF rule. On decision making, the members appear divided between majority and unanimity rule. They are likely to adopt a consensus-based rule on important matters such as lending, but other routine management issues could be decided by majority rule.

The SRPA, which is meant to replace the BSAs, essentially replicates the model of reserve pooling of the European Monetary Cooperation Fund (EMCF). From the Asian perspective, the innovation of the SRPA is that it is meant to be a legally binding and enforceable contract, which would give effective protection to participating members. Constructing an efficient system of surveillance would be crucial to garnering public credibility for the SRPA. For the ASEAN+3 countries to contribute sizable amounts to the fund, they need reassurances that moral hazard will be contained. Unless an effective system of surveillance is established, there is the danger that the SRPA may not function as an efficient liquidity support system.

Surveillance, a major concern ever since the establishment of the CMI, has become critical with the introduction of a reserve pooling arrangement. At present surveillance is informally conducted through ERPD when finance ministers and their deputies meet (once a year for the ministers and twice a year for their deputies). The ERPD will serve as the normal mechanism for monitoring and for exchange of information, but when a request for borrowing is made, it will be decided by majority or unanimity rule. Obviously, this type of peer review and informal exchange on policy coordination will not be sufficient. ASEAN+3 will have to rely on the IMF and other IFIs for surveillance.

Since China and Japan, the two largest contributors to the arrangement, are not likely to borrow from the reserve pool, there is a clear line of demarcation between potential lenders and borrowers. China and Japan are potential lenders and four ASEAN members (Indonesia, Malaysia, the Philippines, and Thailand) are potential borrowers, while South Korea and Singapore could be either lenders or borrowers. Therefore, cooperation between the two major contributors, China and Japan, which has been wanting in recent years, will be crucial to a successful launching of the SRPA.

The reform of the global financial architecture: viability and the role of regional financial cooperation arrangements

The global financial crisis has underscored the fact that the IMF is not structured to manage a capital account or short-run liquidity crisis, whether local or regional. Traditionally, the IMF has had very little to do with the lending operations in G-7 countries. Despite its efforts to broaden its role in multilateral surveillance and policy consultation, the IMF has not been effective in persuading major players, including the G-7 economies, to coordinate their policies during the global financial turmoil.[10] At the same time, the IMF may not have sufficient resources to help ease U.S. dollar liquidity shortages faced by a growing number of emerging economies.[11] This has led the newly created G-20 to attempt to reform the international financial architecture. This section asks whether regional financial arrangements (RFAs) such as those created by ASEAN+3 are compatible with the G-20 reform agenda and, if so, whether the SRPA could be a building block of the new international system.

Several arguments suggest that RFAs could complement the IMF and enhance the efficiency and stability of a new international financial architecture. The first one invokes the European experience with financial and monetary integration. The EMU has contributed to deeper economic integration and stability in Europe. It has become a component of the international financial system. Many in East Asia believe that they could replicate a similar experience. The architects of the CMI shared such a vision. They may or may not succeed, but in view of the European achievement, their endeavor to promote regional economic integration deserves the support of the global community.

The second and perhaps the most frequently raised argument for creating regional financial arrangements is that they may be better adapted to managing a regional capital account or liquidity crisis than the IMF or, at least, that it can play a useful complementary role. The swap arrangements established during the crisis by the ECB with non-euro area members of the EU are an example of how regional cooperation is compatible with IMF interventions. Another example is provided by regional development banks that have long been a partner of the World Bank. The temporary liquidity swap facilities arranged in 2009 between the U.S. Federal Reserve and the central banks of four systemically important emerging economies (Brazil, Korea, Mexico, and Singapore), each for a total of $30 billion, further illustrates the usefulness of alternative channels of emergency assistance.

A third argument refers to a host of institutional weaknesses of the IMF that narrow its role as an institution entrusted with global lending and surveillance. Even with additional resources committed by the G-20, the IMF may fall short of what it needs to rescue emerging and developing economies suffering a global crisis. Regional lenders could join forces with the IMF to provide additional funds for emergency lending. For example, the SRPA could command a large amount of loanable funds. If the CMI members were able to contribute 5 percent of their combined reserves ($4 trillion) and establish adequate surveillance, the pooled reserve would be as large as the IMF facilities. One could argue that regional organizations such as ASEAN+3 should instead contribute more resources to the IMF instead of creating RFAs. The IMF could then benefit from scale economies and dispel any concerns of potential moral hazard that may beset the RFAs. The problem with this view is that the insufficiency of lendable resources is not the only limitation of the IMF.

Currently the IMF is not a global lender of last resort, nor can it coordinate the macro-economic policies of its members. RFAs such as the SRPA can specialize in monitoring and analyzing country- and region-wide economic developments. The IMF could provide technical assistance to ASEAN+3 and participate in various ASEAN+3 fora, including the AFMM. An additional weakness of the IMF is related to its key role as a provider of policy advice and economic analyses. As many emerging economies are moving up the ladder of development, the IMF is becoming one of many private and public providers of market information, economic analyses, and even policy advice. As a result, the role of the IMF as a confidential adviser has declined in importance, much more so in East Asia since the 1997 to 1998 Asian crisis. Furthermore, as Takagi (2008) points out, an IMF mission that comes with a preset agenda offers little to East Asian policymakers.

4 Concluding remarks

The ongoing global economic crisis has highlighted many deficiencies of the existing international financial system that threaten global financial stability. In a globalized financial system, a crisis originating in one country or region can spill over into other countries at lightning speed. As with the case of the U.S. subprime crisis, a crisis in a large economy can be more devastating as it leaves few countries unscathed, whether they are developed or developing. The lesson of the current global financial turmoil is that such a crisis cannot be resolved without policy coordination and mutual support among the affected countries.

Even though some of them, such as South Korea, suffered large capital outflows, all East Asian countries have been reluctant to seek IMF rescue financing again. Unless the international community joins forces to create a new international financial architecture that could ensure global financial stability by preventing future crises or responding in a concerted manner when they do occur, many emerging economies could conclude that their foreign exchange reserves are not enough to cushion external shocks. East Asia's emerging economies may then be tempted to return to the export-led growth strategy, which could sow the seeds for another crisis to be sparked by ever-growing global imbalances and a falling U.S. dollar.

This danger can be pre-empted if the members of ASEAN+3, the United States, and the EU collaborate to elevate the status of the SRPA to a credible regional lender. On its part, ASEAN+3 should consider enlarging the reserve pool in order to have it be taken seriously by the market. Given the large amount of reserves held by the CMI member countries, the size of the BSAs or the SRPA could easily be doubled. This would require specifying policy conditions to be attached to SRPA loans and the setting up of a surveillance mechanism, as previously discussed.

While the creation of the G-20 and its first deliberations indicate some willingness among the large countries to tackle at least some structural deficiencies of the global financial system, as a group the East Asian political leaders have been most conspicuous by their inactivity. They have mostly watched the financial meltdown from the sidelines. The eight members participating in the CMI have been sitting on a total of $4 trillion in foreign exchange reserves. They should not have faced, therefore, any lack of U.S. dollar liquidity. Yet, several did as the bilateral swaps have not been mobilized. Instead, as it faced acute speculative pressure, Korea has arranged for loans from China and Japan outside of the CMI process, and for a swap agreement between its central bank and the U.S. Federal Reserve.

The crisis has had a positive effect since it has led to the decision to multilateralize the BSAs, a welcome step even if it will not be practical until a surveillance process is put in place. The crisis should also encourage East Asian countries to participate actively in reforming the global financial system. The four members of ASEAN+3 participating in the G-20 meetings (China, Indonesia, Japan, and Korea) could work with other members to present a united front. The regional financial cooperative arrangements in East Asia, such as the BSAs and SRPA, even though they may not be effective in providing protection against crises, may be transformed into one building block of a new international financial architecture. For that to happen, it would need to be supported by the international financial community and the IMF should recognize the legitimacy of the BSAs and of the SRPA as a regional crisis manager and lender that is a component of a new international financial architecture.

Notes

1 This chapter draws on section 3 of Park and Wyplosz (2008).
2 ASEAN+3 includes the ten current members of the Association of Southeast Asian Nations (Brunei Darussalam, Cambodia, Indonesia, Laos, Malaysia, Myanmar, Philippines, Singapore, Thailand, and Vietnam) plus Japan, China, and the Republic of Korea.
3 See Takagi (2008). To be fair, the IMF expressed its concerns about the gaping current account deficit of Thailand and recommended tightening of fiscal policy, financial sector reform, and a more flexible exchange rate system before the onset of the crisis. It should be noted, however, that its failure to assess contagiousness of the crisis may have exacerbated the difficulties of resolving the financial meltdown.
4 In the case of South Korea, the creditor country was the U.S. Blustein (2001, p. 143) quotes a remark made by an IMF official, who says, "the U.S. saw this (crisis) as an opportunity … to crack open all these things that for years have bothered them."
5 The argument is formalized in Jeanne and Wyplosz (2003).
6 Initially ASEAN included five countries: Indonesia, Malaysia, Philippines, Singapore, and Thailand.
7 The eight members include the five original members of ASEAN (Indonesia, Malaysia, the Philippines, Singapore, and Thailand) plus China, Japan, and Korea.
8 The five new members of ASEAN do not participate in the Chiang Mai Initiative.
9 China chose swaps between local currencies with Japan, Korea, and Indonesia. With Indonesia, it also has a dollar–local currency swap.
10 Eichengreen (2008) suggests that the U.S. and EU will be unresponsive to an IMF-directed Multilateral Consultation bringing together the U.S., European Union, and others to discuss the credit crisis. "European finance ministers meet as the Ecofin Council, and if they need to reach Mr. Paulson, they know his number. They do not need a Multilateral Consultation to bring them together."
11 Eichengreen (2008) is skeptical about whether the IMF could have a role in aiding emerging economies caught up in the crisis. As he sees it, "Eastern Europe crisis countries may be bailed out by the EU and the ECB, while their East Asian counterparts may receive swaps and credits through the Chiang Mai Initiative. Once again the Fund may end up being sidelined unless it demonstrates that it has a better idea, in this case about how to link emergency lending with policy adjustment."

References

APEC (Asia-Pacific Economic Cooperation) (2008) "Lima Statement on the Global Economy," November, Lima, Peru. Available from www.apec.org/apec/apec_groups/other_apec_groups/finance_ministers_process.html.

ASEAN+3 (ASEAN Plus Three) (2007) "Joint Ministerial Statement of the 10th ASEAN+3 Finance Ministers' Meeting," May 5, Kyoto, Japan. Available from www.mof.go.jp/english/if/as3_070505.htm,

ASEAN+3 (2008) "Joint Ministerial Statement of the 11th ASEAN Plus Three ASEAN Finance Ministers Meeting," May 4, Madrid, Spain. Available from www.aseansec.org/21502.htm.

ASEM (Asia-Europe Meeting) (2008) "Full Text of Statement of the Seventh Asia-Europe Meeting on the International Financial Situation," Beijing, October 24. Available from www.asem7.cn/misc/2008–10/25/content_57409.htm.

Blustein, Paul (2001) *The Chastening: Inside the Crisis that Rocked the Global Financial System and Humbled the IMF*, New York: Public Affairs Books.

Burton, David (2007) "Asia: Ten Years on – Taking Stock and Looking Forward." Speech at the Singapore Press Club, June 5, Singapore. Available at www.imf.org/external/np/speeches/2007/060507.htm.

Dooley, Michael P., David Folkerts-Landau, and Peter Garber (2003) "An Essay on The Revived Bretton Woods System," NBER Working Paper 9971.

Eichengreen, Barry (2008) "Can the IMF save the World?," *Eurointelligence*, October 6. Available at www.eurointelligence.com/Article3.1018+M577a74f2b10.0.html.

Goldstein, Morris (2003) "IMF Structural Programs" in Martin Feldstein (ed.), *Economic and Financial Crisis in Emerging Market Economies*, National Bureau of Economic Research, Chicago, IL: University of Chicago Press.

G-20 (Group of Twenty) (2008) "Declaration of the Summit on Financial Markets and the World Economy," November 15, Washington DC. Available at www.g20.utoronto.ca/2008-leaders-declaration-081115.html.

IMF (International Monetary Fund) (2000) "Progress in Strengthening the Architecture of the International Financial System." A fact sheet, July. Available at www.imf.org/external/np/exr/facts/arcguide.htm.

IMF (2002) "Reform of the International Financial Architecture: A Work in Progress." Remarks by Horst Köhler at the Central Bank Governors' Symposium, July 5. Available at www.imf.org/external/np/speeches/2002/070502.htm.

IMF (2003) "IMF and Recent Capital Account Crises: Indonesia, Korea, Brazil." Independent Evaluation Office, *Evaluation Report*, July 28. Available at www.ieo-imf.org/eval/complete/eval_07282003.html.

Jeanne, Olivier and Charles Wyplosz (2003) "The International Lender of Last Resort: How Large Is Large Enough?" in M.P. Dooley and J.A. Frankel (eds), *Managing Currency Crises in Emerging Markets*, Chicago, IL: University of Chicago Press.

Kindleberger, Charles P. (1965) "Balance of Payments Deficits and the International Market for Liquidity" in *Princeton Essays in International Finance 46*, Princeton University International Finance Section.

Lane, Timothy, Atish Ghosh, Javier Hamann, Steven Phillips, Marianne Schulze-Ghattas, and Tsidi Tsikata (1999) "IMF-supported Programs in Indonesia, Korea, and Thailand: A Preliminary Assessment," *IMF Occasional Paper No. 178*, June.

Manzano, George (2001) "Is There Any Value-added in the ASEAN Surveillance Process?" *ASEAN Economic Bulletin* 18/1.

Park, Yung Chul (2007) "Whither Financial and Monetary Integration in East Asia?," *Asian Economic Papers* 6(3), 95–128.

Park, Yung Chul and Charles Wyplosz (2008) "Monetary and Financial Integration in East Asia: The Relevance of European Experience." Paper presented at the *2008 ASEM FMM Conference: Asia, Europe and the Future of Regional Economic Integration*, June 15, Jeju, Korea.

Takagi, Shinji (2008) "The IMF and East Asia: The Legacy of the Crisis and Actions for the Future," January. Paper prepared for *PAFTAD 32 Conference: The Impact of International Arrangements and Organizations on Development in Asia and the Pacific*, December 17–19, 2007, Hanoi, Vietnam.

Part II

Exchange rate regimes

Old debate, new answers

3 'Global inflation' and 'the proper use of policies under fixed and flexible exchange rates'

A personal perspective on two themes of Alexander's research[1]

Hans Genberg

1 Introduction

Headline inflation rates have increased more or less simultaneously in a number of countries and regions during the past one to two years. Globalization has been mentioned as one of the possible factors responsible for this increase much as it was given as a reason for the subdued inflation rates in the same economies during the previous five to ten years. The term 'global inflation' was used in the late 1960s and 1970s to describe a similar worldwide pattern of inflation rates that emerged at that time. Alexander Swoboda was a prominent contributor to the analysis of the sources and spread of inflation at that time, emphasizing the critical role of the Bretton Woods exchange rate system of fixed exchange rates centered on the US dollar.

In the next section of this chapter I first review the analysis of global inflation during the Bretton Woods system as seen through research by Alexander and colleagues at the Graduate Institute of International Studies in Geneva and with whom I had the fortune of being associated as a fresh PhD out of the University of Chicago. I then discuss whether this analysis can be used to shed light on the current debate about the sources and spread of global inflation pressures.

Section 3 takes up another theme in Alexander's research, namely the proper use of economic policies under fixed and flexible exchange rates. In several writings he had emphasized how the stability of a fixed exchange rate system required monetary policy to be 'assigned' to maintaining external balance and that this result fundamentally did not depend on the degree of capital mobility. Similarly, the logic of a floating exchange rate system required that monetary policy be assigned to another objective, namely internal balance, or price stability as we would call it now. If ensuring external (current account) balance was also a goal of economic policy, some other instrument would have to be found. Fiscal policy was shown to be the appropriate choice.

The appropriate pairing of instruments and objectives was emphasized in analyses of the major 'global imbalance' of the early 1980s, namely the large current account deficit of the United States and the corresponding surpluses of Germany and Japan. At the time there was considerable pressure on the Japanese authorities to appreciate the yen in order to solve the global imbalance. Research by Alexander and myself showed that this policy prescription amounted to an inappropriate pairing of instruments and goals of economic policy. In section 3 I argue that the same error has been perpetuated in the context of the current 'global imbalance' where the Chinese authorities have been urged to appreciate the renminbi. To remedy this error, I propose that policy consultations and advice related to current account imbalances should focus on policies that are likely to have a strong influence on these imbalances and should de-emphasize the notion of exchange rate misalignments.

As befits a Festschrift, and as the reader will recognize, references to the literature in what follows are heavily biased towards articles written by Alexander. As I had the privilege of working closely with him during these years, my own, as well as jointly authored articles also figure prominently. Alternative interpretations of the issues we wrote about were of course published, but the purpose of this chapter is not to survey the entire literature but rather to describe what we believed at the time of writing and what relevance it may have today.

2 Globalization and inflation: then and now

In the past several years considerable attention has been given to the possible influence of globalization on many aspects of economic activity, among them inflation. Taking the IMF's *World Economic Outlook* as a barometer of the interest the international community places on certain topics, one notes that the April 2006 report bore the subtitle *Globalization and Inflation* and the October 2007 report contained an analysis of the meaning and measurement of 'global liquidity.' One set of issues that these reports addresses is the extent to which 'global liquidity' may be seen as a proximate cause of inflation in the world, and whether 'globalization' changes the nature of the impulses to inflation and their transmission across economies.

Then

These questions were the focus of intense debates and research back in the mid-1970s. At the Graduate Institute of International Studies, a research project led by Alexander provided a fitting venue for contributing to these debates as part of our attempts to analyze and explain how the Bretton Woods (BW) system of fixed exchange rates functioned. Recall that annual inflation rates in the main industrialized economies had increased steadily in the 1960s and into the early 1970s from an average of around 3 percent in the early part of this period to over 9 percent on the eve of the oil supply shocks that came to dominate discussions in the mid-1970s. The increase in inflation coincided with a similar increase in global liquidity, or in world money growth as it was frequently referred to at the time (see Figure 3.1 for an illustration). The correlation suggested that there might be a causal relation between the two phenomena. Of course there was also a correlation between inflation and money growth at the individual country level,

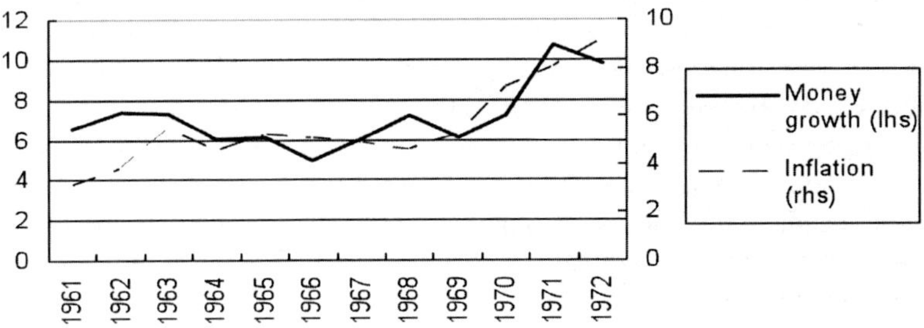

Figure 3.1 Inflation and money growth in G-10 economies.

so a debate ensued between 'global monetarists,' i.e. those who argued that inflation in the world economy could be usefully analyzed by focusing on the determinants of global demand and supply of money, and 'local,' for want of a better word, monetarists who focused analysis principally on experiences in each economy separately.[2] Alexander and I belonged to the first group.

The theoretical case for a focus on global monetary factors rather than on individual countries derived from a view of the monetary adjustment mechanism in a fixed exchange rate system which at the time became known as the monetary approach to the balance of payments. We had both been influenced by Bob Mundell and Harry Johnson at the University of Chicago where this approach had been applied to issues of international adjustment and monetary policy under fixed exchange rates by Rudi Dornbusch, Jacob Frenkel, Mike Mussa, and many others.

A characteristic of the 'monetary approach' was a view that the international adjustment mechanism could be usefully analyzed by assuming that markets for goods and assets were highly integrated internationally. In such a world, a change in money demand or money supply in one country would only succeed in influencing domestic interest rates – and hence aggregate demand and inflation – to the extent that it would influence world interest rates. For very small open economies of negligible effective size, monetary policy initiatives by the central bank or changes in money demand would in the extreme case only have an impact on the balance of payments. The evolution of inflation would be entirely due to global phenomena.[3]

The international transmission mechanism was often described in terms of Hume's price specie flow mechanism whereby domestic monetary expansion would in a first instance lead to increases in domestic prices. This in turn would bring about a balance of trade deficit and a reserve outflow which would increase prices abroad and partially offset those that had previously occurred at home. While this was theoretically convenient, it implied a time–series relationship between money and inflation in small open economies – i.e. that money should Granger-cause inflation – that was not always observed.[4] Hence I would argue that a more robust, and certainly more rapid, transmission mechanism was the result of the integration of asset markets. On this interpretation, an increase in liquidity in the U.S. market would lead to a decrease in interest rates throughout the fixed rate system and the consequences for prices, output, and the quantity of money would depend on the speed of adjustment of these variables to the monetary stimulus and could very well be different across economies.

While the extreme assumption of perfect integration of goods and asset markets was unlikely to have been completely accurate, empirical evidence that we and others gathered did not contradict the global monetarist interpretation of the onset of inflation in the later years of the BW system,[5] but much of it begged the question what process determined the evolution of the world money supply, and in particular what was the role of the U.S. as center country of the Bretton Woods system. To answer this question Alexander built on his earlier work on the euro–dollar market and developed a model that implied that the money supply process in the BW system was inherently asymmetric in view of the habit of non-U.S. central banks to hold their reserves in U.S. Treasury bills, which implied that the effect on the U.S. money supply of balance of payments disequilibria were effectively sterilized.[6] For this reason, the U.S. became the undisputed center of the BW system, not only by its economic size but also because of how the BW system operated. In fact, it could be characterized as a de facto dollar standard. The asymmetry highlighted in Alexander's model did not appear to be contradicted by the facts.[7]

As a number of major central banks adopted floating exchange rates in the mid-1970s, the theoretical case for looking at global inflation and global liquidity seemed to disappear. Purchasing power parity theory implied that exchange rate changes should accommodate inflation differentials, so the concept of world inflation would lose its meaning.[8] Likewise, not only did national monetary aggregates start to lose favor among academics and central banks, but the notion of a world money supply or global liquidity was no longer believed to be relevant, as individual countries could pursue their own monetary policy independently. The logic and rationale for the adoption of floating exchange rates meant that what went on in the rest of the world did not need to be factored into monetary policy considerations of individual central banks. Indeed, looking only at the domestic output gap and the deviation from inflation from the target would (much) later be considered as sufficient indicators of the need of policy adjustments.

Now

Fast forward to the present. As noted in the opening paragraph of this section, during the past two to three years increasing attention has been given to the possibility that inflation is influenced by global factors, even in the current environment of floating exchange rates, and that the notion of global liquidity is useful for analytical purposes.

There are several strands to the arguments. The least controversial refers to the increased role of common shocks combined with similar reactions to such shocks by national monetary authorities. The obvious and topical example would be an increase in the prices of food and energy relative to other goods and services. If central banks react to such relative price increases in a similar manner, for example, focusing on core inflation measures and thereby excluding them from the price index used in determining monetary policy responses, then the increase in headline inflation will look similar across countries.[9] It could furthermore be described as being due to global rather than local factors.

Another uncontroversial reason for inflation to be considered a regional rather than a country-specific issue would exist if exchange rates were fixed or heavily managed. An obvious example would be a monetary union like the euro area, although even here one must be mindful of relative price changes that lead to differences in inflation rates across member economies. Less formal exchange rate management is sometimes ascribed to many emerging and developing countries which are said to suffer from 'fear of floating.' According to the logic of a fixed exchange rate system, such countries would import the monetary conditions set in the center country, often the U.S., and these in turn would lead to a certain commonality of inflation rates.

Neither of these two arguments implies that individual central banks *could not* control domestic inflation if they so desired, only that there are reasons why they choose not to. Borio and Filardo (2007) have put forward a more controversial argument, according to which the *ability* of central banks to control inflation is reduced by globalization. They contrast the prevailing 'country-centric' approach in which inflation is driven only by domestic factors – the output gap and the domestic policy interest rate – with a 'globe-centric' approach where global factors are potentially dominant. In brief, their conceptual framework departs from the usual model in which economies are identified by the imperfect substitutability between goods produced at home and abroad. They instead invite us to consider a world in which goods produced in different economies are different varieties of the same differentiated good, where markets in any given location are contestable, and where production facilities and certain factors of production may be footloose. Under such conditions they argue that 'a mapping between country-specific excess demand and a country's inflation rate is not fully justified. It is global excess demand for the goods in question that is relevant' (p. 5). In their framework, exchange rate changes do not appear to play an important role in determining inflation outcomes over a horizon that is relevant for counter-cyclical monetary policy. This may be due to a number of factors: the random-walk nature of exchange rate changes which appears to be out of tune with 'fundamentals' in the short to medium term, the limited pass-through of exchange rate changes to prices leading to deviations from the 'law-of-one price,' or the widespread use of hedging to make production decisions relatively insensitive to exchange rate changes.

Borio and Filardo provide empirical evidence that does not contradict their globe-centric view of the inflation process. Using a relatively traditional Phillips curve framework, they show that measures of global excess demand are as important as measures of domestic excess demand for individual countries' inflation rates, and in some cases even more important. While they caution that their results are preliminary, they point out that the implications of the globe-centric approach for how we should model inflation and how we should think about monetary policy may be far-reaching. They note that 'questions could ultimately be raised about the very effectiveness of domestic monetary policy. To the extent that, in a proximate sense, domestic inflation became increasingly influenced by global capacity constraints, this could weaken the near-term efficacy of domestic monetary policy levers, because of their limited (i.e. domestic) reach' (p. 21). Furthermore, '[t]he power of policy could be complicated further by the implications of financial globalization, which could be weakening the ability of central banks to influence domestic real interest rates, especially longer-term rates, independently of global conditions' (p. 21).

Time will tell whether the Borio–Filardo view will stand up to further empirical and theoretical scrutiny. In the meantime it is, I believe, an important challenge to the conventional model of the inflation process, and it suggests that when we consider monetary policy there may now be a case for distinguishing not between local vs. global monetarists but between local vs. global New Keynesians.

3 The proper use of policies under fixed and flexible exchange rates

Monetary policy and the choice of exchange rate regime

A recurring theme in Alexander's writings and in his teaching to GIIS students has been that domestic economic policy choices must be consistent with the constraints and economic logic of the exchange rate regime a country has chosen. Failing this, goals may not be reached or, worse, crises and conflicts may arise. In a fixed exchange rate context he emphasized how monetary policy could not be relied on to influence domestic income or prices other than in the short run, or using his own words: 'tying monetary policy to the balance of payments is seen to be the only governing principle for monetary policy consistent with maintenance of a fixed exchange-rate system in the long run' (Swoboda 1973, p. 152). The same article explained how the presence of imperfect capital mobility, non-traded goods, and sticky prices did not in any way alter the basic conclusion. They only altered the speed with which the economy would reach the long-run equilibrium. An earlier article (Swoboda 1971) had elaborated on this point by explaining why even in the complete absence of capital mobility, monetary policy would be ineffective in a fixed exchange rate context.

While the need to focus monetary policy on external balance had already been emphasized in the work of Mundell and others, the full implications were not widely recognized in the mid-1970s. I recall attending many conferences in Europe (the annual Konstanz conference was one of the highlights) where there were lively debates about the relevance of the constraint on monetary policy effectiveness posed by a fixed exchange rate regime. The implications of the monetary approach to the balance of payments were questioned by colleagues with a more closed economy mindset, those I referred to as 'local monetarists' in the previous section. References were made to less than perfect capital mobility, portfolio balance models of capital flows, non-traded goods, and so on in these debates to argue that monetary policy could still be used to target domestic inflation even if the exchange rate was fixed. It was useful to be able to refer to Alexander's articles to counter these arguments.

The limited impact of monetary policy in a fixed exchange rate regime was drilled into many cohorts of Institute students in the obligatory open economy macro course (or 'International Monetary Economics' as it was called at the time) that Alexander (and in some years I or yet in other years both of us) taught. I would like to think that the lessons learned at the minimum helped in job interviews that many of the students had with the IMF, which over the years led to a substantial contingent of Institute students being employed in Washington. Whether they led to better IMF programs or better monetary policies in member countries I will have to let others comment on.

In terms of the choice of exchange rate regime the emphasis on the clear internal logic of either fixed or flexible regimes led Alexander to favor clear-cut, later called corner, solutions, i.e., either fixed rates or freely floating rates as opposed to the middle-of-the-road solutions. In a joint paper entitled 'Fixed Rates, Flexible Rates, of the Middle of the Road: A Re-examination of the Arguments in View of recent Experience' (Genberg and Swoboda 1983), we elaborated on this view, arguing that clear rules for monetary policy are necessary for any exchange rate to perform satisfactorily, and it is easier to define such rules when the exchange rate regime is well defined. The paper was presented at one of the Wingspread conferences organized by Bob Aliber. John Williamson was there, and I recall that when he saw the title of the paper, he was hopeful that Alexander and I had finally seen the light (John believed firmly in middle-of-the-road solutions), but his opinion changed quickly when he heard our presentation.

The actual choice of exchange rate regime by governments in the past two decades displays a tendency towards a bipolar arrangement at the two ends along a line from very hard pegs to freely floating, in particular for economies with open capital accounts (Fischer 2007). The bipolar arrangement has grown out of a realization by the authorities that intermediate regimes tend to experience crises of confidence and credibility, bringing on speculative attacks and their ultimate demise. Although to my knowledge Alexander did not predict the actual evolution of exchange rate regimes, his insistence that stability of a chosen regime requires strict adherence by policy makers to the logic of that regime remains as valid as ever.

Misalignment of currencies or misalignment of policies

In the 1980s

In the mid-1980s there was much discussion of the current account imbalances in the world economy. As Figure 3.2 illustrates, the U.S. current account deficit

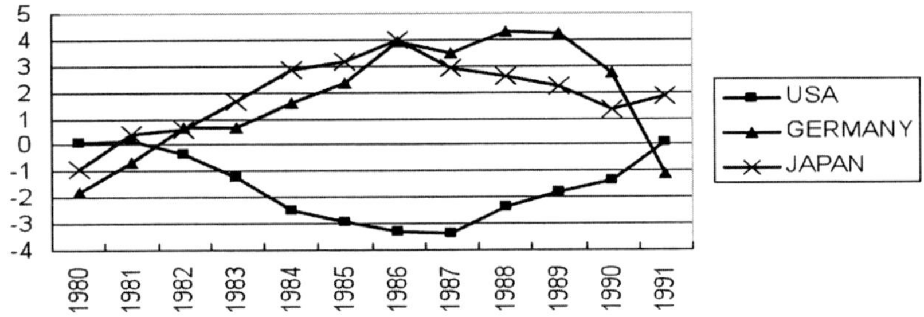

Figure 3.2 Current account balances as a percentage of GDP.

increased steadily throughout the beginning of that decade from being roughly balanced at the beginning to a deficit of slightly over 3 percent of GDP in 1986 and 1987. Corresponding surpluses were recorded in Germany and Japan in particular. As the imbalances built, questions started to be raised about their sustainability, and about currency misalignment and manipulation.

Implicit, and sometimes explicit, in many policy discussions was a belief that exchange rate changes should be used to influence the current account, so it became popular to ask how far the dollar would have to fall (it had appreciated substantially during the first half of the 1980s) for the current account positions to be reversed. The partial equilibrium elasticity model was used to give answers.

The suggestion that exchange rates should be changed by intervention, by 'talking down' the dollar or 'talking up' the yen, or by other policies with the aim to influencing current account imbalances struck Alexander and me as being contrary to the proper use of economic policies under floating exchange rates. In Genberg and Swoboda (1987) we showed that in the context of the original Mundell–Fleming model the proper policy assignment under flexible exchange rates is for *fiscal* policy to ensure external balance (a balanced current account) and for monetary policy to ensure internal balance (price stability). We also extended the argument to a, then, more modern analytical framework which incorporated an aggregate supply as well as an aggregate demand side.[10] By carrying out the analysis in a general equilibrium model (however simple it may seem from a current perspective), we quite naturally

> emphasized … the need to focus policy discussions on the appropriate setting of policy *instruments* and not on the values of endogenous variables [exchange rates] … Hence, one should not ask what value of the dollar is appropriate in the light of a [current account target], but rather what are the most effective tools … and what are suitable values for the implied policy instruments.
>
> (Genberg and Swoboda 1989, p. 27)

In 2008

Policy discussions surrounding the current account imbalances that have emerged in the recent past have shared many of the features of the discussions in the 1980s. Many of the early assessments made misalignment of exchange rates responsible for the imbalances, and protectionist legislation has been proposed to deal with the implied unfair competition. In addition, considerable effort went into calculating the exchange rate adjustment required to correct the U.S. current account deficit. Under pressure from major shareholders the IMF has devoted large amounts of resources to the calculation of equilibrium exchange rates, and reports on Article IV consultations are required to contain some assessment of the appropriateness of the exchange rate level.

More recently it has been recognized that the early, almost exclusive focus on exchange rate adjustment was misplaced and that one needs to discuss solutions in terms of 'the appropriate setting of policy instruments and not the values of endogenous variables.' Quite appropriately, fiscal policies and policies that aim to influence savings behavior directly have received most attention. One can only wonder why the emphasis on exchange rate adjustments dominated the debate for several years before a more balanced assessment appeared.

Part of the reason may be that the main watchdog of the international monetary system is hampered by a formulation of its mandate that in my view puts undue emphasis on exchange rate policy. Article IV, Section 3(b) of the IMF's Articles of Agreement states that 'the Fund shall exercise firm surveillance over the *exchange rate policies* of members' (emphasis added). This has had the result that the IMF has been judged on how it has carried out this particular task rather than on how it has carried out the task of 'oversee[ing] the international monetary system in order to ensure its effective operation' (Articles of Agreement, Article IV, Section 3(a)). An assessment of the latter would require a more nuanced and wide-ranging analysis which focuses on the Fund's surveillance over all aspects of economic policies, not only exchange rate policies.[11] Stanley Fischer, Governor of the Bank of Israel, expressed a similar opinion in his Mundell–Fleming lecture at the Eighth Annual Jacque Polak Research Conference last November. There he wondered why the new IMF Decision of Bilateral Surveillance relates to '*exchange rate policies* that result in external instability, regardless of their purpose' (emphasis added) rather than to "*policies* that result in external instability, regardless of their purpose."' Perhaps it is time to reformulate Article IV of the IMF's Articles of Agreement by replacing the emphasis on *exchange rate* policies with a formulation of the type 'the Fund shall exercise firm surveillance over the economic policies of members.'

4 Concluding remarks

Globalization, global imbalances, global inflation are all terms that have been frequently used to describe important aspects of the current state of the world economy. In this brief chapter I have argued that the concepts are not new and lessons from an earlier analysis can be helpful in putting current concerns into perspective. Professor Alexander Swoboda at the Graduate Institute of International Studies in Geneva, Switzerland contributed important elements to that earlier analysis, and the conclusions he reached are well worth keeping in mind when we contemplate solutions to current problems. This is particularly the case when we discuss choices of exchange rate/monetary policy regimes and when we contemplate the use of economic policies to correct international payments imbalances.

Notes

1 I would like to thank Andrew Filardo and Michael Salemi for valuable comments on a first draft of this chapter.

2 From today's perspective the focus on monetary analysis as the principal source of inflation may seem somewhat quaint, but thirty years ago it was relatively mainstream, even though there was also a spirited debate between monetarists of both types on the one hand and economists who emphasized 'cost-push' and sociological explanations for the resurgence of inflation on the other. In the UK this debate was conducted forcefully by Michael Parkin and David Laidler and their colleagues at Manchester University, with whom the Geneva research group maintained contact at conferences and joint seminars.

3 Of course, it was recognized that Balassa-Samuelson type effects could lead to differences in inflation rates across countries, but that was not something over which the central bank had any control.

4 Genberg (1976).

5 Genberg and Swoboda (1977).

6 Swoboda (1978).

7 Genberg and Swoboda (1981, 1993).

8 In the event, it turned out that deviations from PPP became even larger in the floating rate period (at least in the early part thereof) than it had been during the previous fixed rate period. Genberg (1978).

9 To the extent that central banks have output objectives as well as inflation objectives, the different impact on real income in net importing countries vs. net exporting countries would elicit differences in monetary policy responses to food and energy price shocks, thereby also reducing the cross-country similarity of headline inflation rates.

10 Genberg and Swoboda (1989).

11 For a further analysis see Swoboda (2007).

References

Borio, C. and A. Filardo (2007) 'Globalisation and Inflation: New Cross-country Evidence on the Global Determinants of Domestic Inflation.' BIS Working Paper No. 227, May.

Fischer, S. (2007) 'Exchange Rate Systems, Surveillance, and Advice.' Mundell–Fleming lecture at the Eighth Annual Jacques Polak Research Conference at the IMF, Washington DC, 15 November. Available at www.bis.org/review/r071203c.pdf.

Genberg, H. (1976) 'Aspects of the Monetary Approach to Balance of Payments Theory: An Empirical Study of Sweden.' In Jacob A. Frenkel and Harry G. Johnson (eds), *The Monetary Approach to the Balance of Payments*. London: Allen & Unwin, pp. 298–325.

Genberg, H. (1978) 'Purchasing Power Parity under Fixed and Flexible Exchange Rates,' *Journal of International Economics* 8, 247–276.

Genberg, H. and A. Swoboda (1977) 'Causes and Origins of the Current Worldwide Inflation.' In Erik Lundberg (ed.), *Inflation Theory and Anti-inflation Policy*. London: Macmillan Press, pp. 72–93.

Genberg, H. and A. Swoboda (1981) 'Gold and the Dollar: Asymmetries in World Money Stock Determination, 1959–71.' In R. Cooper, P. Kenen, J. de Macedo, and J. van Ypersele (eds), *The International Monetary System under Flexible Exchange Rates: Global, Regional, and National*, Essays in honor of Robert Triffin. Cambridge: Ballinger, 1981, pp. 235–257.

Genberg, H. and A. Swoboda (1983) 'Fixed Rates, Flexible Rates, of the Middle of the Road: A Re-examination of the Arguments in View of Recent Experience.' Discussion Papers in International Economics 8803, Graduate Institute of International Studies, July. In R. Aliber (ed.), *The Reconstruction of International Monetary Arrangements*. London: Macmillan Press, pp. 92–116.

Genberg, H. and A. Swoboda (1987) 'The Current Account and the Policy Mix under Flexible Exchange Rates.' IMF Working Paper No. 87/70.

Genberg, H. and A. Swoboda (1989) 'Policy and Current Account Determination under Floating Exchange Rates.' International Monetary Fund Staff Papers, Vol. 36, March, pp. 1–30.

Genberg, H. and A. Swoboda (1993) 'The Provision of Liquidity in the Bretton Woods System.' In M. Bordo and B. Eichengreen (eds.), *A Retrospective on the Bretton Woods System*. Chicago, IL: The University of Chicago Press, pp. 269–306.

IMF (2006) *World Economic Outlook: Globalization and Inflation*. Washington, DC: International Monetary Fund, April.

IMF (2007) *World Economic Outlook: Globalization and Inequality*. Washington, DC: International Monetary Fund, October.

Swoboda, A. (1971) 'Equilibrium, Quasi-equilibrium, and Macro-economic Policy under Fixed Exchange Rates.' *Quarterly Journal of Economics* 85, 162–171.

Swoboda, A. (1973) 'Monetary Policy under Fixed Exchange Rates: Effectiveness, the Speed of Adjustment and Proper Use.' *Economica*, New Series 158 (May), 136–154.

Swoboda, A. (1978) 'Gold, Dollars, Euro-dollars, and the World Money Supply under Fixed Exchange Rates.' *American Economic Review* 68(4), 625–642.

Swoboda, A. (2007) 'International Monetary and Financial Architecture in an Integrating World Economy.' In *The Swiss National Bank 1907–2007*. Zurich: Swiss National Bank, pp. 781–814.

4 Inflation targeting and debt crises in the open economy

A note

Olivier Jeanne

1 Introduction

The first time I met Alexander Swoboda was about ten years ago when he was visiting the Research Department of the IMF. Alexander and I collaborated, together with Jeromin Zettelmeyer and Michael Mussa, on an all-encompassing paper on reforming the international financial architecture (Mussa *et al.* 2000). This paper had a big impact – on me at least, since I am still working on the questions that we discussed at that time. This chapter is therefore naturally related to international financial architecture, namely a certain new "conventional wisdom" about the appropriate exchange rate regimes for developing countries. At the risk of oversimplifying, I would define its core elements as follows: (1) inflation targeting is the best nominal anchor for an autonomous monetary policy; (2) however, some countries may prefer to adopt the currency of another country rather than develop an inflation-targeting regime of their own.

This view is consistent with the "polar" or "corner" view of exchange rate regimes, to which Alexander Swoboda was an early contributor (Swoboda 1986; Eichengreen 1994; Fischer 2008). But the new conventional wisdom goes further than simply emphasizing the inherent fragility of a fixed but adjustable exchange rate peg in a world of capital mobility: it also outlines a long-run future for the international monetary system, as a set of inflation-targeting currency areas linked to each other by floating exchange rates. It is not even clear that the world needs coordination mechanisms or institutions to manage such a "system" to the extent that the gains from international monetary coordination are small or difficult to achieve (Rose 2007).

I am going to cast a somewhat critical look on this "new conventional wisdom," but before I do so, let me clarify beforehand that this chapter is not meant as a defense of old-style fixed currency pegs. Fixed but adjustable currency pegs have demonstrated their instability and macro-financial costs on many occasions. By contrast, floating exchange rate *cum* inflation-targeting regimes have so far largely fulfilled the expectations of their proponents. They are more stable than fixed pegs, and they have produced better macro-economic outcomes in the emerging market countries that have adopted them (Rose 2007).

But I think that there are issues related to financial stability that are left unresolved by the inflation targeting paradigm (as it stands).[1] In this chapter I argue that when there is a risk of systemic debt crisis, "flexible inflation targeting"[2] may have implications that seem different from what is usually understood by inflation targeting. I also argue that even in a world composed of inflation-targeting currency areas, international cooperation can play a useful role in insuring countries against financial shocks, so that there remains scope for multilateralism in managing international monetary and financial matters. My arguments are based on a very simple model, to which I now turn.

2 Model

I consider a small open economy in which excessive debt can lead to widespread bankruptcies and a loss of output. Domestic monetary policy can help the domestic economy by inflating away some of the debts (assumed to be denominated in domestic currency).

For simplicity, I assume that there are only two periods ($t = 1, 2$) and one good. The law of one price applies,

$$P_t = S_t + \varepsilon_t, \tag{1}$$

where S_t is the exchange rate at time t (the price of domestic currency in terms of foreign currency) and ε_t is a noise term. In this simple one-good model, ε_t could be interpreted as a shock to the foreign price level or to trading costs, but in a more general multi-goods model it could be interpreted as a shock to the real exchange rate.

Domestic agents have the following utility,

$$u(c, \pi) = c - a\pi^2, \tag{2}$$

where c is period-2 consumption, π is the inflation rate between 1 and 2, and parameter a is the domestic aversion to inflation. The aversion of domestic agents to inflation is simply assumed (it is not micro-founded). The desired inflation rate is normalized to zero without restriction of generality. One question we will look at is whether there is a case for delegating monetary policy to a conservative central banker who is more averse to inflation than the population.

There are two types of domestic agents: entrepreneurs and investors. Entrepreneurs have an investment opportunity in period 1, which they finance by borrowing from investors. For simplicity I assume that there is one investor per entrepreneur. Total population is normalized to 1, so aggregate and per capita variables will be the same.

Each entrepreneur can make an indivisible investment k in period 1 which yields

$$y = Ak, \tag{3}$$

in period 2, where the level of productivity, A, is stochastic. I assume, for simplicity, that A can take two values. Productivity is normally high, $A = A_H > 1$, but with probability p it could be low, $A_L < 1$. The world riskless interest rate is normalized to zero, and the domestic investment opportunities are profitable *ex ante* ($E(A) = (1 - p) A_H + pA_L > 1$). Productivity is perfectly correlated across entrepreneurs, so that a shock to A is an aggregate shock.

Entrepreneurs have no funds in period 1, implying that each entrepreneur must borrow k. I assume that each domestic investor is endowed with $w = k$ so that there is no need for capital inflows to finance domestic investment. The case with capital inflows introduces complications that are interesting but not necessary to make the main points of this chapter.[3] Thus, in period 1, each domestic investor lends k to each domestic entrepreneur.

The entrepreneur promises to repay $d = Rk$ in domestic currency to the investor. Note that debt is nominal: the repayment is specified in terms of domestic currency. The value of the domestic currency is set by the domestic central bank. The period-1 nominal price is irrelevant and normalized to 1. Thus, the period-2 nominal price is equal to 1 plus the inflation rate ($P_2 = 1 + \pi$). The central bank sets π in period 2.

The lending relationship is affected by a friction *à la* Townsend (1979). If the entrepreneur is insolvent ($P_2 y < d$), then there is a bankruptcy in which the creditor recovers $y - \gamma$, where γ is the deadweight cost of a bankruptcy. The entrepreneur recovers nothing in a bankruptcy. Thus, the equilibrium gross interest rate on the debt, R, includes premia for the risks of inflation and default.

A systemic default occurs when the representative entrepreneur is insolvent, that is, if $P_2 y < d$. Using $P_2 = 1 + \pi$, $y = Ak$ and $d = Rk$, this condition can be rewritten as

$$\pi \leq \pi^*(A),$$

where the threshold $\pi^*(A)$ is defined by

$$\pi^*(A) = \frac{R}{A} - 1. \qquad (4)$$

The threshold $\pi^*(A)$ is the minimum level of inflation to avoid a systemic default. If $A_L < R < A_H$ (which is true in equilibrium, as shown in the appendix), then

$$\pi^*(A_H) < 0 < \pi^*(A_L). \qquad (5)$$

This means that if productivity is high the central bank can set the inflation rate at the desired level (zero) at no cost in terms of output. But if productivity is low, the central bank must raise the inflation rate above the desired level in order to avoid a systemic default.

The central bank sets the inflation rate so as to maximize an objective function. For example, it could maximize domestic welfare, defined as the sum of the utilities of domestic investors and entrepreneurs. It is easy to see that domestic welfare is a linear-quadratic function of output per capita and inflation,

$$U = y - a\pi^2. \tag{6}$$

Expression (6) is obtained by summing up $u(c, \pi)$ across domestic investors and entrepreneurs and using the fact that period-2 aggregate consumption is equal to aggregate output (since the country does not borrow or lend abroad in period 1).

Note that (6) is the same type of objective function as in Barro and Gordon's (1983) seminal paper about the time inconsistency problem in monetary policy. The difference with the Barro-Gordon model is that output is influenced by inflation through a financial friction rather than through nominal stickiness. Inflation can increase output, following a bad productivity shock, by avoiding a systemic default.

The aggregate supply schedule is shown in Figure 4.1. Note that the impact of inflation on supply is highly non-linear. If productivity is low and there is a systemic debt crisis, the central bank must raise the inflation rate above a critical threshold in order to have a real impact on the economy. Increasing the inflation rate marginally above the desired level has no effect. This non-linearity implies that the central bank must choose between two corner solutions in a systemic debt crisis: one with high inflation and high output, and one with low inflation and low output.

3 Inflation targeting and debt crises

Before proceeding with a discussion of exchange rate regimes, I would like to digress a little on what this model has to say about inflation targeting. The

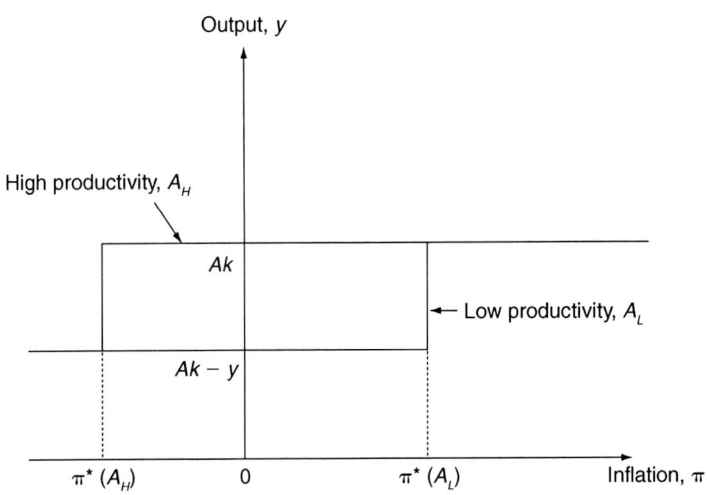

Figure 4.1 Aggregate supply.

equilibrium of the model is derived in the appendix under the assumption that the central bank maximizes domestic welfare (6). As suggested by the discussion above, the central bank's policy reaction function is to implement zero inflation if productivity is high, and a positive rate of inflation (to avoid generalized default) if productivity is low:

$$\begin{cases} \pi = 0 & \text{if } A = A_H, \\ \pi = \pi^*(A_L) > 0 & \text{if } A = A_L. \end{cases} \tag{7}$$

This is the optimal policy reaction if the central bank cares sufficiently about output relative to inflation, i.e., if the inflation aversion parameter a is not too high relative to the output cost of systemic bankruptcy:

$$a\pi^*(A_L)^2 < \gamma. \tag{8}$$

An interesting feature of this model is that, unlike the Barro-Gordon model, it does not give rise to a time consistency problem. If the policy reaction function (7) is optimal *ex post*, then it is also the optimal policy rule *ex ante*. Thus, there is no reason, in this model, to delegate monetary policy-making to a conservative central banker *à la* Rogoff (1985) who is more averse to inflation than the population.[4] Doing so would generate a downward bias in inflation: the conservative central banker will tend to be insufficiently responsive to systemic credit crises, even from an *ex ante* perspective.

How does the policy reaction function (7) compare with an inflation-targeting regime? It is obviously different from *strict* inflation targeting, which would imply that the inflation rate is maintained at zero no matter what happens to output. However, this policy reaction may be interpreted as *flexible* inflation targeting as defined by Svensson. The policy reaction function (7) is exactly what one gets if the central bank announces a target inflation rate of zero, allowing for deviations from the target to accommodate concerns about output captured by the objective function (6). And as I argued above, this objective function is the appropriate one, given that there is no reason for the monetary policy-maker to be more conservative than the population.

Flexible inflation targeting thus implies, in this model, that the central bank envisages to tolerate a rate of inflation substantially higher than the target in a systemic credit crisis. Furthermore, the central bank should choose between high inflation and low output based on the preferences of the population, not that of a conservative central banker. This sounds rather different (to me) from the way that most central bankers think of inflation targeting.

Obviously, the model is simplistic and misses important costs of inflation. First, the reputational costs of inflation are not taken into account. This raises the question of how the central bank can make clear that a temporary increase in inflation in response to a debt crisis does not mean that the inflation target is abandoned in the long run. Second, the model does not take into account the moral hazard (or other distortions) that may be generated by the fact that the central bank effectively insures firms against the consequences of bad productivity shocks.[5] The broader point, however, carries through: in a systemic debt crisis, a regime of flexible inflation targeting (properly understood) may put more weight on output stabilization and less weight on inflation than one might think.

4 Exchange rate regimes: the polar view

What are the implications of the model for exchange rates and exchange rate regimes? Using (1) and $P_2 = 1 + \pi$, the second-period exchange rate is given by

$$S_2 = 1 + \pi - \varepsilon_2.$$

Thus, under **flexible inflation targeting**, the exchange rate is floating for two reasons: because of the shocks to the law of one price (ε_2), and because the exchange rate depreciates in a debt crisis resolved by high inflation ($\pi > 0$). Using (6) *ex ante* domestic welfare is given by

$$U^{float} = U^{fb} - pa\pi^*(A_L)^2, \tag{9}$$

where $U^{fb} = E(A)k$ is the first-best level of welfare, i.e., the expected level of output if there is no risk of default.

One may compare the floating regime with the following two regimes:

1 **Full dollarization.** Then $S_2 = 1$, which implies

$$\pi = \varepsilon_2.$$

Inflation is low, but variable, and in a way that it is dictated by foreign conditions. This regime does not offer any insurance against a debt crisis if ε_2 is uncorrelated with A. Domestic welfare is given by

$$U^{dol} = U^{fb} - p\gamma - aVar(\varepsilon). \tag{10}$$

2 **Fixed peg with escape clause.** This regime is a combination of the previous two. The fixed peg $S_2 = 1$ is maintained if productivity is high, and the currency is depreciated to the level ensuring no default if productivity is low. The advantage of this regime, relative to dollarization, is that the exchange rate can be depreciated in response to a large negative productivity shock. Then there is no deadweight loss of output, but the inflation rate is still excessively variable.

$$U^{fix} = U^{fb} - pa\pi^*(A_L)^2 - (1 - p)aVar(\varepsilon). \tag{11}$$

Using (8), (9), (10) and (11), it is easy to see that there is a strict Pareto ranking between the three regimes,

$$U^{float} > U^{fix} > U^{dol}.$$

This ranking simply reflects the benefits of flexibility. Inflation targeting with floating dominates the other two regimes, and a fixed peg with an escape clause is better than full dollarization.

However, the ranking might be different if the credibility of the regimes were less than perfect. To see this, let us assume that the announced regime is implemented with probability μ (the credibility of the regime). With probability $1 - \mu$ the monetary authorities implement a stochastic rate of inflation that is uncorrelated with A. By construction, dollarization is irreversible and so it is perfectly credible ($\mu^{dol} = 1$). But the same is not true for the other two regimes. In the limit where credibility is equal to zero ($\mu = 0$), those regimes compound variable inflation with a high risk of systemic default.

Figure 4.2 shows how domestic welfare depends on the level of credibility under the different regimes. For low credibility, full dollarization dominates, and the reason is precisely that this regime is completely credible. By contrast, for a given sufficiently high level of credibility, inflation targeting dominates. The interesting point is that the intermediate regime (currency peg with escape clause) is always dominated by one of the other two regimes. Thus the country should either float or dollarize, never peg, which is the polar view.

One might argue that the comparison is unfair, because it assumes the same level of credibility for inflation targeting as for the fixed peg. One view is that a floating exchange rate is intrinsically less credible because it does not offer the same clear nominal anchor as a fixed peg, that is,[6]

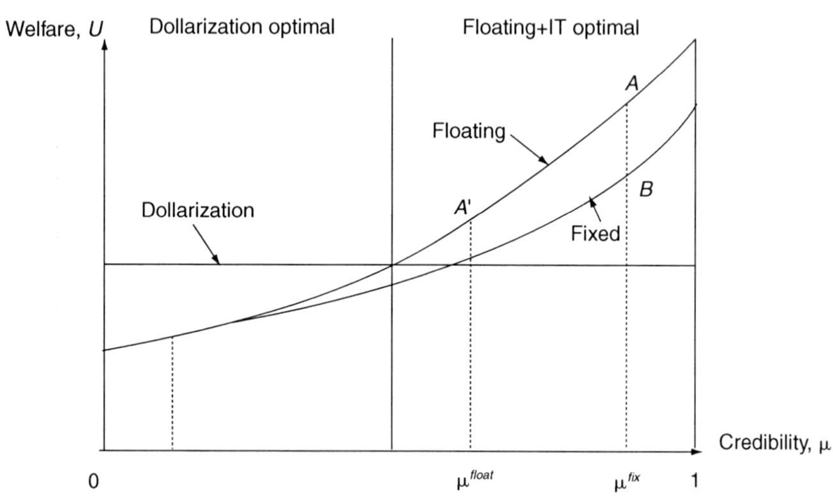

Figure 4.2 Welfare comparison of exchange rate regimes.

$$\mu^{float} < \mu^{fix}.$$

Thus, in terms of Figure 4.2, the appropriate comparison should be between B and A', rather than between B and A, so that a fixed peg could dominate floating.

However, this argument is not very convincing from a theoretical or an empirical point of view. First, one might argue that floating (cum inflation targeting) is intrinsically more credible than a fixed peg precisely because it yields a higher level of welfare – and so is less costly to maintain – for any given level of credibility.[7] Second, the evidence suggests that an inflation targeting regime does a reasonably good job of providing a credible nominal anchor, even in developing countries with a recent history of monetary instability. This is not to say that inflation targeting regimes cannot be vulnerable to the same kinds of vicious circles (in which low credibility feeds on itself in a self-fulfilling way) as fixed pegs. But both theory and experience suggest that they are less prone to those problems.

5 International financial insurance

As a way of concluding this chapter, I would like to question Rose's (2007) idea that international cooperation becomes much less relevant in a world where all countries target inflation and let their exchange rates float. My point will be that even in such a world, there is scope for cooperation to enhance financial stability, and this has implications for exchange rates.

Assume that a number of countries like the one described above have established perfectly credible inflation targeting regimes (Rose's "end of history"). Then the *ex ante* welfare of each country would be given by U^{it}, which is the highest level of welfare we have seen so far. Is it not possible to do better?

The answer is yes, if the productivity risk is diversifiable across countries. Then the welfare of each country could be increased to the first-best level by a crisis insurance mechanism that transfers resources from high-productivity countries to low-productivity countries.[8]

To keep things simple, let us assume that the productivity risk is perfectly diversifiable across countries. Then a fraction p of the countries have low productivity and each one of these countries receives a transfer θ from high-productivity countries. The transfer costs $\frac{p}{1-p}\theta$ to each high-productivity country. Since $E(A) > 1$, it is possible to find a level of θ such that the entrepreneurs in all countries are solvent, i.e.,

$$A_L k + \theta \geq 1,$$

$$A_H k - \frac{p}{1-p}\theta \geq 1.$$

With such an arrangement, all entrepreneurs are guaranteed their expected level of productivity and there is no risk of systemic bankruptcy. Monetary policy, being relieved of the burden of dealing with financial instability, can focus on strict inflation targeting (leading to more stable exchange rates). Hence, the first-best level of welfare, U^{fb}, is achieved by all countries.

This is, again, a simplistic piece of analysis. I am glossing over important issues, such as moral hazard. But I think that there is a more general theme behind this simplistic example. A lot is asked from monetary policy, especially in times of financial instability, and there might be a scarcity of policy instruments relative to the number of objectives – a point also made by Charles Goodhart (Chapter 9, this volume). This is not a weakness of inflation targeting relative to other monetary regimes, but it is certainly a critique of the idea that the inflation targeting framework resolves all the main issues faced by monetary policymakers. There is a need for thinking of monetary policy in the context of a wider framework that also includes financial stability in its objectives. The point I am trying to conclude with is that such a framework may have a strong international, multilateral dimension.

Appendix

The purpose of this appendix is to characterize the equilibriums of the model, and to prove the statements made in the text. We first consider a discretionary equilibrium in which the central bank solves for the optimal inflation rate *ex post* (in period 2). The equilibrium gross interest rate R^* must solve the following fixed-point problem. Given R and A, the optimal policy reaction function $\pi(R, A)$ is the level of inflation that maximizes domestic welfare (6) subject to the supply schedule. Then R^* must satisfy the zero-profit condition of lenders which, using $P_2 = 1 + \pi$, $y = Ak$, and $d = Rk$, can be written as:

$$1 = E\left[(1 - \delta(R, A))\frac{R}{1 + \pi(R, A)} + \delta(R, A)\left(A - \frac{\gamma}{k}\right)\right], \qquad (12)$$

where $\delta(R, A)$ is the dummy variable for a systemic default (equal to 1 if $\pi(R, A) < R/A - 1$, and to zero if not).

The policy reaction function $\pi(R, A)$ maximizes $U = y - a\pi^2$ subject to the supply schedule

$$\begin{cases} y = Ak & \text{if } \pi \geq \pi^*(A) = R/A - 1, \\ y = Ak - \gamma & \text{if } \pi < \pi^*(A). \end{cases}$$

There are two cases to consider:

- $\underline{R \leq A}$: then there is no trade-off between output and inflation; inflation can be set at its desired level at no cost in terms of output ($\pi = 0$ and $y = Ak$).
- $\underline{R > A}$: then there is a trade-off between output and inflation: the central bank either inflates ($\pi = R/A - 1$ and $y = Ak$) or implements the desired inflation target ($\pi = 0$ and $y = Ak - \gamma$). The former course of action is preferred if

$$a\left(\frac{R}{A}-1\right)^2 < \gamma. \tag{13}$$

We necessarily have $R^* > A_L$ since $A_L < 1$. But a priori, R^* could be larger or smaller than A_H. First, let us look for equilibriums in which $R^* \leq A_H$. Then if the risk aversion parameter a is not too high (i.e., condition (13) is satisfied for $A = A_L$), the policy reaction function is given by (7). The lenders' zero-profit condition (12) then reduces to

$$1 = (1-p)R^* + pA_L,$$

which yields a closed form expression for the equilibrium gross interest rate,

$$R^* = 1 + \frac{p}{1-p}(1-A_L). \tag{14}$$

Using this expression and $A = A_L$ to substitute out R^* and A from (13) gives a condition on the exogenous parameters of the model,

$$a < \gamma\left(\frac{(1-p)A_L}{1-A_L}\right)^2. \tag{15}$$

Note that (14) implies $R^* < A_H$ since $E(A) > 1$. Thus, if (15) is satisfied, there is an equilibrium in which the policy reaction function is given by (7).

Can there be an equilibrium in which $R^* > A_H$? In such an equilibrium the creditors receive either Ak (if the central bank inflates) or $Ak - \gamma$ (if the central bank does not inflate). Such an equilibrium does not exist in pure strategies because the right-hand side of (12) does not depend on R. There could exist, however, equilibriums with mixed strategies, in which the central bank randomizes over π in the high-productivity state or the low-productivity state. In those equilibriums the level of R is such that the central bank is indifferent between inflating or not, i.e., condition (13) is an equality. Those mixed-strategy equilibriums are Pareto dominated by the pure strategy equilibrium (7).

Next, let us consider the optimal policy rule, in which the central bank announces *ex ante* a policy function $\pi(R, A)$. Then one can see that a rule cannot yield a strictly higher level of welfare than in the pure strategy equilibrium (7). The only reason that a rule might dominate discretion is that the policy-maker takes into account that R is affected *ex ante* by the rule. However, a rule cannot produce an equilibrium interest rate that is not the same as under discretion. The equilibrium interest rate under the optimal rule cannot be smaller than $A_L < 1$, nor larger than A_H (otherwise it would be dominated by discretion). But if $A_L < R < A_H$, it is easy to see that the optimal rule coincides with the discretionary solution, i.e., inflate if and only if productivity is low. Hence, the equilibrium R must be the same as under discretion. However, a rule could help eliminate the inefficient mixed-strategy equilibriums mentioned above.

Notes

1 Charles Goodhart develops a similar theme (see Chapter 9, this volume). Kumhof *et al.* (2007) show that inflation-targeting regimes may be vulnerable to speculative attacks when there is fiscal dominance and fiscal policy is inconsistent with the inflation target. See also Bordo and Jeanne (2002) for an analysis of the dilemmas faced by monetary policy-makers in credit boom/bust episodes that is closely related to the one in this chapter.

2 As defined by Lars Svensson, i.e., as a targeting rule that maximizes an explicit objective function capturing concerns about the real economy in addition to inflation. See Svensson (2000) for an analysis of flexible inflation targeting in a small open economy.

3 These complications come from the fact that the domestic government may be tempted to expropriate foreign holders of domestic currency debt through inflation. The consequences of this have been discussed elsewhere (see, e.g., Tirole 2002). In particular, foreign creditors may protect themselves from expropriation by denominating their claims in foreign currency, leading to liability dollarization. Of course, dollarization reduces the country's ability to resolve a debt crisis by domestic inflation.

4 As shown in the appendix, there is one caveat to this statement. The commitment to a policy rule may help eliminate a bad equilibrium in which a high probability of debt crisis is self-fulfilling.

5 Those distortions are discussed in Jeanne (2008). To the extent that the insurance does not involve an *ex post* transfer from a third party (but a transfer between the contracting parties), it does not create moral hazard *stricto sensu*. However, the insurance involves an externality that may lead to excessive inflation and inefficient herding in investment. As I argue in my other paper, those distortions are difficult to address in the context of a narrowly defined inflation targeting framework (i.e., in which interest rate setting is not augmented by other policy instruments).

6 See Calvo and Reinhart (2000) for a discussion of various problems posed by floating exchange rates in emerging market countries.

7 This would be the prediction of an escape-clause model with an optimizing policy-maker (aka "second-generation" model of currency crisis) of the type reviewed by Jeanne (2000).

8 Alternatively, the countries could establish in period 1 a fund that bails out the entrepreneurs of the countries that have low productivity in period 2. Although this may be reminiscent of an institution such as the IMF, it is important to keep in mind that the IMF operates under different rules (it lends, does not make transfers; and its lending should be motivated by some balance-of-payments problems rather than domestic financial crises). An analysis of how the IMF can help in the context of my model requires a slightly more involved analysis.

References

Barro, Robert and David Gordon (1983) "A Positive Theory of Monetary Policy in a Natural Rate Model," *Journal of Political Economy* 91, 589–610.

Bordo, Michael and Olivier Jeanne (2002) "Monetary Policy and Asset Prices: Does Benign Neglect Make Sense?," *International Finance* 5, 139–164.

Calvo, Guillermo and Carmen Reinhart (2000) "Fear of Floating," *Quarterly Journal of Economics* 107, 379–408.

Eichengreen, Barry (1994) *International Monetary Arrangements for the 21st Century*, Washington, DC: The Brookings Institution.

Fischer, Stanley (2008) "Mundell–Fleming Lecture: Exchange Rate Systems, Surveillance and Advice," IMF *Staff Papers* 55, 367–383.

Jeanne, Olivier (2000) "Currency Crises: A Perspective on Recent Developments," *Special Papers in International Economics* 20, International Finance Section, Princeton University, Princeton, NJ.

Jeanne, Olivier (2008) "What Inflation Targeting Means in the Credit Crunch," unpublished paper, Johns Hopkins University.

Kumhof, Michael, Li, Shujing, and Isabel Yan (2007) "Balance of Payments Crises Under Inflation Targeting," IMF Working Paper 07/84, Washington, DC.

Mussa, Michael, Alexander Swoboda, Jeromin Zettelmeyer, and Olivier Jeanne (2000) "Moderating Fluctuations in Capital Flows to Emerging Market Economies." In P. Kenen and A. Swoboda (eds), *Key Issues in Reform of the International Monetary and Financial System*, Washington, DC: IMF, pp. 75–142.

Rogoff, Kenneth (1985) "The Optimal Degree of Commitment to an Intermediate Monetary Target," *Quarterly Journal of Economics* 100, 1169–1189.

Rose, Andrew K. (2007) "A Stable International Monetary System Emerges: Inflation Targeting is Bretton Woods Reversed," *Journal of International Money and Finance* 26, 663–681.

Svensson, Lars E. O. (2000) "Open-economy Inflation Targeting," *Journal of International Economics* 50, 155–183.

Swoboda, Alexander (1986) "Credibility and Viability in International Monetary Arrangements," *Finance and Development* 23, 15–18.

Tirole, Jean (2002) *Financial Crises, Liquidity and the International Monetary System*. Princeton, NJ: Princeton University Press.

Townsend, Robert (1979) "Optimal Contracts and Competitive Markets With Costly State Verification," *Journal of Economic Theory* 21, 265–293.

5 Exchange rate regimes and capital mobility

How much of the Swoboda thesis survives?[1]

Barry Eichengreen

1 Introduction

Alexander Swoboda is recognized for many important contributions to exchange rate economics. One of the less known is the fact that he is the father (grandfather? godfather?) of the bipolar view – that is, of the idea that capital mobility creates pressure for countries to abandon intermediate exchange rate arrangements in favor of greater flexibility and harder pegs. Looking back on his contributions to this literature (Swoboda 1986; Genberg and Swoboda 1987a, b), it is hard to know whether to group him with the hawks or the doves.[2] The hawks argue that international capital mobility fatally undermines the viability of intermediate regimes. It makes it more difficult to maintain both monetary independence and an exchange rate target. Insofar as monetary independence has value, the result is the adoption of a more flexible exchange rate. And insofar as the stability offered by an exchange rate target has value, the result is a tendency to seek monetary unification with like-minded partners.

While the doves acknowledge that capital mobility complicates the operation of intermediate arrangements, they resist the conclusion that it creates irresistible pressure to move to the poles. As in other economic settings where agents trade off two objectives, an interior solution may be optimal. In the present context this means striving for a degree of monetary independence that is less than complete and a degree of exchange rate stability that is less than perfect. This interior solution will be characterized by managed flexibility. The exchange rate will have to be more flexible than when capital mobility is absent, in which case it is possible to have monetary independence without compromising currency stability, but free flexibility is not required. The middle may have to be defined more liberally – in addition to pegged but adjustable rates and narrow bands it must now include managed floats and wide bands. Subject to this caveat, however, capital mobility does not imply the need to abandon intermediate regimes.

It is unlikely that one more paper will produce a consensus on these contested issues, which have occupied Alexander Swoboda in the course of a long and productive career. However, if nothing else, another look at the data will help the participants in this debate to refine their priors.

2 Another look at the evolution of exchange rate regimes

In this section I take another look at the evolution of practice with respect to exchange rate regimes, using two popular de facto classifications. The first is produced by the staff at the International Monetary Fund. As described by Bubula and Otker-Robe (2002), this classification combines market exchange rates and other quantitative information with assessments of the nature of the regime drawn by IMF economists in the course of bilateral surveillance. Its advantage is that it is independently constructed; the author cannot be accused of having coded country regimes to his liking. This series has now been updated through 2006. Its disadvantage is that, based as it is in part on input from the IMF's country economists, this series is not easily extended. The second classification is that of Reinhart and Rogoff (2004), who provide a detailed description of their methods. This classification has been updated by the author in collaboration with Raul Razo-Garcia.[3] Somewhat arbitrarily, most of the analysis here is conducted using the Bubula and Otker-Robe calculation.[4] Statements below refer to this classification except where noted to the contrary.

Table 5.1 documents the decline in intermediate regimes since 1990. For the full sample of countries, the share of intermediate regimes (fixed pegs to a single currency, fixed pegs to a basket, currencies pegged within horizontal bands, forward-looking crawling pegs, forward-looking crawling bands, backward-looking crawling pegs, backward-looking crawling bands and other lightly managed floats) falls from about 70 percent in 1990 to about 45 percent in 2004. The evacuees move to hard pegs and floats in roughly equal proportions.

Beneath these regularities are contrasts between the advanced countries, emerging markets, and developing countries.[5] Among the advanced countries, intermediate regimes have essentially disappeared. (The one country still classified as operating a soft peg is Denmark.) This supports the bipolar view for the countries for which it was first developed. Within this subgroup the dominant movement has been toward hard pegs, reflecting monetary unification in Europe.

Although emerging markets have also seen a decline in the prevalence of intermediate arrangements, these regimes still account for more than one-third of the relevant subsample (41 percent in 2006, down from 77 percent in 1990). Here the majority of the evacuees have moved to floats rather than fixes, reflecting the absence of EMU-like arrangements in other parts of the world.[6] But it is apparent that the move away from intermediate regimes among these countries has slowed and even reversed in recent years. The same pattern is evident in Table 5.2 for the Reinhart-Rogoff classification.[7] There is a secular trend away from intermediate regimes, albeit one that has slowed and even reversed in recent years.[8]

The prevalence of intermediate regimes has again declined among developing countries. Where these regimes accounted for two-thirds of the developing country subsample in 1990 (Table 5.1), they account for a little more than half today (55 percent of the total in 2006, down from 64 percent in 1990). As with emerging markets, the majority of those abandoning the middle have moved to floats rather than to hard pegs.

Table 5.1 Evolution of exchange rate regimes: Bubula/Otker-Robe classification (percentage of members in each category)

	Shares																
	1990	*1991*	*1992*	*1993*	*1994*	*1995*	*1996*	*1997*	*1998*	*1999*	*2000*	*2001*	*2002*	*2003*	*2004*	*2005*	*2006*
All countries																	
Hard pegs[1]	16.88	17.31	20.45	17.32	17.78	18.23	18.23	20.33	20.33	25.82	26.37	26.92	26.92	26.92	26.92	26.92	26.92
Soft pegs[2]	67.53	64.74	55.68	56.98	55.00	56.91	56.91	51.10	46.70	39.56	40.11	37.91	38.46	37.91	39.56	43.96	45.60
Floating[3]	15.58	17.95	23.86	25.70	27.22	24.86	24.86	28.57	32.97	34.62	33.52	35.16	34.62	35.16	33.52	29.12	27.47
Total	100	100	100	100	100	100	100	100	100	100	100	100	100	100	100	100	100
Members	154	156	176	179	180	181	181	182	182	182	182	182	182	182	182	182	182
Advanced																	
Hard pegs[1]	4.35	4.35	8.33	8.33	8.33	8.33	8.33	8.33	8.33	50.00	50.00	54.17	54.17	54.17	54.17	54.17	54.17
Soft pegs[2]	69.57	69.57	45.83	50.00	50.00	50.00	58.33	54.17	54.17	12.50	12.50	4.17	4.17	4.17	4.17	4.17	4.17
Floating[3]	26.09	26.09	45.83	41.67	41.67	41.67	33.33	37.50	37.50	37.50	37.50	41.67	41.67	41.67	41.67	41.67	41.67
Total	100	100	100	100	100	100	100	100	100	100	100	100	100	100	100	100	100
Members	23	23	24	24	24	24	24	24	24	24	24	24	24	24	24	24	24
Emerging markets																	
Hard pegs[1]	6.67	10.00	9.68	9.38	9.38	9.38	9.38	12.50	12.50	12.50	15.63	12.50	12.50	12.50	12.50	12.50	12.50
Soft pegs[2]	76.67	66.67	64.52	75.00	68.75	81.25	78.13	56.25	53.13	40.63	37.50	34.38	34.38	34.38	34.38	40.63	40.63
Floating[3]	16.67	23.33	25.81	15.63	21.88	9.38	12.50	31.25	34.38	46.88	46.88	53.13	53.13	53.13	53.13	46.88	46.88
Total	100	100	100	100	100	100	100	100	100	100	100	100	100	100	100	100	100
Members	30	30	31	32	32	32	32	32	32	32	32	32	32	32	32	32	32
Other developing																	
Hard pegs[1]	22.77	22.33	25.62	21.14	21.77	22.40	22.40	24.60	24.60	24.60	24.60	25.40	25.40	25.40	25.40	25.40	25.40
Soft pegs[2]	64.36	63.11	55.37	53.66	52.42	52.00	51.20	49.21	43.65	44.44	46.03	45.24	46.03	45.24	47.62	52.38	54.76
Floating[3]	12.87	14.56	19.01	25.20	25.81	25.60	26.40	26.19	31.75	30.95	29.37	29.37	28.57	29.37	26.98	22.22	19.84
Total	100	100	100	100	100	100	100	100	100	100	100	100	100	100	100	100	100
Members	101	103	121	123	124	125	125	126	126	126	126	126	126	126	126	126	126

Notes

1 Includes arrangements with another currency as legal tender, currency union and currency board and monetary union/monetary association.

2 Includes conventional fixed peg to a single currency, conventional fixed peg to a basket, pegged within horizontal bands, forward-looking crawling peg, forward-looking crawling band, backward-looking crawling peg, backward-looking crawling band and other tightly managed floating.

3 Includes managed floating with no predetermined path for the exchange rate and independently floating.

How will the constellation of regimes look in twenty years' time if present trends continue? This question may be answered by using a simple Markov chain model, as in Masson (2001) and Eichengreen and Razo-Garcia (2006), to estimate the probability of regime transitions. This assumes that the past is a guide to the future and that the probability of being in a regime in the next period depends only on the current regime.[9] For the sample as a whole (Bubula and Otker-Robe classification), the most persistent state is a hard peg, followed by the intermediate and, last, floating regimes (Table 5.3). There is no absorbing state and hence no tendency for countries to converge to a single regime or subset of regimes. The last line of the table shows the distribution of regimes if current trends continue for another twenty years. This suggests that in two decades 30 percent of countries will have pegs, 30 percent will have floats, and 40 percent will have intermediate arrangements. Compared to the current constellation, the share of intermediate regimes will have declined further, but only modestly.

The picture looks different when calculations are done separately for advanced countries, emerging markets, and developing economies. Among the advanced countries, intermediate arrangements are the least persistent while hard pegs are an absorbing state. This, of course, is just another way of saying that no country that joined EMU since 1999 has left.[10] By 2025, the share of floaters is forecast to decline from 40 percent to 30 percent of the advanced country subsample, one imagines through the adoption of the euro by additional countries.[11]

Among emerging markets and developing countries, in contrast, hard pegs are the most persistent regime, followed by intermediate arrangements and then floats; note that this is a different pattern than for the advanced countries.[12] Here there is no strong support for the bipolar view. The Markov chain analysis suggests that the share of emerging markets and developing countries with floating rates will actually be lower in 2025 than today, reversing the trend in recent decades. This reflects the fact that intermediate arrangements are more persistent than flexible regimes in this subsample. They may be adopted infrequently, but once adopted they persist. Thus, this analysis does not suggest that intermediate regimes will disappear any time soon outside the OECD.

At the same time, the contrast between the advanced, emerging and developing countries suggests that there is a tendency to move away from intermediate regimes in the course of economic and financial (and political?) development. To the extent that this is true, one can imagine that the phenomenon of the hollow middle will eventually spread from the now advanced countries to the rest of the world. One interpretation is that economic development, in practice, is associated with financial liberalization and the removal of capital controls, which heighten the fragility of intermediate regimes and prompt movement to the poles. This suggests that if developing countries follow their advanced country counterparts in pursuing financial and capital account liberalization, they will also follow them in abandoning intermediate regimes. Compared to other developing countries, emerging markets both have more open capital accounts and a greater tendency to abandon intermediate regimes (relative openness to foreign investment being how the emerging markets category is defined), consistent with this view.

Table 5.2 Evolution of exchange rate regimes: Reinhart Rogoff classification (percentage of members in each category)

	Shares																	
	1990	*1991*	*1992*	*1993*	*1994*	*1995*	*1996*	*1997*	*1998*	*1999*	*2000*	*2001*	*2002*	*2003*	*2004*	*2005*	*2006*	*2007*
All countries																		
Hard pegs[1]	22.31	20.77	20.46	20.00	21.32	22.14	22.63	23.91	23.40	31.92	31.92	33.33	33.33	33.57	33.57	32.86	32.86	33.57
Soft pegs[2]	46.28	46.92	45.46	48.89	50.74	54.29	56.20	51.45	48.94	40.43	39.72	37.59	34.04	36.43	37.14	40.00	38.57	38.57
Floating[3]	15.70	10.77	10.61	10.37	8.09	10.00	13.14	13.77	17.73	20.57	23.40	24.82	28.37	27.14	27.86	26.43	27.86	26.43
Freely falling	15.70	21.54	23.49	20.74	19.85	13.57	8.03	10.87	9.93	7.09	4.96	4.26	4.26	2.86	1.43	0.71	0.71	1.43
Total	100	100	100	100	100	100	100	100	100	100	100	100	100	100	100	100	100	100
Members	121	130	132	135	136	140	137	138	141	141	141	141	141	140	140	140	140	140
Advanced																		
Hard pegs[1]	4.35	4.35	0.00	0.00	0.00	0.00	0.00	0.00	0.00	47.83	47.83	52.17	52.17	52.17	52.17	52.17	52.17	52.17
Soft pegs[2]	73.91	73.91	56.52	65.22	65.22	65.22	65.22	65.22	65.22	21.74	17.39	13.04	8.70	8.70	13.04	13.04	13.04	13.04
Floating[3]	21.74	21.74	34.78	34.78	34.78	34.78	34.78	34.78	34.78	30.44	34.78	34.78	39.13	39.13	34.78	34.78	34.78	34.78
Freely falling	0.00	0.00	8.70	0.00	0.00	0.00	0.00	0.00	0.00	0.00	0.00	0.00	0.00	0.00	0.00	0.00	0.00	0.00
Total	100	100	100	100	100	100	100	100	100	100	100	100	100	100	100	100	100	100
Members	23	23	23	23	23	23	23	23	23	23	23	23	23	23	23	23	23	23

Emerging markets																		
Hard pegs[1]	10.00	10.00	9.68	10.00	10.00	9.38	9.38	12.50	15.63	15.63	18.75	18.75	15.63	15.63	15.63	12.50	12.50	12.50
Soft pegs[2]	60.00	60.00	61.29	70.00	73.33	68.75	71.88	50.00	50.00	43.75	40.63	34.38	34.38	37.50	40.63	46.88	46.88	50.00
Floating[3]	10.00	6.67	0.00	0.00	0.00	3.13	9.38	21.88	25.00	37.50	40.63	40.63	40.63	46.88	43.75	40.63	40.63	37.50
Freely falling	20.00	23.33	29.03	20.00	16.67	18.75	9.38	15.63	9.38	3.13	0.00	6.25	9.38	0.00	0.00	0.00	0.00	0.00
Total	100	100	100	100	100	100	100	100	100	100	100	100	100	100	100	100	100	100
Members	30	30	31	30	30	32	32	32	32	32	32	32	32	32	32	32	32	32
Other developing																		
Hard pegs[1]	33.82	29.87	30.77	29.27	31.33	32.94	33.74	34.52	32.56	33.72	32.56	33.72	34.88	35.29	35.29	35.29	35.29	36.47
Soft pegs[2]	30.88	33.77	35.90	36.59	38.55	45.88	46.99	47.62	44.19	44.19	45.35	45.35	40.70	43.53	42.35	44.71	42.35	41.18
Floating[3]	16.18	9.09	7.69	7.32	3.61	5.88	8.43	5.95	10.47	11.63	13.95	16.28	20.93	16.47	20.00	18.82	21.18	20.00
Freely falling	19.12	27.27	25.64	26.83	26.51	15.29	10.84	11.91	12.79	10.47	8.14	4.65	3.49	4.71	2.35	1.18	1.18	2.35
Total	100	100	100	100	100	100	100	100	100	100	100	100	100	100	100	100	100	100
Members	68	77	78	82	83	85	83	84	86	86	86	86	86	85	85	85	85	85

Source: Author's estimates using Reinhart and Rogoff's exchange rate classification.

Notes

1 Includes arrangements with no separate legal tender, pre-announced peg or currency boards, and pre-announced horizontal band that is narrower than or equal to +/–2%.

2 Includes de facto pegs, de facto crawling band that is narrower than or equal to +/–2%, pre-announced crawling band that is wider than or equal to +/–2%, de facto crawling band that is narrower than or equal to +/–5%, moving band that is narrower than or equal to +/–2% (i.e., allows for both appreciation and depreciation over time), pre-announced crawling peg, pre-announced crawling band that is narrower than or equal to +/–2%, and de facto crawling peg.

3 Includes managed floating and freely floating arrangements.

Table 5.3 Transition probability from period t to period t + 1

Regime in period t	*Hard peg*	*Intermediate*	*Floating*	*Total observations*
All countries				
Hard peg	98.92	0.31	0.77	648
Intermediate	1.08	91.74	7.18	1,392
Floating	0.37	10.12	89.51	820
Total				2,860
Forecast 2025	31.47	38.97	29.56	
Advanced countries				
Hard peg	100.00	0.00	0.00	105
Intermediate	8.46	86.15	5.38	130
Floating	0.00	2.04	97.96	147
Total				382
Forecast 2025	62.35	5.11	32.55	
Emerging market countries				
Hard peg	98.25	0.00	1.75	57
Intermediate	0.00	88.45	11.55	277
Floating	1.73	12.14	86.13	173
Total				507
Forecast 2025	20.38	41.56	38.14	
Other developing countries				
Hard peg	98.77	0.41	0.82	486
Intermediate	0.41	93.40	6.19	985
Floating	0.00	11.80	88.20	500
Total				1,971
Forecast 2025	23.60	49.35	27.05	

Not everyone will agree that the further relaxation of capital controls is inevitable or even probable. Financial globalization has been reversed before in response to economic and political turbulence. Since renewed turbulence cannot be ruled out, neither can reversals. That said, many observers will agree that financial development, as it proceeds, shifts the balance of costs and benefits between capital account restrictions and capital account liberalization, in part by creating new avenues for evading controls (thereby rendering their effective operation more costly) while dampening at least partially the volatility against which controls are intended to protect. In this view, there is little question that developing countries will eventually follow the developed world in the direction of more openness to capital flows, although there remains the question of how quickly this will happen.

Another interpretation is that the advanced countries have been faster to abandon soft pegs because they have been faster to develop alternatives. Europe's alternative is Economic and Monetary Union (EMU). Two emerging markets (Slovenia and Slovakia) are now members of EMU. There are monetary unions in the developing world, notably in the East Caribbean and West Africa.[13]

That said, most developing countries do not have an appealing monetary union option to lure them away from intermediate regimes, although one day, perhaps, with further economic, financial and political development, they will.

But another alternative to a pegged exchange rate as an anchor for monetary policy is inflation targeting. A number of advanced countries and emerging markets have been able to move away from soft pegs by installing this alternative approach to the formulation and conduct of monetary policy that ensures not only price stability but also a reasonably well-behaved exchange rate. This argument is developed further below.

3 Determinants of exchange rate regime choice

This section inquires into the determinants of exchange rate regime choice. The point of departure for this analysis is the theory of optimum currency areas, which points to country size, openness, and the asymmetry of shocks, among other variables, as shaping the choice between pegging and floating and – in the present context – between hard pegs, intermediate regimes, and floats. It follows a previous attempt by Bayoumi and Eichengreen (1997) to bring that theory to the data. To explore the availability of alternatives to soft pegs, it follows Eichengreen and Taylor (2004) by extending this framework to incorporate the prerequisites for inflation targeting.

The focus is on the variability of the exchange rate between a pair of countries (as implicit in much of the optimum currency area literature). The exchange rate arrangement is measured by the volatility of the nominal bilateral rate over (centered) five-year periods.[14] The results of analyzing real rates are very similar, since price levels display inertia and most of the variability in real rates over periods of five years or less derives from the variability of nominal rates. In focusing on actual exchange rate variability as a measure of the regime, the analysis parallels Ghosh *et al.* (2003). Insofar as actual variability is the most important single consideration in most de facto regime classifications, it is consistent with the analysis in Section 2 above.

The basic specification relates the variability of the exchange rate to two measures of asymmetric shocks: the difference or asymmetry of output shocks (measured as the standard deviation of the difference in the change in logGDP between the two countries), and the similarity or dissimilarity of export structures (as measured by the sum of the absolute differences in the shares of agriculture, mineral, and manufacturing trade in total merchandise trade). In addition, I consider the importance of bilateral trade linkages (measured as exports to the partner country, scaled by GDP, and averaged over the two countries) and the transaction costs associated with having a relatively variable exchange rate (which are assumed to decline with country size, measured here by the log of the product of real GDP of the two countries, in dollars).[15]

There is close conformance between the predictions of the theory and the results for the full sample (column 1 of Table 5.4). Countries with more dissimilar output movements have more variable bilateral rates. Countries whose export

Table 5.4 Determinants of the volatility of the bilateral exchange rate: 1983–2005

Variables	*All countries*					*Advanced*[a]					*Emerging markets*[b]				
	[1]	[2]	[3]	[4]	[5][d]	[6]	[7]	[8]	[9]	[10][d]	[11]	[12]	[13]	[14]	[15][d]
Variability of output	2.3077	1.1822	0.2723	0.2459	–0.0238	0.1227	–0.0372	–0.0326	–0.0208	0.0275	3.0342	1.5940	0.2719	0.2509	0.3122
(SD (lnYi-lnYj))	0.0493	0.0629	0.0216	0.0219	0.0438	0.0295	0.0568	0.0567	0.0567	0.0533	0.0931	0.1013	0.0316	0.0320	0.0641
Dissimilarity of	0.0042	0.0019	0.0007	0.0007	0.0020	0.0021	0.0013	0.0013	0.0013	0.0018	0.0029	0.0022	0.0006	0.0007	0.0009
exports	0.0002	0.0002	0.0001	0.0001	0.0001	0.0001	0.0002	0.0002	0.0002	0.0002	0.0004	0.0004	0.0001	0.0001	0.0002
Trade ratio	–0.0174	–0.0080	0.0017	0.0010	–0.0052	–0.0085	–0.0039	–0.0043	–0.0044	–0.0050	–0.0154	0.0123	–0.0058	–0.0062	–0.0037
	0.0014	0.0021	0.0007	0.0007	0.0010	0.0005	0.0008	0.0008	0.0008	0.0008	0.0027	0.0065	0.0020	0.0020	0.0018
Size of economy	0.0057	0.0053	0.0000	0.0008	0.0084	0.0160	0.0040	0.0032	0.0040	0.0098	0.0288	0.0106	–0.0051	–0.0030	0.0014
	0.0019	0.0026	0.0009	0.0009	0.0014	0.0007	0.0016	0.0017	0.0017	0.0022	0.0047	0.0048	0.0015	0.0016	0.0028
Capital account		–0.0073	–0.0005	–0.0002	–0.0058		–0.0057	–0.0062	–0.0070	–0.0062		–0.0024	0.0055	0.0058	0.0038
openness[c]		0.0009	0.0003	0.0003	0.0005		0.0009	0.0009	0.0010	0.0017		0.0018	0.0006	0.0006	0.0007
Money ratio		–0.1157	–0.0190	–0.0176	0.0026		0.0119	0.0139	0.0130	0.0243		–0.1565	–0.0098	–0.0058	–0.0041
		0.0077	0.0027	0.0027	0.0038		0.0048	0.0049	0.0049	0.0048		0.0153	0.0047	0.0048	0.0057
Openness		–0.0006	0.0000	0.0000	–0.0001		–0.0005	–0.0004	–0.0004	0.0000		–0.0007	0.0000	0.0000	0.0000
		0.0001	0.0000	0.0000	0.0000		0.0001	0.0001	0.0001	0.0001		0.0001	0.0000	0.0000	0.0000

Relative growth of		0.3812	0.0437	0.0428	–0.0024		0.0042	0.0048	0.0051	0.0021		0.3672	0.0445	0.0437	–0.0054
money		0.0050	0.0020	0.0020	0.0088		0.0120	0.0119	0.0119	0.0119		0.0070	0.0025	0.0025	0.0104
Variability of U.S.			1.6766	1.6763	1.5374			–0.1110	–0.1166	–0.5142			1.6648	1.6640	1.6131
dollar exchange rate			0.0054	0.0054	0.0128			0.0438	0.0438	0.0534			0.0069	0.0069	0.0131
Inflation targeting				–0.0122	–0.1225				0.0075	0.0347				–0.0118	–0.0021
				0.0017	0.0079				0.0030	0.0080				0.0028	0.0090
Constant	–0.0049	0.1629	–0.0436	–0.0506	–0.0429	–0.1382	0.0911	0.1115	0.1044	0.0097	–0.2276	0.1167	0.0058	–0.0182	–0.0589
	0.0230	0.0316	0.0108	0.0108	0.0179	0.0092	0.0217	0.0231	0.0232	0.0372	0.0542	0.0596	0.0183	0.0192	0.0307
Observations	24,352	12,600	12,600	12,600	6,375	4,164	1,094	1,094	1,094	734	8,064	6,147	6,147	6,147	2,727
R^2	0.12	0.45	0.94	0.94	0.75	0.24	0.30	0.30	0.30	0.45	0.13	0.43	0.95	0.95	0.88

Notes
a Advanced countries versus advanced countries.
b Emerging markets versus emerging markets.
c Brune's capital account openness index excluding exchange rate structure.
d Estimated by IV.
Standard errors are reported below the coefficients. The model controlling for inflation targeting is estimated by IV. In the IV model, inflation targeting was instrumented using the index of corruption perceptions and the exogenous variables.

structures are more dissimilar have more variable bilateral rates. Larger economies have more variable rates. Countries that trade more with one another, on the other hand, have less variable bilateral rates.[16] These effects all carry over when the sample is split between advanced and emerging market countries. All of them continue to hold when the sample is split between the periods before and after the Asia-Russia-LTCM crisis (c.f. Tables 5.5 and 5.6).[17]

The model can be stress tested by adding additional potential determinants of de facto exchange rate arrangements. Countries with better developed financial markets (as measured by the average across the two countries in the M2/GNP ratio) enjoy more stable exchange rates. Where money growth rates diverge across countries, bilateral rates are more variable. Importantly, when these additional determinants are added, none of the central variables in column 1 is altered in terms of sign or significance.

An additional variable of particular interest is a measure of capital account openness. The results here are surprising, in that pairs of countries with relatively open capital account regimes appear to have *less* variable exchange rates, other things being equal. This is contrary to the notion that capital mobility compels movement toward greater flexibility. But capital account openness is not always significant at conventional confidence levels. It also varies across subsamples: it is negative for advanced countries but mostly positive for emerging markets.[18] For the advanced countries, capital account openness may be picking up aspects of financial development not fully captured by the other independent variables but conducive to financial and currency stability. It may also be picking up omitted political determinants of exchange rate variability, including the institutions of the European Union. In the 1980s these mandated the removal of capital controls as part of the single market program while at the same time providing the EMS as a currency stabilization device; at the end of the 1990s they combined open capital markets with the euro – options that were not available to emerging economies. For the latter, there is more evidence of the tradeoff between capital account openness and exchange rate stability predicted by the bipolar view.

Another contrast arises when the variability of the bilateral exchange rate against the dollar is included to measure the global (or regional) exchange rate regime. For the period 1983 to 1997 there is evidence that pegging to the dollar was an effective way for countries to peg to one another. (To put it another way, it appears that limiting the variability of dollar exchange rates was an effective way of limiting the variability of bilateral rates among third countries.) This effect is more strongly evident among emerging markets than among advanced countries. This will not surprise those who are aware of the historical tendency for Asian countries, in particular, to stabilize intra-regional exchange rates by the use of dollar pegs. After 1997 the results for emerging markets remain basically unchanged (long live de facto dollar pegging), but the coefficient for the advanced countries switches sign. For this subsample, greater stability vis-à-vis one another is now associated with less stability vis-à-vis the dollar. This is the monetary union effect: EMU member states have effectively eliminated exchange rate variability among themselves while at the same time, as a result of the greater size and relatively lesser openness to the outside world of their union, learning to tolerate larger dollar fluctuations.

4 Inflation targeting as an alternative to exchange rate targeting

One of the appeals of pegged exchange rates is thus that they provide an anchor and a practical guide for monetary policy. Their corresponding limitation is that the anchor may not be well suited to the structure of the economy or the shocks to which it is subjected. Small countries are essentially forced to import the monetary policy stance of the larger country or countries to which they peg. Inflation targeting has emerged in recent years as an increasingly popular alternative. A stable price level (or a low rate of inflation) becomes the anchor for monetary policy. To implement this framework the central bank must be granted the independence and clear mandate to commit credibly to low inflation. It then issues an inflation forecast, explains how its policy settings map into the specified target, and provides an explanation for instances where the target is missed.[19] These steps should help to anchor market expectations and provide a mechanism for political accountability. Thus, in addition to independence and a mandate for price stability, transparency is required for the credibility of this regime.[20]

It is sometimes said that floating is not a monetary policy strategy; rather, it is the absence of a strategy. Thus, by providing a substitute strategy, inflation targeting should reduce the pressure to target the exchange rate. This suggests a positive relationship between inflation targeting and exchange rate variability as countries reduce their reliance on pegs for the nominal anchor function. Alternatively, one might argue that, in developing countries in particular, where exchange rate-centered monetary policy strategies are likely to be fragile and lack credibility, adopting a more robust and credible alternative like inflation targeting may in fact reduce exchange rate volatility. Insofar as inflation targeting provides a credible anchor for expectations, investors have less reason to believe that current inflation is a leading indicator of future inflation. As expectations become regressive rather than extrapolative, speculation becomes stabilizing. Exchange rates should then settle down.

The fourth and fifth equations in Table 5.4 – and the corresponding specifications for the country and period subsamples – add a dummy variable that equals unity when at least one of the central banks in a country pair is classified as an inflation targeter. Because inflation outcomes are likely to be affected by the behavior of the exchange rate – to put it another way, because countries do not opt for inflation targeting at random – I instrument inflation targeting using a measure of transparency (taken from Transparency International). Policy transparency is an important dimension of a successful inflation targeting strategy, as noted above: it is important both for managing expectations and providing for political accountability. But not all countries are equally capable of implementing policy transparency; where transparency is integral to the functioning of

Table 5.5 Determinants of bilateral exchange rate volatility, 1983–1997

Variables	*All countries*					*Advanced*[a]					*Emerging markets*[b]				
	[1]	[2]	[3]	[4]	[5][d]	[6]	[7]	[8]	[9]	[10][d]	[11]	[12]	[13]	[14]	[15][d]
Variability of output	2.5722	1.5917	0.2315	0.2318	–0.1014	0.2119	–0.0397	–0.0864	–0.0814	0.1351	3.0765	1.8629	0.2098	0.2124	0.2659
(SD (lnYi-lnYj))	0.0689	0.1009	0.0293	0.0294	0.1020	0.0427	0.1669	0.1539	0.1545	0.2422	0.1279	0.1430	0.0425	0.0425	0.1572
Dissimilarity of	0.0051	0.0024	0.0003	0.0002	0.0013	0.0017	0.0003	0.0003	0.0003	0.0011	0.0039	0.0031	0.0006	0.0005	0.0005
exports	0.0003	0.0004	0.0001	0.0001	0.0003	0.0001	0.0003	0.0002	0.0002	0.0004	0.0006	0.0006	0.0002	0.0002	0.0004
Trade ratio	–0.0239	–0.0110	0.0034	0.0034	–0.0002	–0.0094	–0.0070	–0.0057	–0.0057	–0.0081	–0.0192	0.0400	–0.0368	–0.0368	–0.0744
	0.0022	0.0040	0.0012	0.0012	0.0019	0.0007	0.0013	0.0012	0.0012	0.0012	0.0042	0.0239	0.0070	0.0070	0.0112
Size of economy	0.0195	–0.0032	0.0051	0.0051	0.0065	0.0147	0.0009	0.0078	0.0082	0.0361	0.0751	–0.0007	–0.0049	–0.0053	–0.0284
	0.0027	0.0049	0.0014	0.0014	0.0036	0.0009	0.0033	0.0031	0.0032	0.0107	0.0070	0.0085	0.0025	0.0025	0.0076
Capital account		–0.0020	0.0046	0.0046	0.0017		–0.0031	0.0019	0.0017	0.0271		0.0078	0.0082	0.0082	0.0022
openness[c]		0.0017	0.0005	0.0005	0.0011		0.0012	0.0013	0.0013	0.0078		0.0033	0.0010	0.0010	0.0026
Money ratio		–0.1676	–0.0451	–0.0451	–0.0535		–0.0107	–0.0428	–0.0434	0.0074		–0.1832	–0.0154	–0.0158	–0.0511
		0.0146	0.0042	0.0042	0.0080		0.0096	0.0096	0.0097	0.0172		0.0289	0.0085	0.0085	0.0158
Openness		–0.0020	0.0002	0.0002	–0.0008		–0.0007	–0.0011	–0.0011	–0.0009		–0.0024	0.0000	0.0000	–0.0011
		0.0002	0.0001	0.0001	0.0001		0.0003	0.0003	0.0003	0.0006		0.0003	0.0001	0.0001	0.0002

Relative growth of		0.3737	0.0365	0.0365	0.0157		0.0070	−0.0058	−0.0049	0.0541		0.3582	0.0422	0.0422	0.0024
money		0.0062	0.0021	0.0021	0.0149		0.0243	0.0224	0.0226	0.0630		0.0087	0.0030	0.0030	0.0208
Variability of U.S.			1.7195	1.7196	1.7490			0.6199	0.6262	0.6035			1.6818	1.6826	1.8059
dollar exchange rate			0.0062	0.0062	0.0182			0.0702	0.0719	0.2984			0.0084	0.0085	0.0266
Inflation targeting				0.0008	−0.0282				0.0021	0.0529				0.0069	0.0265
				0.0030	0.0093				0.0051	0.0118				0.0062	0.0124
Constant	−0.1774	0.3245	−0.1082	−0.1082	−0.0437	−0.1134	0.1634	0.0380	0.0330	−0.6455	−0.7352	0.3045	0.0079	0.0120	0.3697
	0.0335	0.0609	0.0175	0.0175	0.0461	0.0114	0.0482	0.0467	0.0483	0.1970	0.0814	0.1058	0.0309	0.0311	0.0949
Observations	15,723	6,944	6,944	6,944	1,039	2,759	444	444	444	84	5,094	3,711	3,711	3,711	507
R^2	0.11	0.46	0.96	0.96	0.92	0.19	0.12	0.26	0.26	0.59	0.13	0.44	0.95	0.95	0.92

Notes

a Advanced countries versus advanced countries only.

b Emerging markets versus emerging markets only.

c Brune's capital account openness index excluding exchange rate structure.

d Estimated by IV.

Standard errors are reported below the coefficients. The model controlling for inflation targeting is estimated by IV. In the IV model, inflation targeting was instrumented using the index of corruption perceptions and the exogenous variables.

Table 5.6 Determinants of bilateral exchange rate volatility, 1998–2005

Variables	*All countries*					*Advanced*[a]					*Emerging markets*[b]				
	[1]	[2]	[3]	[4]	[5][d]	[6]	[7]	[8]	[9]	[10][d]	[11]	[12]	[13]	[14]	[15][d]
Variability of output	1.2351	1.0772	0.4268	0.3720	0.0412	0.0251	−0.0197	0.0037	0.0164	0.0268	2.0793	2.0628	0.5230	0.4344	0.4556
(SD(lnYi-lnYj))	0.0530	0.0612	0.0327	0.0330	0.0483	0.0381	0.0574	0.0546	0.0537	0.0546	0.1198	0.1250	0.0527	0.0538	0.0684
Dissimilarity of	0.0025	0.0019	0.0014	0.0015	0.0021	0.0027	0.0022	0.0023	0.0021	0.0019	0.0014	0.0016	0.0008	0.0009	0.0009
exports	0.0002	0.0002	0.0001	0.0001	0.0001	0.0001	0.0002	0.0002	0.0002	0.0002	0.0003	0.0003	0.0001	0.0001	0.0002
Trade ratio	−0.0101	−0.0043	0.0001	−0.0009	−0.0066	−0.0065	−0.0026	−0.0039	−0.0040	−0.0041	−0.0091	0.0015	−0.0026	−0.0033	−0.0030
	0.0012	0.0016	0.0008	0.0008	0.0011	0.0006	0.0009	0.0009	0.0009	0.0009	0.0022	0.0039	0.0016	0.0016	0.0016
Size of economy	−0.0088	−0.0053	−0.0017	−0.0003	0.0085	0.0197	0.0138	0.0081	0.0101	0.0117	−0.0172	−0.0289	−0.0046	0.0006	0.0007
	0.0017	0.0022	0.0012	0.0012	0.0016	0.0011	0.0021	0.0021	0.0021	0.0023	0.0043	0.0045	0.0019	0.0020	0.0031
Capital account		−0.0133	−0.0059	−0.0063	−0.0093		−0.0101	−0.0106	−0.0098	−0.0091		−0.0173	0.0028	0.0030	0.0026
openness[c]		0.0008	0.0004	0.0004	0.0006		0.0020	0.0019	0.0019	0.0020		0.0016	0.0007	0.0007	0.0008
Money ratio		−0.0655	−0.0054	−0.0028	0.0126		0.0282	0.0289	0.0255	0.0227		−0.1291	−0.0035	0.0024	0.0017
		0.0060	0.0032	0.0032	0.0043		0.0054	0.0051	0.0051	0.0053		0.0115	0.0048	0.0048	0.0057
Openness		−0.0003	0.0000	0.0000	0.0000		−0.0001	−0.0001	0.0000	0.0000		0.0000	0.0000	0.0000	0.0000
		0.0001	0.0000	0.0000	0.0000		0.0001	0.0001	0.0001	0.0001		0.0001	0.0000	0.0000	0.0000

Relative growth of		0.3231	0.0352	0.0309	0.0030		–0.0012	0.0013	0.0014	0.0016		0.3627	–0.0073	–0.0132	–0.0095
money		0.0144	0.0080	0.0079	0.0104		0.0129	0.0123	0.0120	0.0122		0.0250	0.0107	0.0106	0.0115
Variability of U.S.			1.4843	1.4835	1.4604			–0.4854	–0.5061	–0.5230			1.5612	1.5630	1.5467
dollar exchange rate			0.0123	0.0122	0.0160			0.0582	0.0573	0.0586			0.0141	0.0140	0.0150
Inflation targeting				–0.0199	–0.1412				0.0182	0.0331				–0.0204	–0.0122
				0.0021	0.0483				0.0036	0.0082				0.0029	0.0092
Constant	0.2049	0.2853	–0.0015	–0.0038	–0.0107	–0.2032	–0.0506	0.0785	0.0391	0.0070	0.3157	0.5488	0.0085	–0.0400	–0.0438
	0.0210	0.0275	0.0147	0.0146	0.0197	0.0145	0.0316	0.0338	0.0340	0.0379	0.0491	0.0555	0.0231	0.0239	0.0330
Observations	8,629	5,656	5,656	5,656	5,336	1,405	650	650	650	650	2,970	2,436	2,436	2,436	2,220
R^2	0.11	0.26	0.79	0.80	0.67	0.35	0.37	0.43	0.45	0.44	0.11	0.29	0.88	0.88	0.88

Notes

a Advanced countries versus advanced countries only.

b Emerging markets versus emerging markets only.

c Brune's capital account openness index excluding exchange rate structure.

d Estimated by IV.

Standard errors are reported below the coefficients. The model controlling for inflation targeting is estimated by IV. In the IV model, inflation targeting was instrumented using the index of corruption perceptions and the exogenous variables.

social, economic, and political institutions, an inflation targeting regime is more likely to be feasible. Such is the rationale for using transparency as an instrument for inflation targeting. For completeness, I report the results estimated both with and without the instrument.

The contrast between advanced countries and emerging markets is striking. In Table 5.4, inflation targeting enters with a negative coefficient for the emerging markets, as if its stabilizing effect on expectations also stabilizes the exchange rate, although the coefficient loses its statistical significance when instrumental variables are used. That negative effect is driven by post-1997 experience (cf. Tables 5.5 and 5.6). In Table 5.6, which focuses on the 1998 to 2005 period, the negative coefficient on the inflation targeting dummy is statistically significant at standard confidence levels even when instrumented. It is of course in the post-1997 period when most developing country experience with inflation targeting is concentrated. That the coefficients for this subsample are therefore better defined makes sense.

5 Conclusion

The advanced countries have already abandoned the unstable middle. The results here suggest that the growing popularity of inflation targeting may allow an increasing number of emerging markets to follow them without exposing the converts to high levels of exchange rate volatility.

Appendix

Table 5.7 List of countries included in the regressions

Argentina	Iceland	Philippines
Australia	India	Poland
Austria	Indonesia	Portugal
Belgium	Ireland	Russian Federation
Brazil	Israel	Singapore
Bulgaria	Italy	South Africa
Canada	Japan	Spain
Chile	Jordan	Sri Lanka
China	Korea Republic	Sweden
Colombia	Luxembourg	Switzerland
Czech Republic	Malaysia	Thailand
Denmark	Mexico	Turkey
Ecuador	Morocco	United Kingdom
Egypt Arab Republic	Netherlands	United States
Finland	New Zealand	Venezuela
France	Nigeria	
Germany	Norway	
Greece	Pakistan	
Hong Kong China	Panama	
Hungary	Peru	

Notes

1 Prepared for the conference in honor of Alexander Swoboda, Geneva, May 30, 2008. Thanks to Inci Otker-Robe and Harald Anderson for data and to Raul Razo-Garcia for help with the calculations. Sections 2 and 3 are an update and extension of Eichengreen and Razo-Garcia (2006). I thank Raul Razo-Garcia for his input into the larger project of which this chapter is part.

2 A number of others have laid claim to this theory or discovered it independently, such as Crockett (1994) and Eichengreen (1994). But Swoboda came first.

3 There exist still further alternatives, notably those of Ghosh *et al.* (2003), Levy-Yeyati and Sturzenegger (2003, 2007), and Shambaugh (2004).

4 Comparisons suggest that the analysis undertaken here is not particularly sensitive to the measure of de facto exchange rate regime used. This is what we found in Eichengreen and Razo-Garcia (2006). Where it is sensitive is with respect to the choice between measures of de facto and *de jure* regimes. The above arguments apply to de facto regimes. The IMF has long published a series for countries' official (self-announced) exchange rate regimes. Alesina and Wagner (2003) provide an analysis of why *de jure* and de facto regimes might differ.

5 The definition of advanced countries coincides with the definition of industrial countries in *International Financial Statistics*. Following Bubula and Otker-Robe (2002), emerging markets are defined as the countries included in the Emerging Market Bond Index Plus (EMBI+), the Morgan Stanley Capital International Index (MSCI), Singapore, Sri Lanka and Hong Kong SAR. Taiwan is excluded from the sample of emerging countries to make the results comparable to Bubula and Otker-Robe (2002). The resulting sample consists of twenty-four advanced countries, thirty-two emerging market countries, and 126 developing countries.

6 Note that BOR's floats include managed floats but not "tightly managed floats," which are classified as intermediate regimes, consistent with the idea that there really has been an increase in flexibility.

7 The tabulations here differ very slightly from those in Eichengreen and Razo-Garcia (2006) because new data became available in some cases for earlier years (on, *inter alia*, black and parallel exchange rates). In other cases, countries are classified as operating de facto pegs and de facto crawling pegs using five-year windows, so the updating can in a few instances have implications for prior years.

8 For what it is worth, the emerging markets classified as having moved to intermediate regimes using the Reinhart-Rogoff procedures are Nigeria in 2004 (managed exchange rate to de facto band), Malaysia (preannounced peg to de facto crawling peg),the Philippines (managed to de facto crawling band) and Thailand (freely floating to de facto crawling band) in 2005, and Argentina (managed to de facto crawling band) in 2007.

9 Appendix 2 of Eichengreen and Razo-Garcia (2006) describes the derivation of these matrices. Appendix 3 of that paper also presents modified matrices constructed on the basis of estimates of how various covariates affect the likelihood of regime transitions. Those matrices together with assumptions about the evolution of the covariates allow us to relax the assumption that transition probabilities are independent of country characteristics, and they allow us to apply alternative assumptions about how the key characteristics evolve over time.

10 Something that the author has argued will most likely remain the case (Eichengreen 2007).

11 Not too much should perhaps be made of this point, which is a function of the fact that a growing number of European countries adopted the euro starting in 1999. Implicit here is the question of whether this tendency for countries to gravitate toward the Euro area could shift into reverse in the future.

12 This difference is reinforced by developments in the past two years (see note 8 above).

13 See, e.g., Van Beek *et al.* (2000) and Masson and Pattillo (2004).
14 Centering becomes important when a measure of inflation targeting is added below, since this measure is year- as well as country-specific. But the results are robust to different ways of calculating period averages. Thus, I have estimated the same basic equations, as in columns 1–3, 5–7, and 10–12 of Table 5.4, with all the same conclusions. There is also the fact that for a number of year/country-pair observations bilateral exchange rate variability is zero. The obvious solution to this problem is estimating by Tobit. Again, doing so makes for no substantial difference in results.
15 Note that the number of countries included is now smaller because information on some of these correlates is lacking (year 2006 is omitted for the same reason). The country sample is given in Table 5.4. At the same time the number of observations is greater, owing to the focus on bilateral relationships. Data are from the International Monetary Fund's *Direction of Trade* and *International Financial Statistics*, *Penn World Tables*, Statistics Canada's *World Trade Analyzer*, the World Bank's *World Development Indicators*, and the OECD's *Main Economic Indicators*. Given the focus on bilateral relationships, it is worth addressing the question of whether the observations are independent of one another, as required for classical statistical inference. While it is true that changes in bilateral rates are not independent (e.g., the change between the dollar and euro and between the euro and yen), the standard deviations of these rates – which is what are considered here – are still independent, insofar as covariances differ across country pairs.
16 These effects are statistically significant at standard confidence levels.
17 That crisis having been a potential watershed in exchange rate arrangements.
18 Similar findings are reported in Bayoumi and Eichengreen (1997), where the coefficient on this variable is shown to vary across subperiods.
19 Formally, inflation targeting may be defined as a monetary policy operating strategy with four elements: an institutionalized commitment to price stability as the primary goal of monetary policy; mechanisms rendering the central bank accountable for attaining its monetary policy goals; the public announcement of targets for inflation; and a policy of communicating to the public and the markets the rationale for the decisions taken by the central bank. Institutionalizing the commitment to price stability lends credibility to that objective and gives the central bank the independence needed to pursue it. Mechanisms for accountability make this pursuit politically acceptable and impose costs on central banks that are incompetent or behave opportunistically. Announcing a target for inflation and articulating the basis for the central bank's decisions allows these mechanisms to operate.
20 As credibility is gained, it becomes possible for the central bank to deviate from the inflation target temporarily as needed to dampen short-run fluctuations in output and employment without undermining belief in its commitment to price stability. This then provides more policy flexibility than a simple exchange rate peg. Hence "flexible inflation targeting."

References

Alesina, Alberto and Alexander Wagner (2003) "Choosing (and Reneging on) Exchange Rate Regimes," NBER Working Paper No. 9809 (June).

Bayoumi, Tamim and Barry Eichengreen (1997) "Optimum Currency Areas and Exchange Rate Volatility: Theory and Evidence Compared." In Benjamin J. Cohen (ed.), *International Trade and Finance: New Frontiers for Research*, Cambridge: Cambridge University Press, pp. 184–215.

Bubula, Andrea and Inci Otker-Robe (2002) "The Evolution of Exchange Rate Regimes since 1990: Evidence from De facto Policies," IMF Working Paper No. 02/155 (September).

Crockett, Andrew (1994) "Monetary Implications of Increased Capital Flows." In *Changing Capital Markets: Implications for Monetary Policy*, Kansas City: Federal Reserve Bank of Kansas City.

Eichengreen, Barry (1994) *International Monetary Arrangements for the 21st Century*, Washington, DC: The Brookings Institution.

Eichengreen, Barry (2007) "The Break-up of the Euro Area," NBER Working Paper No. 13393 (September).

Eichengreen, Barry and Raul Razo-Garcia (2006) "The International Monetary System in the Last and Next 20 Years," *Economic Policy* 47, 393–442.

Eichengreen, Barry and Alan Taylor (2004) "The Monetary Consequences of a Free Trade Area of the Americas," in Antoni Esevadeordal, Dani Rodrik, Alan Taylor, and Andres Velasco (eds), *Integrating the Americas: FTAA and Beyond*, Cambridge, MA: David Rockefeller Center Series on Latin American Studies, Harvard University, pp. 189–226.

Genberg, Hans and Alexander Swoboda (1987a) "Fixed Rates, Flexible Rates, or the Middle of the Road: A Reexamination of the Arguments in View of Recent Experience." In Robert Z. Aliber (ed.), *The Reconstruction of International Monetary Arrangements*, London: Macmillan, pp. 92–116.

Genberg, Hans and Alexander Swoboda (1987b) "Changes fixes ou flottants: les leçons de l'après-Bretton Woods," in *Relations internationales, Politique économique et Méthodologie: Essais en l'honneur de Jacques l'Huillier*, Geneva: Georg, pp. 155–176.

Ghosh, Atish, Anne-Marie Gulde, and Holger Wolf (2003) *Exchange Rate Regimes: Choices and Consequences*, Cambridge, MA: MIT Press.

Levy-Yeyati, Eduardo and Federico Sturzenegger (2003) "To Float or to Fix: Evidence on the Impact of Exchange Rate Regimes on Growth," *American Economic Review* 93, 1173–1193.

Levy-Yeyati, Eduardo and Federico Sturzenegger (2007) "Fear of Floating in Reverse: Exchange Rate Policy in the 2000s," unpublished manuscript, Universidad Torcuato Di Tella and Harvard University.

Masson, Paul (2001) "Exchange Rate Regime Transitions," *Journal of Development Economics* 64, 571–586.

Masson, Paul and Catherine Pattillo (2004) *The Monetary Geography of Africa*, Washington, DC: The Brookings Institution.

Reinhart, Carmen and Kenneth Rogoff (2004) "The Modern History of Exchange Rate Arrangements: A Reinterpretation," *Quarterly Journal of Economics* 119, 1–48.

Shambaugh, Jay (2004) "Exchange Rate Regime Classification," www.dartmouth.edu/~shambau/.

Swoboda, Alexander (1986) "Credibility and Viability in International Monetary Arrangements," *Finance and Development* 23, 15–18.

Van Beek, Frits, Jose Roberto Rosales, Mayra Zermeno, Ruby Randall, and Jorge Shepherd (2000) "The East Caribbean Currency Union," Occasional Paper No. 195, Washington, DC: IMF.

6 Exchange rate regimes and external adjustment

New answers to an old debate

Atish R. Ghosh, Marco E. Terrones, and Jeromin Zettelmeyer[1]

1 Introduction

During the birth and infancy of the Bretton Woods system, the debate on exchange rate regimes was dominated by systemic arguments and concerns. The fathers of Bretton Woods believed that a centrally supervised system of fixed exchange rates was critical for postwar prosperity, as it would shield international trade both from exchange rate volatility and from exchange rate manipulation by individual countries. Against this view, a classic 1953 article by Milton Friedman argued that exchange rate volatility was a symptom rather than a cause of economic imbalances. Fixing the exchange rate would not remove these problems but merely suppress them, until they eventually erupted, in the form of a currency crisis, or painful domestic adjustment. Flexible exchange rates, in contrast, provided a mechanism for adjustment on an ongoing basis. "Changes in it occur rapidly, automatically, and continuously and so tend to produce corrective movements before tensions can accumulate and a crisis develop." Friedman also argued that with good macro-economic management, exchange rates were unlikely to be very volatile, and very unlikely to burden trade in goods and services, which could avail itself from futures markets to hedge exchange rate risk.

More than half a century after Friedman's article, and over thirty years after the end of the Bretton Woods era, many of these claims have been clearly proven either right or wrong. On the one hand, floating exchange rates did in fact turn out to be quite volatile – more so than Friedman had anticipated. A celebrated article by Michael Mussa (1986) showed that flexible exchange rate regimes display much higher *real* exchange rate variability than pegged regimes – especially in advanced economies, where exchange rates are driven mainly by capital flows. On the other hand, Friedman turned out to be right in his conjecture that flexible exchange rates would, at most, impose a modest burden on trade. Although currency unions retained their fans and triumphed in continental Europe, flexible exchange rates did not hinder the growing trade and financial integration of Europe, North America, and Japan.

However, there has been no closure on Friedman's central claim – namely that flexible exchange rate regimes would, for most countries, permit smoother adjustment of external imbalances. This omission is surprising because there is an enormous theoretical and empirical literature on the implications of the exchange rate regime for other aspects of macro-economic performance and policy-making – including Alexander Swoboda's many contributions to this subject.[2] Will a particular regime help a country stabilize from high inflation? Which regime is most conducive to economic growth? Which will do a better job in isolating the economy against specific types of shocks, given the structure of the economy? While the link between exchange rate regimes and external stability briefly returned to the forefront following the emerging market crises between 1995 and 2001, this was often cast in terms of vulnerabilities to various types of crisis, including currency crises, debt crises, and banking crises. The relationship between the exchange rate regime and external adjustment – Friedman's original claim – has received much less attention.

A welcome exception is a provocative recent paper by Menzie Chinn and Shang-Jin Wei (2008). Their main finding is that current account balances under flexible regimes seem to be no less persistent than under fixed regimes. Chinn and Wei (2008) also provide a simple interpretation: while nominal exchange rate flexibility may contribute to real exchange rate *volatility*, it does not seem to contribute to real exchange *adjustment*, in the sense that it does not seem to make the real exchange rate more mean-reverting. If this is true, it would seem to undermine the empirical basis for Friedman's argument.[3]

Is this the last word, and should we dismiss Friedman's case for flexible exchange rates as superficially plausible, but ultimately wrong? In this chapter, we argue that this would be premature, as the answer to the question of whether floating regimes facilitate external adjustment appears to be sensitive to how exactly the question is asked. We first show, using a different classification of exchange rate regimes, that Chinn and Wei's finding is indeed robust, in the sense that on average, current accounts in floating regimes do not appear to exhibit greater mean reversion than in fixed regimes. However, if the question is posed differently – namely whether floating regimes are associated with smaller external imbalances than fixed regimes – than the answer turns out to be supportive of Friedman's views. Furthermore, large current account imbalances (as captured by subsequent abrupt reversals) are far less frequent, and tend to be less disruptive under flexible regimes.

How can these facts be reconciled with Chinn and Wei's findings regarding current account persistence? A possible answer points in the direction of nonlinearities in the adjustment of current account imbalances. We show that current account dynamics differ depending on whether current accounts are in deficit or in surplus, and on whether imbalances are large or small. Flexible exchange rate regimes seem to be associated with faster adjustment of both *small* deficits and surpluses, and, in particular, of large *surpluses*. In contrast, flexible exchange rates do not lead to faster adjustment of *large deficits*: here, intermediate regimes exhibit by far the lowest persistence, perhaps reflecting currency crises. We conclude that, when allowing for these threshold effects, exchange rate regimes seem to be highly relevant for current account dynamics, in ways that generally support Friedman's thesis.

2 Does nominal exchange rate flexibility lead to faster external adjustment?

Following Chinn and Wei (2008), we estimate current account *persistence* using a simple first order autoregressive model,

$$CA_{it} = \rho_0 + \rho_1 CA_{it-1} + \nu_{it} \tag{1}$$

where CA_{it} stands for the current account-to-GDP ratio in country i and year t. The closer ρ_1 is to one, the slower the adjustment in response to shocks, i.e., the more persistent is the current account.

To see whether the persistence of the current account is influenced by the exchange rate regime, equation (1) can be augmented with an exchange rate regime variable and an interaction term between this variable and the current account balance:[4]

$$CA_{it} = \rho_0 + \rho_1 CA_{it-1} + \rho_2 XRR_{it} + \rho_3 (XRR_{it} \times CA_{it-1}) + \nu_{it} \tag{2}$$

where XRR_{it} takes on the value 0 for floating regimes, 1 for intermediate regimes, and 2 for fixed regimes. We estimate (1) and (2) with annual data for 151 countries from 1980 to 2007,[5] using pooled OLS, fixed effects, and both fixed and time effects.[6,7] To allow for heterogeneity across country samples, we show results separately for advanced countries, emerging market countries, and other developing countries.[8] Results are presented in Table 6.1. The coefficient of interest is the interaction term between the exchange rate regime and the lagged current account. If floating regimes help countries adjust – that is, make current accounts less persistent – we would expect this coefficient to be positive and statistically significant.

As it turns out, the coefficient is almost never statistically significant, and has inconsistent signs across country groups. For developing countries the sign is positive, indicating that current accounts are more persistent the more fixed the regime, as predicted by Friedman. However, this effect is (borderline) statistically significant for only one country group – emerging markets – and only when country-fixed effects are included. For advanced countries the coefficient is negative (albeit very small and statistically insignificant).

Hence, by and large, Table 6.1 confirms the "negative" findings of Chinn and Wei (2008), who show that the main result is robust in a number of dimensions: different definitions of the de facto exchange rate regime; stratification of the regression sample by regime, adding additional controls, and attempting to deal with the endogeneity of regimes. As far as our borderline significant result for emerging markets is concerned, this could be driven by our specific regime definition (the IMF de facto classification) or – more interestingly – represent a robust finding for this particular country group (which is not considered by Chinn and Wei). This remains to be explored in future work.

How should the lack of interaction between current account persistence and the exchange rate regime be interpreted? Chinn and Wei rerun equation (2) for

Table 6.1 Current account persistence (dependent variable: current account, in percent of GDP)

	Pooled		*FE*		*FE/TE*	
	(a)	*(b)*	*(a)*	*(b)*	*(a)*	*(b)*
All						
$CA_{t-1}{}^1$	0.645***	0.453*	0.448***	0.227	0.444***	0.220
	(0.094)	(0.265)	(0.101)	(0.235)	(0.1)	(0.232)
$CA_{t-1}{}^1 \times$ XRR[2]		0.131		0.156		0.159
		(0.129)		(0.113)		(0.112)
XRR^2		–0.126		0.195		0.264
		(0.425)		(0.447)		(0.433)
Observations	3,700	3,700	3,700	3,700	3,700	3,700
Advanced countries						
$CA_{t-1}{}^1$	0.944***	0.968***	0.801***	0.811***	0.795***	0.805***
	(0.017)	(0.032)	(0.03)	(0.056)	(0.028)	(0.067)
$CA_{t-1}{}^1 \times XRR^2$		–0.023		–0.010		–0.011
		(0.027)		(0.046)		(0.053)
XRR^2		–0.015		–0.346		–0.391
		(0.139)		(0.207)		(0.242)
Observations	701	701	701	701	701	701
Emerging markets						
$CA_{t-1}{}^1$	0.703***	0.574***	0.634***	0.419***	0.607***	0.379***
	(0.045)	(0.109)	(0.061)	(0.113)	(0.062)	(0.107)
$CA_{t-1}{}^1 \times XRR^2$		0.091		0.148*		0.155**
		(0.076)		(0.079)		(0.07)
XRR^2		0.07		–0.047		0.304
		(0.242)		(0.345)		(0.311)
Observations	984	984	984	984	984	984
Other developing markets						
$CA_{t-1}{}^1$	0.588***	0.300	0.407***	0.128	0.407***	0.129
	(0.099)	(0.289)	(0.104)	(0.242)	(0.103)	(0.242)
$CA_{t-1}{}^1 \times XRR^2$		0.196		0.196		0.196
		(0.148)		(0.121)		(0.122)
XRR^2		0.545		0.794		0.705
		(0.839)		(0.837)		(0.819)
Observations	2,015	2,015	2,015	2,015	2,015	2,015

Notes

1 Current account balance as percent of GDP, lagged.

2 De facto exchange rate regime according to IMF, *XRR*, where 0 = floating, 1 = intermediate, and 2 = fixed.

Robust/clustered standard errors in parentheses. The symbols, *, **, and *** indicate statistical significance at the 10%, 5%, and 1% level, respectively. The FE regression includes country dummies and the FE/TE regression includes country and time dummies.

real effective exchange rates instead of current account, and find, again, that nominal exchange rate regimes are irrelevant for real exchange rate adjustment. If this is true, it is not surprising that current accounts persistence is not modified by the exchange rate regime. But is it reconcilable with Mussa's (1986) finding which showed that real exchange rate variability is highly sensitive to the exchange rate regime? It surely is, if all that flexible exchange rates do is to increase noise, i.e. to act on the variance error term of the real exchange rate adjustment equation, rather than on the persistence parameter.

In short, based on this evidence, the answer to Friedman's empirical conjectures seems to be that although nominal exchange rates may make real exchange rates more flexible, they do not generate flexibility of the useful kind, at least from the perspective of the "real" economy. They mainly add noise, and hence are not conducive to faster current account adjustment.

3 Do flexible exchange rate regimes lead to smaller external imbalances?

Before writing off Friedman's argument, however, it is useful to look at the empirical evidence from a different angle, namely to look at the size of external imbalances across exchange rate regimes. Arguably, this is an even more direct test of Friedman's claim that flexible exchange rates encourage "corrective movements before tensions can accumulate and a crisis develop" than testing the persistence properties of the current account balance.

Table 6.2 presents some facts about the distribution of current account deficits and surpluses across regimes and country groups. It shows that on average, and for every country group except for emerging markets, current account balances are much smaller in absolute size in floating regimes than in fixed regimes. In addition, there is a monotonic relationship between regimes and current account imbalances, with the size of absolute deviations rising the more fixed the regime. Importantly, emerging markets are only a seeming exception to this pattern, as fixed regimes are associated both with very large average deficits and large average surpluses, which tend to cancel across countries. Once the sample is stratified in terms of deficit countries and surplus countries, the association between regime "rigidity" and current account imbalances is visible for all country groups except the advanced countries with surpluses, and is very strong in both emerging markets and other developing countries.

Although Table 6.2 is suggestive, it is too crude to serve as a "test" of Friedman's hypothesis, particularly because it does not tell us whether the accumulation of larger average imbalances is a problem in any sense among the countries with fixed regimes. To address this point, we use criteria commonly used in the literature on current account reversals (among others, Milesi-Ferretti and Razin 1997, 1998; Freund 2005; Freund and Warnock 2005; Eichengreen and Adalet 2005) to identify episodes of sudden, large reversals in the current account.[9] If Friedman is right that flexible rates encourage corrective movements in the current account before imbalances get very large and disruptive adjustments occur, we should be observing two things. First, large, sudden current account reversals should be much less frequent in flexible regimes. Second, on average, current account reversals should occur starting from larger initial imbalances if

Table 6.2 Current account balances (de facto exchange rate; sample statistics)

	Current account balance			*Deficits*			*Surpluses*		
	Mean	*Standard deviation*	*Obs.*[1]	*Mean*	*Standard deviation*	*Obs.*[1]	*Mean*	*Standard deviation*	*Obs.*[1]
All countries									
All	–3.6	10.3	3851	–7.2	9.2	2768	5.7	6.6	1083
Fixed	–4.6	11.6	1492	–9.0	10.3	1061	6.2	6.3	431
Intermediate	–3.2	9.9	1901	–6.4	8.7	1400	5.7	7.4	501
Floating	–2.0	6.4	458	–5.0	4.9	307	4.2	4.1	151
Advanced countries									
All	0.2	5.7	728	–3.6	3.1	404	4.9	4.6	324
Fixed	1.9	5.7	174	–3.7	3.5	65	5.3	3.9	109
Intermediate	–0.6	5.4	370	–3.4	2.9	237	4.5	5.2	133
Floating	0.0	5.8	184	–3.9	3.2	102	5.0	4.3	82
Emerging markets									
All	–1.6	6.0	1024	–4.5	3.8	696	4.6	5.0	328
Fixed	–0.8	7.6	305	–5.5	4.7	180	5.9	5.6	125
Intermediate	–2.1	5.4	608	–4.4	3.5	446	4.2	4.7	162
Floating	–0.8	3.1	111	–2.7	1.7	70	2.4	2.1	41`
Other developing countries									
All	–5.9	12.4	2099	–9.3	11,0	1668	7.2	8.5	431
Fixed	–6.8	12.6	1013	–10.2	11.3	816	7.0	7.6	197
Intermediate	–5.0	12.9	923	–8.6	11.3	717	7.7	9.5	206
Floating	–5.1	7.4	163	–7.1	6.2	135	4.6	5.0	28

Notes

The sample comprises 151 countries (27 advanced countries, 40 emerging market economies, and 84 developing countries) over the 1980 to 2007 period.

1 Number of observations.

Table 6.3 Current account reversals (sample statistics by country groups and de facto exchange rate[1])

	Number	*Frequency*	*Mean*	*Median*	*Top 25%*	*Bottom 25%*
Advanced countries						
Surplus reversal						
Fixed exchange rate	6	3.45	7.85	7.65	9.16	4.76
Intermediate exchange rate	7	1.89	4.44	4.16	4.83	3.22
Floating exchange rate	2	1.09	3.72	3.72	4.26	3.19
Deficit reversal						
Fixed exchange rate	1	0.57	–6.28	–6.28	–6.28	–6.28
Intermediate exchange rate	20	5.41	–5.98	–5.47	–3.81	–8.18
Floating exchange rate	2	1.09	–4.65	–4.65	–3.39	–5.92
Emerging markets						
Surplus reversal						
Fixed exchange rate	11	0.83	10.41	9.41	14.81	7.16
Intermediate exchange rate	15	0.98	8.82	7.73	11.72	5.28
Floating exchange rate	0	0.00	–	–	–	–
Deficit reversal						
Fixed exchange rate	10	0.76	–11.40	–9.66	–8.52	–12.48
Intermediate exchange rate	29	1.89	–8.64	–7.97	–6.35	–9.94
Floating exchange rate	0	0.00	–	–	–	–
Other developing countries						
Surplus reversal						
Fixed exchange rate	12	0.91	11.52	9.90	14.17	7.03
Intermediate exchange rate	16	1.05	11.66	6.60	14.53	5.40
Floating exchange rate	3	1.09	6.63	6.31	8.51	5.08
Deficit reversal						
Fixed exchange rate	60	4.55	–20.60	–14.29	–9.57	–21.70
Intermediate exchange rate	45	2.94	–20.79	–13.14	–9.94	–22.09
Floating exchange rate	8	2.92	–10.42	–9.93	–9.09	–11.92

Notes

Reversals are defined as in Freund (2005). A minimum threshold of 2 (–2) was used to identify surplus (deficit) reversals for advanced countries. A minimum threshold of 4 (–4) was used to identify surplus (deficit) reversals for emerging markets and other developing countries.

1 Sample statistics (means and percentiles) refer to the level of the current account at the time of the reversal.

2 For advanced countries: number of reversal years in each exchange rate regime group as a percentage of total number of observations for advanced countries. For emerging and other developing countries: number of reversal years in each exchange rate regime/country group as a percentage of total number of observations in both country groups.

regimes are fixed. As it turns out, both of these predictions are strongly supported by the data (Table 6.3 and Figure 6.1).

Table 6.3 shows, first, that with only one exception (large surpluses in "other" developing countries) large imbalances have been far more frequent in fixed and/or intermediate regimes than in floating regimes. Indeed, in the emerging market sample, there have been no large imbalances as defined here – whether from surpluses or from deficits – in floating exchange rate regimes. Even more significantly, as is shown in both Table 6.3 and Figure 6.1, the average imbalances prior to the current account reversal were much larger, in all country groups, under fixed regimes compared to floating regimes. Pre-reversal surpluses tend to be about twice as large in fixed regimes as in floating regimes, while pre-reversal deficits in fixed regimes on average exceed pre-reversal deficits in floating regimes by 40 to 70 percent. When comparing intermediate regimes and floating regimes, the ratios are smaller (though still positive) for advanced countries, and about the same for developing countries. Hence, this provides strong support in favor of Friedman's contention that under fixed regimes (and, to a perhaps lesser extent, intermediate regimes) imbalances are allowed to fester and grow much more than under flexible regimes.

We also found some evidence suggesting that current account deficit reversals are more costly under fixed regimes. Following Eichengreen and Adalet (2005), Table 6.4 compares changes in growth – defined as the difference between three-year average growth after a reversal and growth in the reversal year – across the three regimes. The more floating (or less fixed) the regime, the lower the growth cost or (in the case of surplus reversals) the larger the growth benefit. These findings are not surprising, as less fixed regimes are associated with smaller adjustments (see second column of Table 6.4) and lower initial imbalances, and the empirical literature on current account reversals suggests a robust link between the size of the initial imbalances and the output cost of reversals (Freund and Warnock 2005).[10] This leads to the question whether adjustment under flexible regimes is less costly even controlling for the size of external imbalances (for example, because it allows relative prices to adjust more easily in the presence of nominal rigidities). This remains to be explored in future work.

4 Reconciling the findings: nonlinearities and threshold effects

How can these results be reconciled with the earlier finding that the exchange rate regimes do not affect the dynamics of the current account? One interpretation that would be consistent with both sets of results is that the effects of the exchange rate regime on the current account vary with the size of the current account. In particular, it could be that less flexible regimes increase the persistence of current account deficits or surpluses as long as these are moderate – leading to larger imbalances on average – but at the same time are associated with less persistence, in the form of large current account reversals, once current

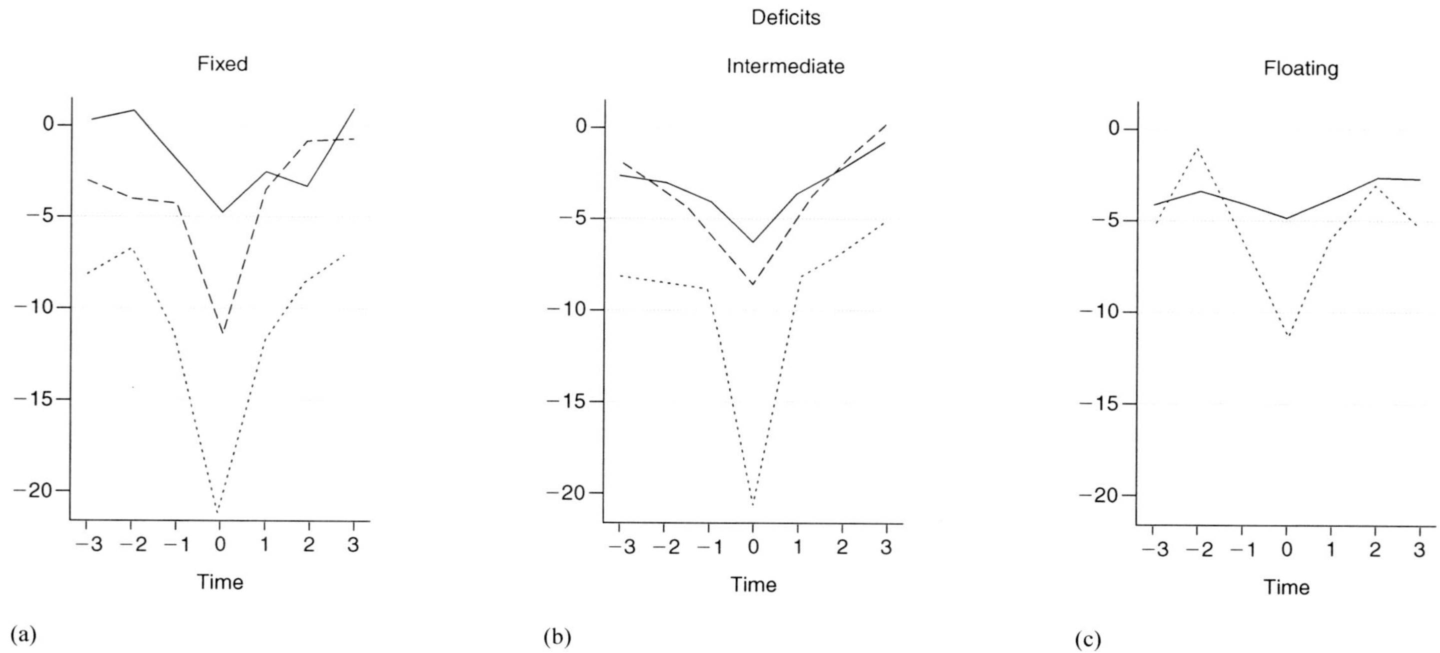
Deficits
Fixed
Intermediate
Floating
0
−5
−10
−15
−20
−3 −2 −1 0 1 2 3
Time
(a)
(b)
(c)

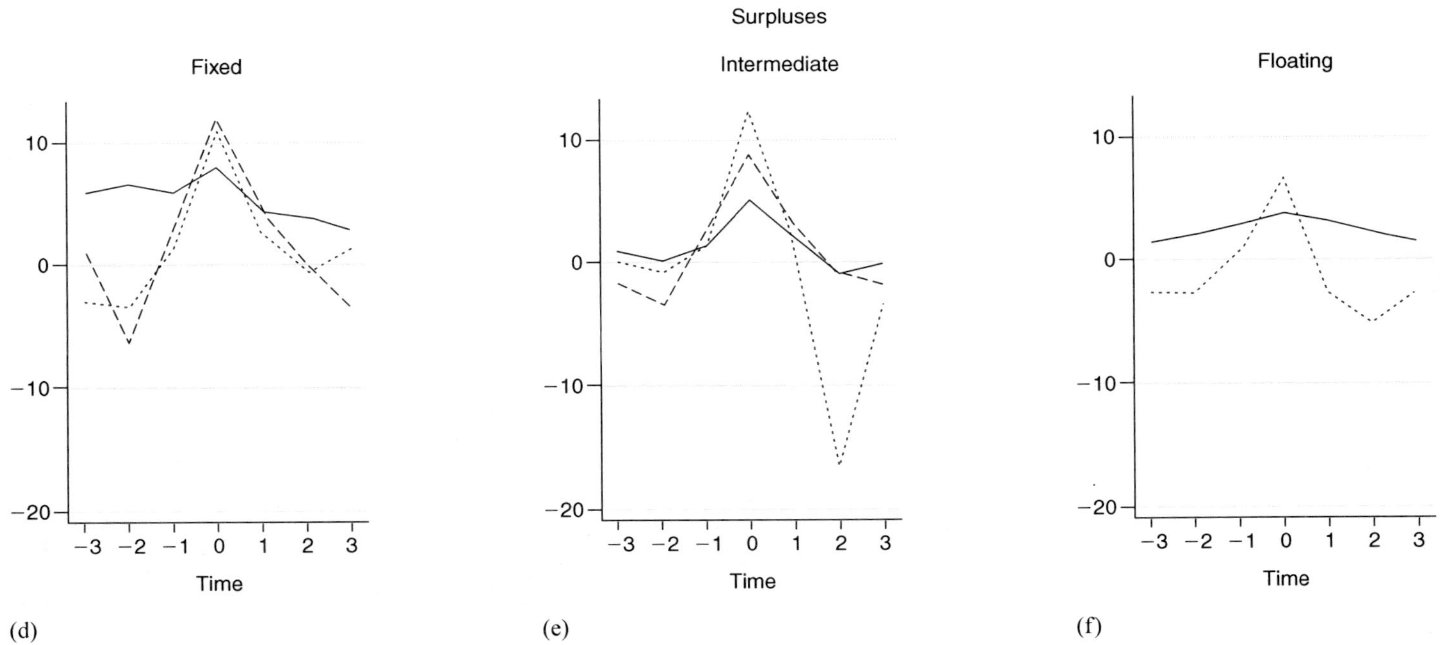

Figure 6.1 Current account reversals (cross-country means by de facto exchange rate regimes and country groups).

Notes
Solid line: industrials; dashed line: emerging economies; dotted line: developing countries.
The period of the reversal is denoted here by time=0

Table 6.4 Cost of current account reversals (medians, by de facto exchange rate regime)

	Δgy^{1}	ΔCA^{1}
Surplus reversal	0.31	–8.38
Fixed exchange rate	–0.56	–9.38
Intermediate exchange rate	0.21	–7.50
Floating exchange rate	2.23	–5.18
Deficit reversal	–0.80	6.25
Fixed exchange rate	–1.30	7.36
Intermediate exchange rate	–0.95	5.84
Floating exchange rate	–0.19	4.16

Notes

Reversals are defined as in Freund (2005). A minimum threshold of 2 (–2) was used to identify surplus (deficit) reversals for advanced countries. A minimum threshold of 4 (–4) was used to identify surplus (deficit) reversals for emerging markets and other developing countries.

1 Change in output growth and current account balance as percent of GDP, respectively. Changes refer to the difference between the three-year average after the reversal and the period of the reversal.

account balances exceed certain thresholds. In other words, our findings could be suggestive of "threshold effects," or more generally, of nonlinearities in the interaction between current account dynamics and exchange rate regimes, which are not picked up in linear regressions along the lines of Table 6.1.

Table 6.5 presents a preliminary attempt to test for the presence of such threshold effects. We allow for nonlinearities – or more precisely, for breaks in linear relationships – of two kinds. First, we distinguish between current account dynamics when balances are in surplus and when they are in deficit. There is no reason to think that these should be the same, particularly when we are interested in the reversals of large imbalances (unlike current account deficits, the reversal of surpluses cannot be forced on a country by a currency crisis). Second, we try to test for threshold effects by including an interaction term between past current accounts and a variable that indicates if the current account is in a large deficit (less than 25th percentile of the current account distribution) or surplus (more than 75th percentile of the distribution). To avoid overloading the model with interaction terms, we run the regressions separately for fixed, intermediate, and floating regimes. As the pooled OLS estimates are likely to be misspecified in this context, we show only fixed effects estimates, with and without controlling for country and time effects.

The results are highly instructive, and may be summarized as follows.

First, threshold effects do not seem to matter for floating regimes (at least for the threshold that is assumed here). Neither does the distinction between surplus and deficit dynamics matter. Regardless of whether the current account is in surplus or in deficit, and regardless of whether these surpluses or deficits are large or small, the autoregressive coefficient in flexible regimes is always in the order or 0.4 to 0.5.

Table 6.5 Nonlinear effects in current account persistence (dependent variable: current account, in percent of GDP, all countries)

	FE		*FE/TE*	
	Deficit	*Surplus*	*Deficit*	*Surplus*
1. Fixed				
$CA_{t-1}{}^{1}$	0.644***	0.503***	0.648***	0.505***
	(0.057)	(0.05)	(0.058)	(0.051)
$CA_{t-1}{}^{1} \times 1(CA_{t-1} \leq q.25)^{2}$	–0.108	–	–0.108*	–
	(0.066)	–	(0.064)	–
$CA_{t-1}{}^{1} \times 1(CA_{t-1} \geq q.75)^{2}$	–	0.297***	–	0.303***
	–	(0.103)	–	(0.103)
Observations	1298	1298	1298	1298
2. Intermediate				
$CA_{t-1}{}^{1}$	0.569***	0.163	0.578***	0.136
	(0.051)	(0.134)	(0.047)	(0.121)
$CA_{t-1}{}^{1} \times 1(CA_{t-1} \leq q.25)^{2}$	–0.365***	–	–0.395***	–
	(0.138)	–	(0.137)	–
$CA_{t-1}{}^{1} \times 1(CA_{t-1} \geq q.75)^{2}$	–	0.605***	–	0.666***
	–	(0.165)	–	(0.16)
Observations	1683	1683	1683	1683
3. Floating				
$CA_{t-1}{}^{1}$	0.489***	0.404***	0.509***	0.404***
	(0.073)	(0.138)	(0.066)	(0.126)
$CA_{t-1}{}^{1} \times 1(CA_{t-1} \leq q.25)^{2}$	–0.147	–	–0.167	–
	(0.148)	–	(0.135)	–
$CA_{t-1}{}^{1} \times 1(CA_{t-1} \geq q.75)^{2}$	–	0.015	–	0.041
	–	(0.18)	–	(0.152)
Observations	373	373	373	373

Notes

1 Current account balance as percent of GDP, lagged.

2 1(.) is the indicator function that takes value 1 if the argument of the function is true and 0 otherwise; q.x refers here to quantile x based on the full sample of current account balances (3,354 observations).

Robust/clustered standard errors in parentheses. The symbols, *, **, and *** indicate statistical significance at the 10%, 5%, and 1% level, respectively. The FE regression includes country dummies and the FE/TE regression includes country and time dummies.

Second, threshold effects do matter in both fixed and intermediate regimes, where they are statistically highly significant. The sign of the effect depends on whether deficits or surpluses are present. With current accounts in deficit, threshold interaction effects are negative and quite large, suggesting that in pegged/intermediate regimes, large deficits unwind much faster than small deficits. By contrast, when the current account is in surplus, threshold interaction effects are large and positive, suggesting that once surpluses have become very large, they are highly persistent under these regimes.

Third, taking into account these threshold effects, there are large and significant differences in the persistence properties of fixed, intermediate, and floating regimes as follows:

- *Large surpluses* are much more persistent in fixed and intermediate regimes than in floating regimes. Adding the coefficients on the main effects and the interaction terms, we obtain a persistence parameter for about 0.8 for fixed/ intermediate regimes and about 0.4 for floating regimes. If we base the comparison only on the statistically significant coefficients, the persistence parameter is 0.8 for fixed regimes, 0.6–0.7 for intermediate regimes, and 0.4 for floating regimes.
- In contrast, *large deficits* exhibit *less* persistence in intermediate regimes than in floating regimes. Adding the coefficients on the main effects and interaction terms, the persistence parameter is about 0.2, whereas it is 0.3–0.5 in floating regimes and 0.5–0.6 in fixed regimes (depending on whether or not insignificant interaction terms are considered). The fact that the persistence parameter in the case of large deficits is lowest for intermediate regimes may reflect the fact that these include soft pegs that are most likely to experience currency crises (Table 6.3 showed that by far the greatest number of current account reversals were concentrated in this category).
- Finally, for *moderate surpluses and deficits*, current accounts are in most cases less persistent under flexible regimes than under fixed and intermediated regimes, with persistence coefficient 0.4–0.5 in flexible regimes and about 0.6 in fixed and intermediate regimes. The only exceptions are small surpluses in intermediate regimes, which have a small persistence parameter which is insignificantly different from zero, perhaps because there are few observations in this category.

5 Conclusions

More than fifty-five years after the publication of Milton Friedman's famous essay advocating a system of flexible exchange rates, the question of whether exchange rate flexibility contributes to the prevention and orderly resolution of external imbalances remains controversial. While much of the policy community nowadays appears to embrace Friedman's view, flexible exchange rates do not, on average, seem to speed up the rate at which current accounts revert to their means (Chinn and Wei 2008). This constitutes prima facie evidence against Friedman's hypothesis.

However, as we have shown in this chapter, Friedman's hypothesis does enjoy considerable empirical support when looked at from a slightly different angle, namely based on cross-country evidence on the size of current account imbalances and the frequency of large current account reversals. Large current account reversals very rarely occur under flexible regimes. Furthermore, when they do occur, they involve much lower initial imbalances than current account reversals that take place in intermediate and fixed regimes. This is precisely what Friedman seems to have had in mind when he argued that flexible exchange rates "tend to produce corrective movements before tensions can accumulate and a crisis develop."

How, then, can the two pieces of evidence be reconciled? Our answer points to nonlinearities in the adjustment of the current account, both across surpluses and deficits, and in relation to the size of current account imbalances. We have shown, first, that *large* current account surpluses are much more persistent in fixed and intermediate regimes than in floating regimes. The difference is substantial, with persistence coefficients in fixed regimes of about twice the size of those in floating regimes. Second, *small* and moderate surpluses and deficits are also more persistent in floating and intermediate regimes than in floating regimes, although the difference is not as large (persistence parameters of about 0.6 compared to 0.4–0.5). Only in the case of *large deficits* do floating regimes not exhibit the lowest persistence. Intermediate regimes, in particular, appear to be much less persistent here. We interpret this as reflecting sharp current account reversals, perhaps via currency crises, which tend to occur most frequently in intermediate regimes compared to both floats and (harder) pegs.

In conclusion, the evidence presented in this chapter supports Friedman's 1953 view regarding the role of flexible exchange rates in the prevention and resolution of current account imbalances. Both large current account imbalances and large reversals are far less prevalent under floating regimes. Furthermore, there is evidence that *small* current account imbalances are less persistent under flexible regimes than under fixed and intermediate rates. This is not true for *large* current account *deficits*, which appear to be far less persistent under intermediate regimes than under floating regimes; however, these faster reversals appear to reflect precisely the kind of abrupt, delayed adjustment that Friedman wanted to avoid. Finally, the evidence appears particularly supportive of present-day Friedmanesque views regarding the role of flexible exchange rates in the reduction of global imbalances, as *large* current account *surpluses* tend to be highly persistent in fixed and intermediate regimes, and much less persistent in floating regimes. While Chinn and Wei (2008) may be right that policy pronouncements about the virtues of floating rates have in this context been largely "faith-based" in the past, this faith seems ultimately to be borne out by the evidence.

Notes

1 The views in this chapter are the authors' only, and should not be attributed to the International Monetary Fund. We thank, without implication, Olivier Jeanne, Jonathan Ostry, Alexander Swoboda, Charles Wyplosz, and seminar participants at the IMF and the Geneva Graduate Institute for International and Development Studies for comments and discussions. This chapter is part of a larger project examining the macro-economic implications of exchange rate regimes.

2 Alexander's research in this area has focused mostly on the implications of exchange rate regimes for monetary and fiscal policies; see, in particular, Swoboda 1971, 1973; Genberg and Swoboda 1983, 1987, 1989; Mussa *et al.* 2000; and Genberg (Chapter 3, this volume) for a survey. For a comprehensive treatment of the macro-economic implications of the exchange rate regime, see Ghosh *et al.* (2003), who find strong evidence that the commitment to a pegged exchange rate contributes to better inflation

performance owing to monetary discipline and credibility effects. On growth, they find few robust results, though there is evidence that countries with hard pegs (currency boards) grow faster (Wolf *et al.* 2008). By contrast, Levy-Yeyati and Sturzenegger (2003), using a de facto classification, find that pegged exchange rates are associated with slower growth. Rogoff *et al.* (2004) survey the empirical literature and, using a different de facto classification, argue that the main inflation benefit of pegging accrues to developing countries. In contrast, they find effects on growth only for advanced economies (which is higher for floating regimes).

3 Evidence in Ghosh *et al.* (2003, ch. 5), however, suggests that floating exchange rates help offset inflation differentials, contributing to lower real exchange rate volatility – especially for developing countries and at longer horizons.

4 This variable codes pegged, intermediate, and floating regimes based on the IMF's de facto classification. This classification seeks to describe the actual behavior of the central bank in managing the exchange rate (as opposed to its stated commitment, which is captured by the de jure classification). While all de facto classifications (Levy-Yeyati and Sturzenegger, Reinhart and Rogoff (2004), and Shambaugh (2004)) differ from each other,; the IMF de facto classification has a high degree of consensus with the other classifications. Chinn and Wei use two alternative de facto classifications, namely those by Sturzenegger and Levy-Yeyati (2003) and Reinhart and Rogoff (2004), with similar results.

5 Chinn and Wei (2008) employ a larger dataset comprising over 170 countries during the 1971 to 2005 period.

6 The standard estimation of models with lagged dependent variables, however, can produce biased estimates of the coefficients when the number of time series observations, T, is small – in particular, the OLS estimator is biased upwards and the FE and FE/TE estimators are biased downwards. Judson and Owen (1999) argue that even with T close to 30, as in our case, the bias could reach as much as 20 percent of the true value of the coefficients. Despite this, they find that the FE and FE/TE perform no worse than other methods including GMM.

7 In most cases we found evidence of significant country and time effects, suggesting that pooled OLS might be inappropriate.

8 The advanced economies comprise the core OECD countries plus Hong Kong, Israel, and Singapore. The emerging markets comprise the remaining countries listed in either JPMorgan's EMBI Global Index (2005) or the International Finance Corporation's Major Index (2005). Finally, other developing countries comprise the remaining countries.

9 In particular, we say that a country experiences a current account reversal if: (1) the current account deficit (surplus) exceeds γ percent of GDP before the reversal; (2) the average deficit (surplus) improves (deteriorates) by γ percent of GDP over three years; (3) the maximum (minimum) deficit (surplus) in the five years after the reversal is not larger (smaller) than the minimum (maximum) deficit (surplus) in the three years before the reversal; and (4) the deficit (surplus) improves (deteriorates) by at least one-third. We set $\gamma = 2$ for the advanced countries and $\gamma = 4$ for the emerging economies and other developing countries. These rules follow those used by Freund (2005) in her analysis of current account deficit reversals.

10 See also Edwards (2004), who provides some direct evidence for linking flexible rates to smaller output costs of deficit reversals in developing countries.

References

Chinn, Menzie and Shang-Jin Wei (2008) "A Faith-based Initiative: Do we Really Know that a Flexible Exchange Rate Regime Facilitates Current Account Adjustment?," unpublished draft, Department of Economics, University of Wisconsin.

Edwards, Sebastian (2004) "Financial Openness, Sudden Stops and Current Account Reversals," NBER Working Paper No. 10277. Cambridge, MA: National Bureau of Economic Research.

Eichengreen, Barry and Muge Adalet (2005) "Current Account Reversals: Always a Problem?," NBER Working Paper No. 11634. Cambridge, MA: National Bureau of Economic Research.

Friedman, Milton (1953) "The Case for Flexible Exchange Rates," in M. Friedman, *Essays in Positive Economics*. Chicago, IL: The University of Chicago Press, pp. 157–203.

Freund, Caroline (2005) "Current Account Adjustment in Industrial Countries," *Journal of International Money and Finance* 24, 1278–1298.

Freund, Caroline and Frank Warnock (2005) "Current Account Deficits in Industrial Countries: The Bigger they Are, the Harder they Fall?," NBER Working Paper No. 11823. Cambridge, MA: National Bureau of Economic Research.

Genberg, Hans and Alexander Swoboda (1983) "Fixed Rates, Flexible Rates, and the Middle of the Road: A Re-examination of the Arguments in View of Recent Experience." Discussion Papers in International Economics 8803, Graduate Institute of International Studies, July. Published in R. Aliber (ed.), *The Reconstruction of International Monetary Arrangements*. London: Macmillan Press, pp. 92–116.

Genberg, Hans and Alexander Swoboda (1987) "The Current Account and the Policy Mix under Flexible Exchange Rates," IMF Working Paper WP/87/70. Published in J. A. Frenkel and M. Goldstein (eds), *International Financial Policy: Essays in Honor of Jacques J. Polak*. Washington, DC: International Monetary Fund, 1993, pp. 420–454.

Genberg, Hans and Alexander Swoboda (1989) "Policy and Current Account Determination under Floating Exchange Rates." IMF *Staff Papers* 36 (March), 1–30.

Ghosh, Atish, Anne-Marie Gulde, and Holger C. Wolf (2003) *Exchange Rate Regimes: Choices and Consequences*. Cambridge, MA: MIT Press.

Judson, Ruth and Ann Owen (1999) "Estimating Dynamic Panel Data Models: A Guide for Macroeconomists," *Economic Letters* 65, 9–15.

Levy-Yeyati, Eduardo and Sturzenegger, Federico (2003) "To Float or to Fix: Evidence on the Impact of Exchange Rate Regimes on Growth," *American Economic Review* 93 (4), 1173–1193.

Milesi-Ferretti, Gian Maria, and Assaf Razin (1997) "Sharp Reductions in Current Account Deficits: An Empirical Investigation," NBER Working Paper No. 6310.

Milesi-Ferretti, Gian Maria, and Assaf Razin (1998) "Current Account Reversals and Currency Crises: Empirical Regularities," NBER Working Paper No. 6620.

Mussa, Michael (1986) "Nominal Exchange Rate Regimes and the Behavior of Real Exchange Rates: Evidence and Implications," *Carnegie-Rochester Conference Series on Public Policy* 25 (autumn), 117–214.

Mussa, Michael, Paul R. Masson, Alexander K. Swoboda, Esteban Jadresic, Paolo Mauro, and Andrew Berg (2000) *Exchange Rate Regimes in an Increasingly Integrated World Economy*, Occasional Paper No. 193. Washington, DC: International Monetary Fund.

Reinhart, Carmen and Kenneth Rogoff (2004) "The Modern History of Exchange Rate Arrangements: A Reinterpretation," *Quarterly Journal of Economics* 119 (1), 1–48.

Rogoff, Kenneth, Aasim Husain, Ashoka Mody, Robin Brooks, and Nienke Oomes (2004) *Evolution and Performance of Exchange Rate Regimes*, Occasional Paper 229. Washington, DC: International Monetary Fund.

Shambaugh, Jay (2004) "The Effects of Fixed Exchange Rates on Monetary Policy," *Quarterly Journal of Economics* 119 (1), 301–352.

Swoboda, Alexander (1971) "Equilibrium, Quasi-equilibrium, and Macro-economic Policy under Fixed Exchange Rates," *Quarterly Journal of Economics*, 85, 162–171.

Swoboda, Alexander (1973) "Monetary Policy under Fixed Exchange Rates: Effectiveness, the Speed of Adjustment and Proper Use," *Economica*, New Series 158 (May) 136–154.

Wolf, Holger, Atish Ghosh, Helge Berger, and Anne-Marie Gulde (2008) *Currency Boards in Retrospect and Prospect*. Cambridge, MA: MIT Press.

7 China's exchange rate impasse and the weak U.S. dollar[1]

Ronald McKinnon and Gunther Schnabl

In assessing Alexander Swoboda's great influence on economics, two themes stand out: the determinants of global inflation, particularly in the 1970s, and the choice of an exchange rate regime consistent with domestic monetary and fiscal policies. Although seemingly narrowly focused on China, our contribution to Alexander's fête straddles both themes. Since 2004, China has been backed into a situation where the renminbi is expected to go ever higher against the dollar, and this one-way bet has led to a loss of domestic monetary control. Combined with a more general flight from the U.S. dollar, the resulting monetary explosion in China contributes to the worldwide increase in primary commodity prices – with excess liquidity reminiscent of the global inflation generated by the weak dollar in the 1970s.

1 Introduction

Because China's trade surplus (net saving surplus) has rapidly spiraled upwards since 2000, its overall current account surplus reached \$359 billion in 2007.[2] This covers almost half of the much larger U.S current account deficit of \$750 billion – and if recent trends continue could cover more than half. Of course, this trade imbalance can only be corrected in the longer term if China's *net* saving – i.e., saving minus investment – falls, and the inverse occurs in the U.S. (the silver lining in the housing crisis?).

In the near term, however, China faces a financial conundrum. Owing to political pressure from the U.S., since July 21, 2005 the renminbi's peg to the dollar has crawled steadily upwards at about 6 percent per year, and this rate of appreciation is expected to continue or even accelerate. Because of this one-way bet in the foreign exchange markets, since 2004 more than 100 percent of China's huge current account surplus has been financed by building up official exchange reserves.

Clearly, China with its ever-rising official exchange reserves contrasts sharply with other large surplus-saving countries such as Germany and Japan, whose surpluses on current account are matched by private short-term and long-term capital outflows. Could foreign exchange restrictions be the problem? By 2007, China had effectively eliminated foreign exchange controls on capital *outflows* by industrial corporations and financial institutions, while individuals receive generous allowances for foreign travel. Although now free to diversify by investing outside of the country, the private (non-state) sector refuses to do so. On the contrary, China's State Administration of Foreign Exchange (SAFE) is still struggling, somewhat vainly, to restrict the deluge of "hot" money inflows.

What is behind this abnormality? Because all participants in the foreign exchange markets now expect that the renminbi will continue to appreciate against the dollar, they are reluctant to hold dollar assets. This reluctance is accentuated even more when American interest rates are abnormally low, as they now are, with the U.S. Federal Funds rate at just 2 percent.

So at this juncture in international finance, we distinguish between two meanings of the concept of "global imbalance." First, the great saving imbalances across countries that are reflected in the large trade (saving) deficit of the U.S. and large trade (saving) surpluses of China, Japan, Germany, oil exporters, and a host of smaller countries. Second, the further massive imbalance in financial intermediation for China's huge current account surplus with the U.S. Instead of a "normal" outflow of private capital to finance China's trade surplus, China's central bank accumulates vast amounts of foreign exchange – some of which is invested in U.S. Treasury bonds.

Of the two types of global imbalance, saving–investment imbalance across countries is at once the best-known and most intractable in the short run. For 2007, Figure 7.1 shows the huge net current account surplus of China amounting to over 10 percent of its GDP, and the large current account deficit of the U.S. of about 5 percent of its much larger GDP necessitating borrowing elsewhere around the world as well. However, rebalancing by reducing excess saving in the large creditor countries while increasing net saving in the U.S. is certainly

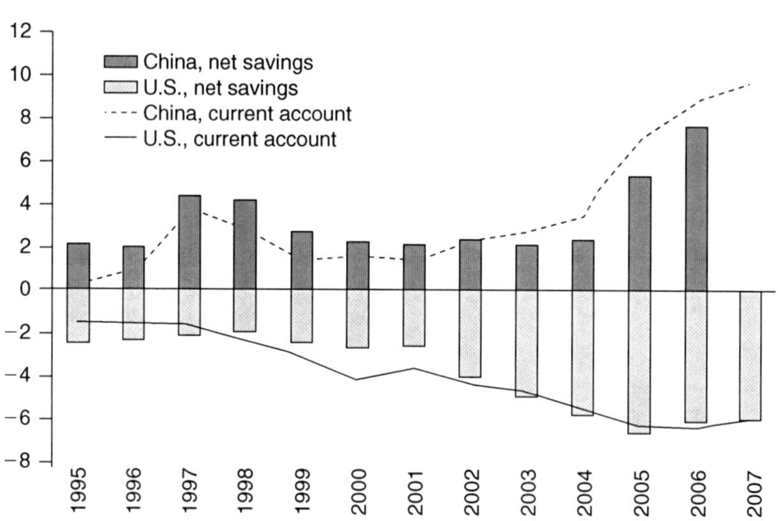

Figure 7.1 Saving–investment balance and current account, China and the U.S (source: IMF).

possible in the longer run, and this international rebalancing can (best) be done without changing nominal exchange rates (McKinnon 2007a). Although very important, this global rebalancing of net saving propensities is intractable without being preceded by currency stabilization.

Consequently, we focus initially on the sub-problem of unbalanced international financial intermediation and loss of monetary control in China. Because of the one-way bet on renminbi appreciation as aggravated by the extraordinary cuts in U.S. interest rates since August 2007, the People's Bank of China (PBC) has had to intervene massively to buy dollars with domestic base money. However, to better understand China's current monetary impasse, we first consider a brief history of China's foreign exchange policies since its market-oriented liberalization began in 1979.

2 Three phases of the yuan–dollar exchange rate

At the risk of oversimplifying, Figure 7.2 partitions the evolution of China's exchange rate regime into three phases: *currency inconvertibility* and exchange depreciation before 1994, the *fixed dollar exchange rate* from 1995 to July 21, 2005, and the subsequent appreciation by a *predictable upward crawl* through mid-2008.

Phase 1

Before 1994, China's currency was inconvertible in the strong sense of the word. There were multiple exchange rates (an official rate and floating swap rates for new exports of manufactures in different parts of the country), exchange controls on both current and capital account transactions, and both exports and imports

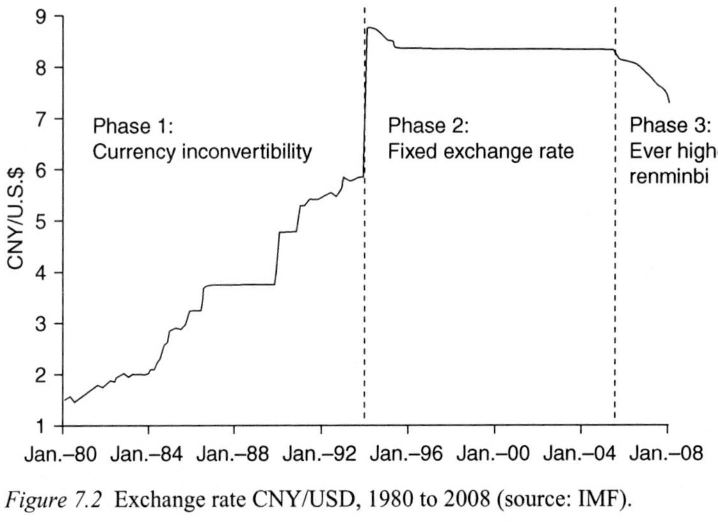

Figure 7.2 Exchange rate CNY/USD, 1980 to 2008 (source: IMF).

had to be funneled through state trading companies. Throughout the 1980s, this so-called "airlock system" insulated domestic relative prices still influenced by central planning from those prevailing on world markets – except for a few fledgling Special Economic Zones (SEZs) on the East Coast.

So without free arbitrage between domestic and foreign prices, how the official exchange rate was set was arbitrary. Figure 7.2 shows only the official exchange rate's path from 1.5 yuan per dollar back in 1979 and increased (devalued) in steps to 5.8 yuan per dollar by the end of 1993. However, the incentives for exporting or importing were not much affected – nor was the domestic price level. And tight exchange controls prevented "hot" money flows. The official rate was not economically very meaningful.

Phase 2

China's banner year for sweeping financial reforms both in domestic taxation and in the organization of foreign trade was 1994. The Chinese authorities abolished exchange controls on current account transactions (exporting, importing, interest, and dividends) and unified the exchange rate. Separate and more favorable exchange rates for manufactured exports were abolished. By 1996, China had formally satisfied the International Monetary Fund's Article VIII on current account convertibility.

The new consolidated official rate was set at 8.7 yuan per dollar in 1994, which was closer to the average of the previous swap rates. True, this represented a substantial devaluation of the official rate from 5.8 yuan per dollar, but the period 1993 to 1995 was a period of high inflation in China. Figure 7.3 shows that the nominal depreciation of the official rate was about the same order of magnitude of the excess of China's inflation over that prevailing in the United

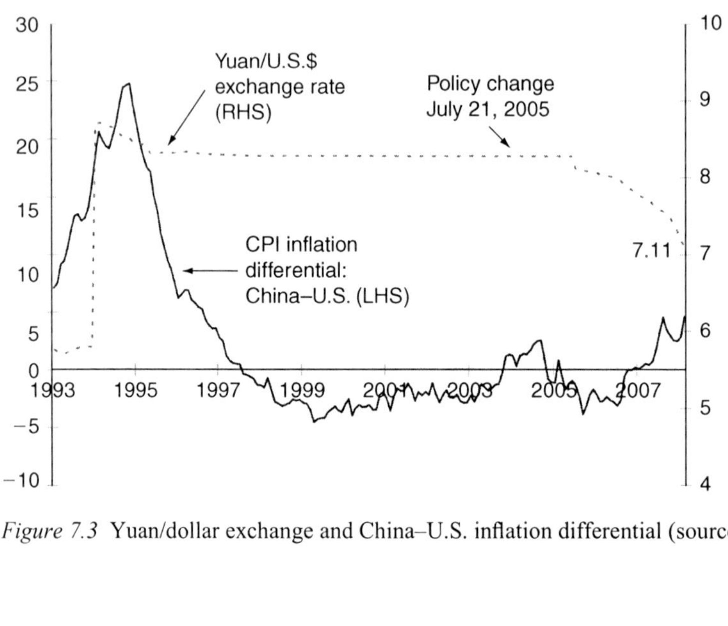

Figure 7.3 Yuan/dollar exchange and China–U.S. inflation differential (source: IMF).

States (as much as 20 percent in 1994). With the currency unification, real depreciation – if any – was minimal.

By 1995, the nominal exchange rate had settled down to about 8.28 yuan per dollar and was held there for ten years – our Phase 2. The main motivations for so fixing the exchange rate were twofold. First, in the previous phase of currency inconvertibility going back to 1979 when liberalization began, China had suffered from a "roller coaster" ride in the rate of real output growth and in inflation rates – peaking out with the high inflation of 1993 to 1995 (Figure 7.4). With only an embryonic domestic capital market and with the progressive relaxation of central planning and direct price controls, the PBC had great trouble anchoring the overall price level by domestic means alone. Thus the unification of the exchange rate regime in 1994, and the move to full current account convertibility in 1994 to 1996, presented an opportunity to adopt a more stable external nominal anchor. Figure 7.4 shows that, as the exchange rate remained fixed at 8.28 yuan/dollar until July 21, 2005, cycles of inflation and real output growth in China eased – while inflation came down to the American level by 2004.

Indeed, in the great Asian crisis of 1997 to 1998, sharp devaluations by neighboring countries – not only the well-known crisis five,[3] but also by Japan, Taiwan, and Singapore – imposed strong deflationary pressure on China. But Premier Zhu Rongji wisely ignored advice to let the renminbi become more "flexible" and depreciate in tandem. Instead, he held on to the fixed exchange rate anchor and engaged in a great "one-trillion" dollar fiscal expansion, largely through infrastructure investments, over the next four years. In the crisis, China's exchange rate and fiscal policies saved the East Asian economy from further imploding – and allowed the neighboring countries to recover more quickly.

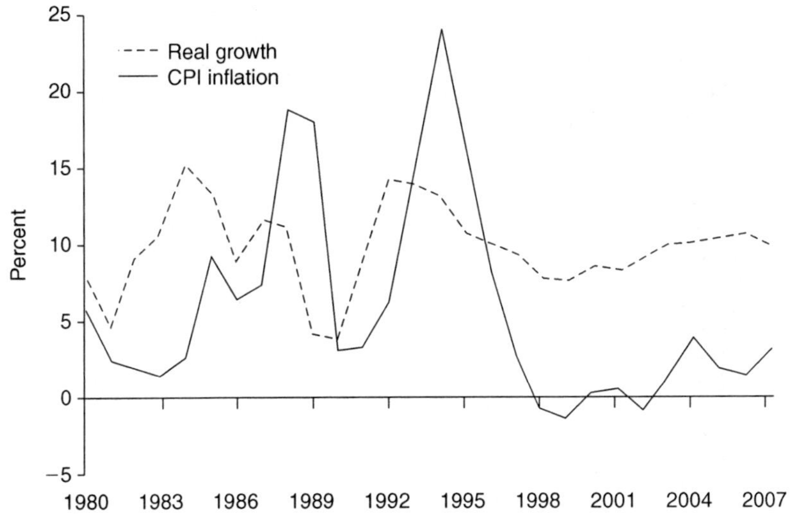

Figure 7.4 Real GDP growth and consumer price inflation, China, 1980 to 2007 (source: IMF).

China's policy of fixing the nominal exchange rate at 8.28/dollar, within a narrow band of ±.3 percent for daily fluctuations, gained credibility.

In Phase 2, the fixed exchange rate's success as an anchor for China's price level was as much a guideline for domestic monetary policy as an instrument. True, continual PBC purchases of foreign exchange, modest by today's standards, were the main instrument for increasing the monetary base. However, before 2004 when the renminbi was not expected to appreciate, these purchases generally amounted to less than 100 percent of the growth in base money (Table 7.1). Thus substantial sterilization operations were not necessary. In this fixed rate period, the rapid increase in the demand for base money from China's very high GDP growth, coupled with an income elasticity of money demand greater than one, more or less balanced the rapid increase in money supply.

However, the monetary control mechanism was not only the exchange rate itself. To prevent overheating, there remained a panoply of supporting direct controls over bank credit – including reserve requirements, credit quotas, lending restrictions by sector, and so on. But for controlling inflation, the renminbi's exchange rate against the dollar was the effective intermediate target.

Why didn't China rely more heavily on domestic financial indicators? With rapid financial transformation and very high saving, the velocity of money – whether defined by M1, M2, or M3 – was (is) too unpredictable for any monetary aggregate to be useful as an intermediate target. And the velocity of money, defined as GDP/M, becomes even more difficult to predict when nominal GDP itself is subject to large revisions. Indeed, nominal GDP was revised sharply

Table 7.1 Foreign reserve holdings and base money of the PBC, 1990–2007

	Reserves	*Base money*	*Reserves/ base money*	*Δ Reserves*	*Δ Base money*	*Δ Reserves/ Δ base money*
1990	82.0	638.7	12.8%	41.5	147.6	28.1%
1991	140.0	793.1	17.6%	57.9	154.4	37.5%
1992	133.0	922.8	14.4%	–6.9	129.7	–5.3%
1993	155.0	1,314.7	11.8%	21.9	391.9	5.6%
1994	445.1	1,721.8	25.9%	290.2	407.1	71.3%
1995	667.0	2,076.0	32.1%	221.8	354.2	62.6%
1996	956.2	2,688.9	35.6%	289.3	612.9	47.2%
1997	1,345.2	3,063.3	43.9%	389.0	374.4	103.9%
1998	1,376.2	3,133.5	43.9%	31.0	70.3	44.1%
1999	1,485.8	3,362.0	44.2%	109.6	228.5	48.0%
2000	1,558.3	3,649.2	42.7%	72.5	287.2	25.3%
2001	1,986.0	3,985.2	49.8%	427.8	336.0	127.3%
2002	2,324.3	4,513.8	51.5%	338.3	528.7	64.0%
2003	3,114.2	5,284.1	58.9%	789.9	770.3	102.5%
2004	4,696.0	5,885.6	79.8%	1,581.8	601.5	263.0%
2005	6,344.0	6,434.3	98.6%	1,648.0	548.7	300.3%
2006	8,577.3	7,775.8	110.3%	2,233.3	1,341.5	166.5%
2007	12,217.1	9,243.3	132.2%	3,639.8	1,467.5	248.0%

Source: IMF, OECD. Billion CNY.

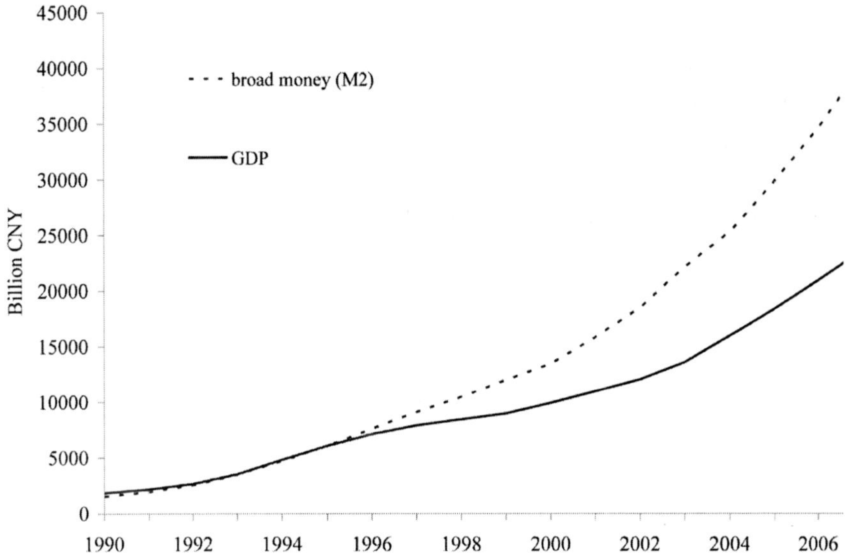

Figure 7.5 Broad money (M2) and nominal GDP, China, 1990 to 2007 (source: OECD, WEO).

upward in 2006. Although Figure 7.5 shows that M2 still grew much faster than nominal GDP, the authorities could have no firm idea of what was "too fast" and thus inflationary.

Still, could the Chinese monetary authorities not target inflation more directly? The absence of a well-developed domestic bond market, and the presence of rigid interest rate pegs for bank deposits and loans, militated against using conventional open market operations to target some key internal interest rate – as per the Taylor Rule – to control the macro-economy as in the U.S. or the euro area. The "New Keynesian" Taylor Rule itself presumes that the authorities have fairly accurate information on the ebb and flow of excess capacity over the business cycle, which could not be the case in China's era of extremely high – but somewhat unpredictable real – economic growth. Thus, the fixed dollar exchange rate was the preferred intermediate monetary target for stabilizing the price level. In Japan's similar era of extraordinary real economic growth and financial change from 1949 to 1971, the domestic price level was safely anchored by pegging the yen at 360 to the dollar (McKinnon and Ohno 1997).

To summarize Phase 2, the ten-year fix at 8.28 yuan per dollar was seen as a way of implementing monetary policy, made possible by the currency unification in 1994 and the move to current account convertibility in 1994 to 1996. It was very successful in anchoring the domestic price level through 2004 (Figure 7.3) and smoothing fluctuations in real economic growth (Figure 7.4). Contrary to what is often alleged,[4] the fixed exchange rate was not a device to cunningly "undervalue" the renminbi so as to create a mercantile advantage by artificially stimulating exports.

Phase 3

What then pushed China off its fixed-rate anchor on July 21, 2005?

First, after 2003, unexpected current account surpluses, coupled with large inflows of foreign direct investment, led to balance-of-payments surpluses. Figure 7.1 shows the sudden spurt in China's multilateral current account surplus from 2 percent of GDP in 2003 to more than 10 percent in 2007. (In Japan's high-growth era of the 1950s and 1960s under a fixed exchange rate, significant inflows of FDI had been prohibited and domestic savings and investments were in better balance.) And the U.S. was the recipient of much of China's surge in manufactured exports. China's bilateral trade surplus with the U.S. (Figure 7.6) reached 1.1 percent of America's GDP in 2006 – twice as large as Japan's. The loss of jobs in U.S. manufacturing disturbed American politicians.

Second, China's balance-of-payments surpluses were misinterpreted by economists and politicians everywhere as an exchange rate problem, i.e., the renminbi was artificially "undervalued," and the more rapid buildup of official exchange reserves in 2003 to 2005 (Table 7.1) was taken as per se evidence of unfair currency manipulation. Hence the American political pressure on China to begin appreciating the renminbi: our Phase 3. Led by Senators Charles Schumer of New York and Leslie Graham of North Carolina, the U.S. government threatened to sanction China by imposing import tariffs unless it appreciated. And on July 21, 2005 it appreciated discretely by 2.5 percent, and subsequently has been appreciating by about 6 percent per year with the disruptive effects on international capital flows discussed above.

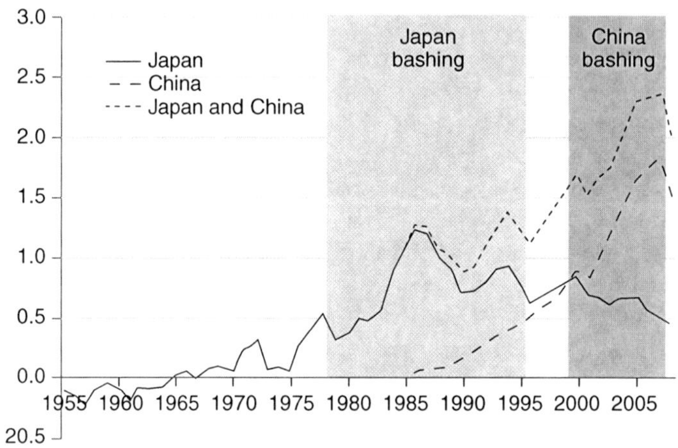

Figure 7.6 Bilateral trade balances of Japan and China versus the U.S. (percent of U.S. GDP) (source: IMF).

The expectation of the further appreciation of the renminbi coupled with the sharp fall in U.S. interest rates, the Federal Funds rate fell from 5.25 percent in August 2007 to just 2 percent in mid-2008, have become the crucial determinants of the huge accumulation of official exchange reserves in China (Table 7.1, Figures 7.7 and 7.8). Despite massive sterilization efforts by the PBC to prevent the monetary base from exploding, inflation could not be fully contained.

Figure 7.9 shows that consumer price inflation in China increased in 2004 with low U.S. interest rates, but then fell in 2005 to 2006 when U.S. interest rates rose so as to reduce capital inflows into China. However, after August 2007 when U.S. interest rates started to decline again, the inflationary outlook for China and the world changed dramatically. Official reserve accumulation further accelerated, raw material and food prices soared, and monetary growth in China became increasingly difficult to contain by various sterilization measures. By May 2008, Chinese consumer price inflation had climbed above 8 percent (Figure 7.9).

With domestic consumer prices rising, Chinese wage increases are putting additional upward pressure on the international dollar prices for Chinese manufactures. By 2007 to 2008, China had been transformed from being a deflationary force on the world economy into an inflationary one. The combination of internal inflation and an appreciating renminbi is now raising the dollar prices of Chinese manufactured goods shipped to the U.S. Figure 7.10 shows that before 2007 the (slightly) falling dollar prices of goods imported from China helped to keep U.S. and world inflation surprisingly low for some years – sometimes

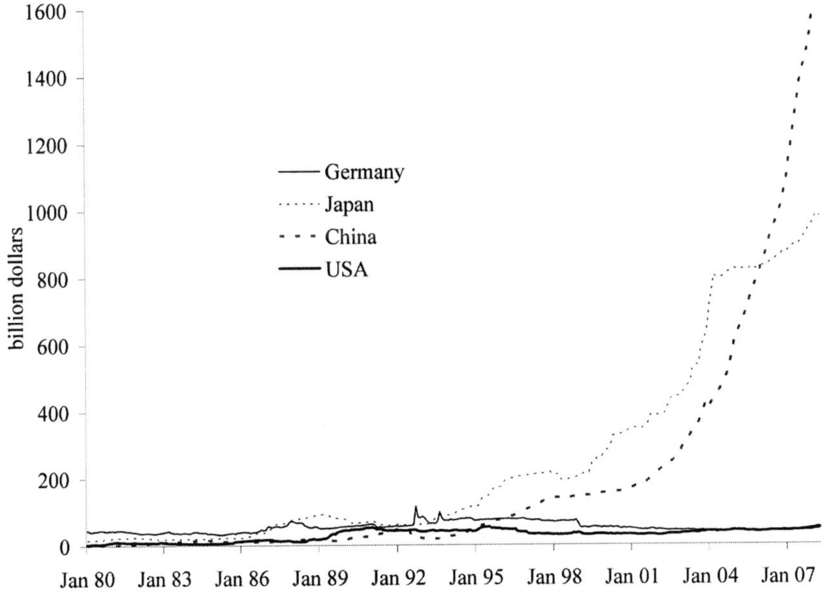

Figure 7.7 Foreign reserves of China, Japan, Germany, and the U.S., 1990 to 2007 (source: IMF, Peoples Bank of China).

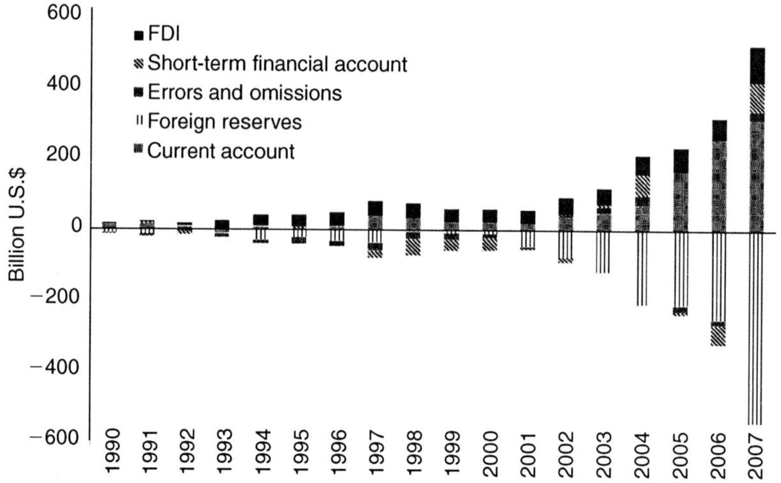

Figure 7.8 Balance of payments, China, 1990 to 2007 (source: IMF, SAFE; 2007 approximated).

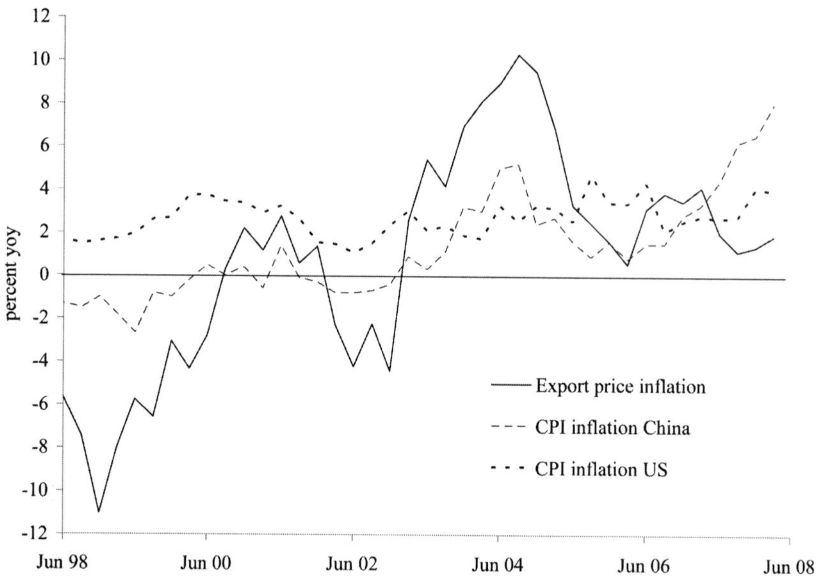

Figure 7.9 Inflation, China and the U.S., 1998 to 2008 (source: Ecowin database).

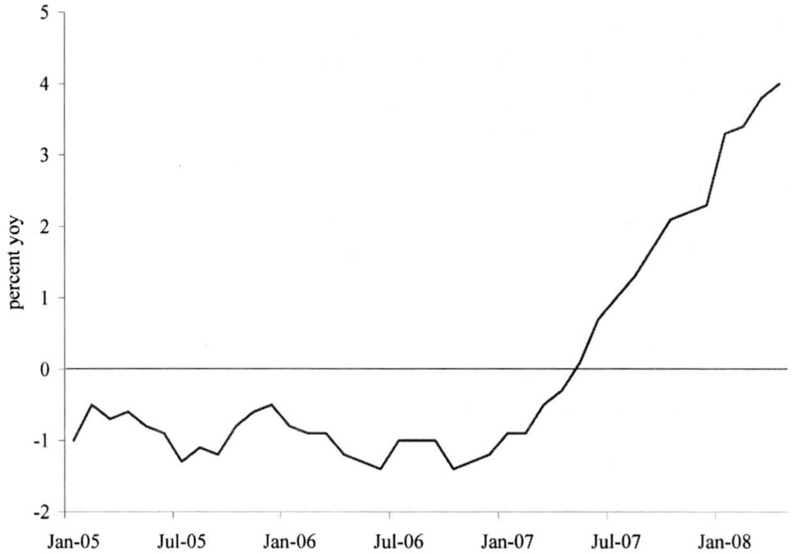

Figure 7.10 U.S. price inflation over imports from China, 2005 to 2008 (source: Ecowin database).

known as the "great moderation." By 2007 to 2008, however, the figure shows the dollar prices of Chinese goods shipped to the U.S. spiking upward. Combined with loose monetary policy in the U.S., the center country under the world dollar standard, worldwide inflation has been unleashed.

True, even without internal inflation, China's rapid growth could well have bid up the prices of primary products – food, oil, and industrial raw materials. However, the loss of monetary control in "peripheral" economies – not only in China but in other emerging markets – accentuates the demand for primary products. As in the 1970s, behind this worldwide inflationary pressure is (was) unduly loose monetary policy by the U.S. coupled with American attempts to devalue the dollar for mercantilist reasons. The resulting capital flight from the U.S. leads emerging markets into overly expansionary monetary policies as they try to resist appreciation of their individual currencies (Swoboda 1978; McKinnon 1981; Hoffman and Schnabl forthcoming). However, the collective effect is undue monetary expansion in the world as a whole with inflation that eventually rebounds back on the U.S. itself.[5]

3 Overcoming three misconceptions about currency stabilization

Because China's current monetary and exchange rate impasse – with its one-way bet in the foreign exchange markets – is overheating its economy with unwanted inflation, its government is inhibited from taking appropriate actions to reduce its ballooning net trade (saving) surplus. Obvious steps for reducing "excess" net saving – such as cutting taxes and increasing government social expenditures – would have a near-term inflationary impact. Less obvious is the impact on net saving of forcing (or encouraging) much higher dividend payouts from China's corporate sector; but, under certain conditions, that too could be expansionary.

Meanwhile, China's current account surplus, uncovered by outflows of private capital, continually worsens the monetary impasse. Figure 7.11 shows the recent "frenzied" buildup of exchange reserves so far in 2008 reaching US$100 billion per month, which is much higher than the monthly current account surplus. Because foreigners misinterpret the trade surplus and accumulating official exchange reserves to be evidence of an undervalued currency, they call for further appreciation of the renminbi. This foreign pressure strengthens the expectation that the renminbi will be higher in the future, thus causing more inflows of hot money.

What is the best way to escape from this conundrum? China can not end its exchange rate impasse, and the worldwide monetary turmoil that goes with it, on its own. With proper foreign cooperation, however, the monetary impasse from the one-way bet in the foreign exchange markets could be resolved quite quickly. Thus, currency stabilization should *precede* measures to correct the saving–investment imbalance – which may take months or years to be effective both in China and abroad.

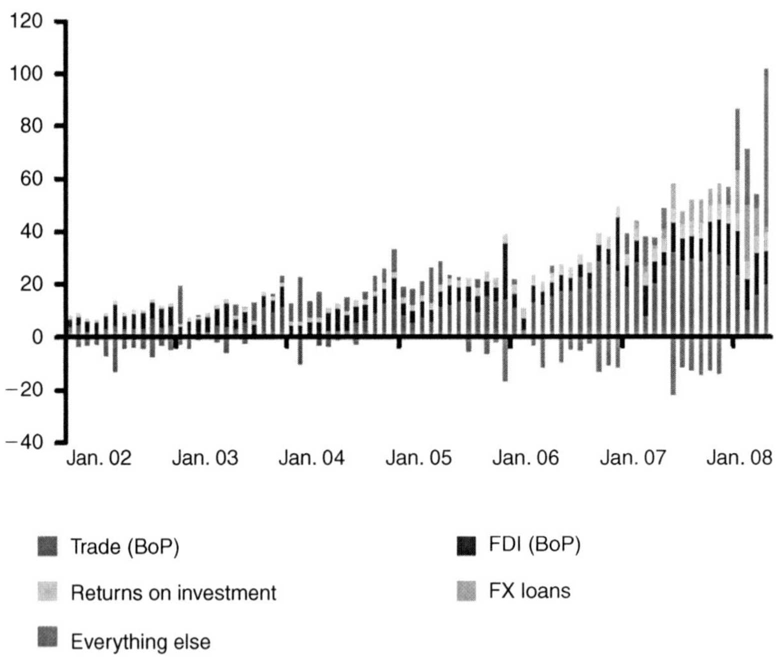

Figure 7.11 Monthly foreign reserve buildup, China, 2002 to 2008 (source: Standard Chartered).

Nevertheless, to be successful, the political economy of any international agreement likely requires both as a package deal. China pushing to get the renminbi up can only be stopped if China proposes definite fiscal measures to reduce its future saving surpluses – possibly in conjunction with U.S. efforts to reduce America's saving deficiency, and overly loose domestic monetary policy leading to a weak dollar.

Populist politics aside, what inhibits China and the U.S. (representing the interests of the industrial economies more generally) from agreeing on such a package deal that would be of such great mutual benefit? Three common misconceptions in economic theory on the role of the exchange rate inhibit any political agreement to stabilize China's currency. Let us consider each in turn.

Misconception #1: The exchange rate can affect the trade balance

Many, if not most, economists believe that a country's net trade balance can be controlled by manipulating the level of its exchange rate. However, a current account surplus (dominated by a trade surplus) just reflects a surplus of saving over investment at home – and the converse abroad. Thus, how a discrete appreciation of a creditor country's currency will eliminate its saving surplus is neither obvious nor unambiguous. True, its goods would become more expensive to foreigners – the relative price effect. But, in an economy open to international capital flows, domestic investment would fall because appreciation makes the country a more expensive place in which to produce. In addition, because China owns huge stocks of foreign currency claims (largely dollars), a negative wealth effect from having the dollar fall against the renminbi would further reduce domestic expenditures – including for imports. This decline in imports offsets the dampening effect of higher foreign currency prices for exports so as to leave any change in the net trade balance small and ambiguous (Qiao 2007).

To illustrate this exchange rate–trade balance misconception, it is instructive to revisit the consequences of Japan pushing to get the yen up more than three decades earlier starting with the Nixon shock of August 1971. The yen rose episodically from 360 to the dollar in early 1971 to touch 80 to the dollar in April 1995. "Despite" this enormous cumulative appreciation, Japan's net trade surplus rose from being negligible in the 1960s to average about 2 percent of GDP in the 1970s, peaked out at about 5 percent in the late 1980s, and remains close to 4 percent of GDP in 2008 with the yen at 100 to 110 to the dollar. Massive currency fluctuations had no systematic impact on Japan's net trade (saving) balance.

However, the great nominal appreciations of the yen against the dollar, which Japan more or less welcomed during the worldwide inflation of the 1970s, eventually unhinged Japan's macro-economy (McKinnon and Ohno 1997). In the late 1980s, the syndrome of the ever-higher yen provoked bubbles in Japan's stock and land markets along with a falling WPI. When the bubbles broke in 1990 to 1991 followed by a further sharp rise in the yen in 1994 to 1995, Japan was thrown into deflationary slump: its infamous "lost decade" of 1992 to 2002.

Foreign exchange risk created (and still sustains) a near-zero interest liquidity trap that renders monetary policy virtually impotent for stimulating domestic spending (Goyal and McKinnon 2003). Although Japan has had modest export-led GDP annual growth of 2 to 3 percent since 2002, a deflationary hangover continues: wages and per capita consumption are stagnant (McKinnon 2007b).

Misconception #2: Ongoing exchange rate appreciation reduces inflation

The second, but more subtle, misconception is that ongoing exchange appreciation can reduce domestic price inflation – or, at the very least, insulate the economy from international inflation. China gets much gratuitous advice to appreciate faster in order to "fight inflation." This admonition is certainly true in the long run, as Japan's unfortunate experience with eventual deflation from yen appreciation attests. However, for a country emerging from a fixed nominal exchange rate where domestic and foreign rates of price inflation had been more or less aligned, the near-term effect of a well-telegraphed transition to an appreciating currency can be highly inflationary – as with China's current monetary impasse. In the near-term transition, the inflationary impact from the loss of monetary control can overwhelm the deflationary impact of a higher level of the exchange rate.

Again, let us refer to Japan's earlier experience with this transition problem. Under the Bretton Woods system of fixed exchange rate parities, the yen had been successfully fixed at 360 to the dollar from 1949 to August 1971, so that price inflation in tradable goods (WPI) between the U.S. and Japan were similar. As early as 1970, however, market participants began to project that the dollar might be depreciated. Hot money began to flow out of the U.S. into European countries as well as Japan (despite its capital controls). In order to prevent more precipitate appreciation, in 1971 to 1972 the Bank of Japan intervened heavily in the foreign exchange markets with a rapid buildup of foreign exchange reserves and a surge in domestic money growth. By 1974, annualized WPI inflation in Japan became higher than in the U.S.: 31.3 percent versus "just" 18.9 percent in the U.S. Only in the late 1970s did Japanese inflation fall below American – the "long-run" relative deflationary effect of a higher yen that most economists expect. But the length and strength of the near-term inflationary transition was surprising. China is still in the inflationary "near term" which, with no change in present circumstances of arm-twisting to get the renminbi up, could continue for an uncomfortably long time.

Are there circumstances where China should acquiesce to continual renminbi appreciation? Clearly if the center country under the world dollar standard continues to inflate too much, the People's Bank of China would have little choice but to acquiesce to a managed ongoing appreciation of the renminbi against the dollar. However, the current rate of appreciation is too rapid for securing either near-term monetary control in China or long-term price-level alignment with the U.S.

Misconception #3: Floating the rate would equilibrate the foreign exchange market

"Flexibility" is a nicer word than floating. Could not the PBC simply withdraw from the foreign exchange market and let the exchange rate be determined by private market makers – much in the way that the euro's value against the dollar is determined? No, because this proposed solution presumes that a determinate market exchange rate – which could balance the demand and supply of dollars in terms of renminbi – actually exists if the PBC were to exit the market. Unlike the Europe–U.S. situation, however, China faces an ongoing *currency mismatch* leading to the syndrome of "conflicted virtue" (McKinnon and Schnabl 2004; McKinnon 2005) which prevents private market-makers from clearing the excess supply of dollars.

What causes the mismatch that undermines the case for floating? The renminbi, like the currencies of other developing economies, is not used significantly for international borrowing or lending; but China couples this gap in its capital markets with an enormous saving (trade) surplus. Thus dollar, rather than renminbi, claims on foreigners continually pile up within the economy. (The dollar is the "default" international money.) Natural private market-makers such as Chinese banks – or even insurance companies and pension funds – all have their liabilities to depositors, policy-holders, and so forth, denominated in renminbi. Thus, even if the yuan/dollar rate fluctuated only randomly, Chinese financial institutions would be exposed to too much exchange risk (relative to their limited capital) to allow dollar assets continually to pile up on their balance sheets. At some point, they would stop buying new dollar claims associated with the ongoing trade surplus. Consequently, a free float would result in an indefinite upward spiral of the renminbi against the dollar – with no well-defined balance point where Chinese financial institutions become sufficiently willing buyers of dollar assets to halt their further depreciation.

This third misconception is linked to the first. A floating but appreciating renminbi would not predictably reduce China's trade surplus, and dollars would continue to pour into the economy. On the other hand, if China was not a creditor country because foreign trade (net saving) was close to being balanced, then no substantial internal currency mismatch would exist and an uneasy float could be possible.[6]

However, the issue is somewhat broader. Suppose China did not have a chronic saving surplus, but its bond markets were still not well developed at different terms to maturity, and there were residual capital controls (as in most developing economies). Then forward markets for private hedging against currency risk become difficult to organize and expensive. So, willy-nilly, if the government attempted to float the rate, it would soon be drawn back to smooth exchange fluctuations – if only at higher frequencies – in order to reduce the risks seen by exporters and importers. This "fear of floating" is well documented by Reinhart (2000) and Calvo (2002).

4 Toward a credibly fixed exchange rate

Overcoming these three misconceptions about the exchange rate is crucial for stabilizing China's monetary system. For a developing country like China on the periphery of the dollar standard, the exchange rate is best considered as just an extension of domestic monetary policy – and not an instrument of trade policy. This monetary approach to the exchange rate suggests that China should reset the yuan/dollar exchange rate and adjust domestic monetary policy through time to keep it stable, as was the case between 1995 and 2004, i.e., phase 2 in Figure 7.2.

What should this new rate be? The precise level of the new rate is much less important than having it credibly stable into the indefinite future. However, with the unfortunate recent history of bashing China to get the rate up, an international understanding or more formal agreement to end China pushing is now necessary for any new fix to be sufficiently credible to eliminate the one-way bet on future renminbi appreciation. If such an agreement were forthcoming "today" (mid-2008), the PBC should simply pick today's rate of 6.8 yuan per dollar as the central rate – within the conventional narrow band of ±0.3 percent – to be continued forward.

Ending China bashing through a political agreement is not as far-fetched as it might first seem. After almost twenty-five years of Japan pushing to get the yen up, in April 1995 U.S. Treasury Secretary Robert Rubin announced a new "strong dollar policy," and Japan bashing ceased. The U.S. Federal Reserve Bank and Bank of Japan then intervened jointly several times in the summer of 1995 to quash any further appreciations of the yen. Although this strong dollar policy saved Japan from further deflationary ruin, it was just a ceiling on the yen and not a stable fix. Subsequent large fluctuations in the yen/dollar rate, when domestic holdings of dollar assets from Japan's being an international creditor are large, have destabilized the Japanese financial system and tightened its low interest rate liquidity trap. But this interest rate story is a digression for another time (McKinnon 2007b).

In the Chinese case, it would be sufficient to stabilize the renminbi if foreign pressure to appreciate ceased. Then the PBC itself could reset the yuan/dollar rate so as to eliminate the one-way bet on ongoing appreciation. A massive outflow of *private* capital largely intermediated by Chinese banks, insurance companies, pension funds, and so forth would surely follow as these institutions would be more than happy to diversify into foreign assets once the one-way bet was eliminated. With normal private sector financial international intermediation for China's huge current account surplus, the PBC may stop purchasing dollar assets on a large scale. Indeed, if the new capital outflow exceeded the current account surplus, the PBC might have to sell some of China's absurdly high dollar reserves to keep the renminbi fixed against the dollar at the newly reset rate. In any event, the PBC could regain control over the domestic money supply while reducing reserve requirements on domestic banks. Inflation would come down and the efficiency of domestic financial intermediation would improve.

The credit crunch in U.S. financial markets would be eased as private capital flowed back to the U.S.

Finally, once its domestic monetary and exchange rate system was stabilized, China could then proceed deliberately to reduce excess domestic saving relative to its huge domestic investment without worrying about exacerbating near-term inflation. But to analyze desirable long-term changes in China's tax, spending, and dividend policies would be a major exercise in public finance beyond the scope of this chapter.

Notes

1 Many thanks to Nick Hope for his insights.
2 *Quarterly Update*, February 2008, World Bank Office, Beijing.
3 Indonesia, Korea, Malaysia, the Philippines, and Thailand.
4 See, for example, Dooley *et al.* (2004) for misinterpreting China's fixed exchange rate, and those of smaller Asian countries, as a more or less deliberate attempt to undervalue their currencies.
5 Notice that when Alexander Swoboda was writing about the dollar's standard's inflationary transmission mechanism in the late 1970s, the important "peripheral" countries forced into undue monetary expansion were in Western Europe and Japan. But now the strong euro system has curbed European monetary expansion and Japan is mired in a near-zero interest rate liquidity trap. So the main avenues of excess "world" money creation are in individual Asian countries outside of Japan.
6 The non-feasibility of a pure float applies symmetrically to a chronic debtor economy whose debts are denominated in foreign currencies, say, dollars, that continue to pile up from ongoing trade deficits. Again there is an internal currency mismatch where domestic foreign currency debtors are threatened with bankruptcy should the domestic currency depreciate – and the threat thereof could easily precipitate a run-out of the domestic currency. This was the case in the great Asian crisis of 1997 to 1998 as the five countries involved had run trade deficits for several years and built up large (private) dollar debts.

References

Calvo, Guillermo and Carmen Reinhart (2002) "Fear of Floating." *Quarterly Journal of Economics* 117, 379–408.

Cline, William (2005) *The United States as a Debtor Nation*. Washington, DC: Institute for International Economics.

Dooley, Michael, David Folkerts-Landau, and Peter Garber (2004) "An Essay on the Revived Bretton-Woods-System." *International Journal of Finance and Economics* 4, 307–313.

Goyal, Rishi and Ronald McKinnon (2003) "Japan's Negative Risk Premium in Interest Rates: The Liquidity Trap and Fall in Bank Lending." *The World Economy* 26, 339–363.

Green, Stephen (2008) "On the Ground (in China)." *Standard Chartered Bank*, February 11.

Hoffman, Andreas and Gunther Schnabl (2008) "Monetary Policy, Vagabonding Liquidity and Bursting Bubbles in New and Emerging Markets – An Overinvestment View." *The World Economy* 31 (9), 1226–1252.

McKinnon, Ronald (1981) "Currency Substitution and Instability in the World Dollar Standard." *American Economic Review* 72 (3), 320–333.

McKinnon, Ronald (2005) *Exchange Rates under the East Asian Dollar Standard: Living with Conflicted Virtue*. Cambridge, MA: MIT Press.

McKinnon, Ronald (2007a) "U.S. Current Account Deficits and the Dollar Standard's Sustainability: A Monetary Approach." *CESifo Forum* 4, 12–23.

McKinnon, Ronald (2007b) "Japan's Deflationary Hangover: Wage Stagnation and the Syndrome of the Ever-weaker Yen." *Singapore Economic Review* 52 (3), 309–334.

McKinnon, Ronald and Kenichi Ohno (1997) *Dollar and Yen. Resolving Economic Conflict between the United Stated and Japan*. Cambridge, MA: MIT Press.

McKinnon, Ronald and Gunther Schnabl (2004) "A Return to Soft Dollar Pegging in East Asia? Mitigating Conflicted Virtue." *International Finance* 7 (2), 169–201.

Qiao, Hong (2007) "Exchange Rates and Trade Balances under the Dollar Standard." *Journal of Policy Modeling* 29, 765–782.

Reinhart, Carmen (2000) "The Mirage of Floating Exchange Rates." *American Economic Review* 90, 65–70.

Swoboda, Alexander (1978) "Gold, Dollars, Euro-dollars, and the World Money Stock under Fixed Exchange Rates." *American Economic Review* 68 (4), 625–642.

Part III

Central banking

A revolution under way?

8 Monetary policy and exchange rates

Theory and practice

Stefan Gerlach and Cédric Tille

1 Introduction

The design of monetary policy, and the associated choice of exchange rate regime, played a prominent role in Alexander's lectures at the Institute in the late 1970s, which one of us attended between 1978 and 1983. This focus reflected the collapse of the Bretton Woods system in 1971. Prior to that profound change, central banks typically fixed the exchange rate, subject to infrequent realignment. The breakdown of that framework required central banks to figure "what to do next" with monetary policy. They broadly faced two main options: they could fix the exchange rate with respect to another currency than the U.S. dollar, or instead opt for an independent policy, but then had to decide on the exact strategy in setting a nominal anchor. The European Community offers a clear illustration with a number of attempts to create a new exchange rate arrangement, starting with the "snake in the tunnel" in 1972, which aimed at limiting exchange rate movements between European currencies (the "snake"), while allowing them to move against the dollar as a group (the "tunnel"). The "tunnel" component soon collapsed following the floating of the U.S. dollar in 1973. Furthermore, monetary policy in the participating currencies reacted to the drastic rise in oil prices in 1973 in incompatible ways, leading to sharp exchange rate fluctuations among European currencies and entrances and exits from the snake.[1] This failure led in turn to the establishment of the European Monetary System in 1979. In sum, positive and normative exchange rate questions had a high profile in academic discussions in Geneva and elsewhere in the late 1970s.

In this chapter, we first review how the literature on the appropriate monetary policy regime in an open economy, and its close connection to the exchange rate regime, has developed over the past thirty years. We then discuss some considerations that play a role in the practical choice of the policy regime. Section 2 takes a theoretical perspective. We first review the open economy extension of the celebrated analysis of Poole (1970), which very much constituted the standard toolbox used to think about the exchange rate regime in the late 1970s. We next present the main message from a range of recent contributions relying on state-of-the-art "dynamic stochastic general equilibrium" models. These models entail limitations along several dimensions, with most contributions, for instance, taking central bank credibility for granted. Section 3 then reviews several points of practical relevance, namely the role of the exchange rate as a nominal anchor, financial integration, the role of institutions, and exit strategies. Section 4 illustrates these practical aspects by a case study of Hong Kong, and Section 5 concludes.

2 Monetary policy in the open economy: theoretical considerations

Modelling then: Poole in the open economy

The main challenge facing the central bank in an open economy is to achieve both internal and external stabilization, as discussed in Mundell (1968). The central bank thus needs to design its policy, taking account of the impact on the exchange rate as well as on international capital flows. The analysis assumes that the central bank's ultimate objective is to stabilize the business cycle, and focuses on which intermediate objective was best suited. In particular, should the central bank stabilize the interest rate or smooth fluctuations of exchange rates? The standard paradigm used to think about the issue in the late 1970s was Boyer's (1978) open economy extension of Poole's (1970) celebrated closed economy analysis of the central bank's choice between operating with an interest rate or money stock objective.[2] The framework inherits the main aspects of the Poole model: the analysis is static, and prices are assumed to be sticky and determined by aggregate demand (thus, direct exchange rate effects on prices were disregarded). By stabilizing aggregate demand, the central bank can therefore stabilize inflation.

The analysis emphasizes how the optimal policy depends on the exact nature of the shocks affecting the economy. Specifically, a flexible exchange rate is preferable when the economy is mostly subject to aggregate demand shocks. A rise in aggregate demand boosts GDP and the demand for money, leading interest rates to rise in order to ensure monetary equilibrium. Higher interest rates in turn attract capital inflows, leading under floating exchange rates to an appreciation of the currency that reduces export competitiveness and aggregate demand. In equilibrium, the aggregate demand shock has no impact on aggregate output as it is exactly offset by the exchange rate appreciation. By contrast, a fixed exchange rate requires the central bank to accommodate the capital inflow through a monetary expansion, leading to a rise in output.

The policy prescription is reversed if monetary shocks are predominant. Under floating exchange rates, an increase in velocity shock leads to a reduction in the interest rate as the demand for money demand falls. Capital then flows out of the country, attracted by the higher returns in foreign currency. This triggers a depreciation of the exchange rate, leading to an increase in output by improving the trade balance. Under a fixed exchange rate, however, such a shock has no impact on economic activity, as the incipient depreciation of the exchange rate would force the central bank to tighten monetary policy. With the exchange rate remaining unchanged, exports and output are kept constant.

In sum, the open economy extension of the Poole analysis showed that stabilizing real activity called for a flexible exchange rate to act as a shock absorber in the presence of real demand shocks, but for a fixed exchange rate to automatically undo the impact of monetary shocks.[3] Since there was no reason to believe that only one type of shock mattered, the policy conclusion was that some intermediate degree of exchange rate flexibility was generally desirable. Absent any estimates of the relative importance of shocks, that was the only policy conclusion that could be drawn, limiting the operational insights from the analysis.

While celebrated, the analysis was subject to a number of shortcomings. In line with the mainstream models at the time, it overlooked the role of expectations, as well as the eventual adjustment of prices in the medium run. Another limitation is the lack of micro-foundations for the underlying aggregate demand and money demand relationships, as stressed by Obstfeld and Rogoff (1996, p. 632).

Modelling now: uses and limits of the exchange rate

The ultimate goal of monetary policy

The limitations outlined above have led to the development of "dynamic stochastic general equilibrium" (DSGE) models in macro-economics. These models cast the analysis in a framework that explicitly accounts for the dynamic response to shocks at various horizons. This shift also occurred in open economy macroeconomics, with Obstfeld and Rogoff (1996, ch. 10; 2002) presenting a tractable version of these models. The framework includes three main ingredients that were lacking in earlier analysis. First, the general equilibrium model is based on explicitly optimizing behavior by consumers, workers, and firms. Second, the model provides a well-grounded metric for evaluating alternative policies, in the form of the welfare criterion that agents maximize. Third, while the assumption of sticky prices remains at the core of the analysis – otherwise monetary policy has no impact on real economic activity – firms set prices in a forward-looking fashion, taking full account of the various possible shocks and the rule under which monetary policy is conducted.[4]

A contribution by such DSGE models is to clarify the nature of the problem facing central banks, both in the short and the long run. In the long run the role of monetary policy is to provide a stable nominal anchor. This prescription was already apparent in the 1970s and 1980s when several central banks opted for a stable expansion of some monetary aggregate. While this monetary targeting strategy broke down due to instability of the link between monetary aggregates and inflation, the prescription for a stable anchor remains at the core of more recent strategies such as inflation targeting.

While monetary policy should smooth economic fluctuations in the short run, DSGE models stress that this stabilization should be understood in terms of movements around an efficient benchmark. Earlier contributions assumed that the central bank aimed at stabilizing the level of output, with steady growth being the optimal allocation. By contrast, the recent literature shows that the ultimate goal of monetary policy is to bring the economy around the obstacle of price rigidities. If prices and wages could be adjusted immediately to shocks, the economy would respond to these shocks in an efficient way. For instance, a slowdown in productivity would lead to a reduction in output. While at first such a recession could appear suboptimal, it is indeed the best possible response to the fact that producing output has become more costly.[5] The failure of prices and wages to adjust is then costly, as it prevents the economy from reacting in an efficient way to shocks. Because of their ability to affect economic activity in the presence of nominal rigidities, central banks have a role to play in alleviating this problem. The best they can achieve is to generate a response of economic variables identical to the one that would be achieved under flexible prices.[6] Stabilization policy is then interpreted in terms of gaps from the flexible price allocation. As the efficient allocation can entail substantial fluctuations in response to shocks, the policy prescription is for a stabilization in relative terms – that is, around the flexible price allocation – and not necessarily in absolute terms.

Exchange rates and relative prices

One of the most prominent distinctions between closed and open economy macro-economics is the central role of relative prices in the latter. In the context of the analysis of monetary policy, this puts the efficiency – or lack thereof – of international relative prices at center stage. Consider, for instance, a productivity improvement in a country. If prices are free to adjust, the prices of the goods produced in that country fall, making them cheaper than goods produced in other countries.

In the presence of price rigidities, a central question is whether monetary policy can generate these efficient responses in international relative prices. Specifically, the analysis stresses the central role of exchange rate pass-through; that is, the extent to which movements in exchange rates affect the price consumers pay for imported goods.

The literature first considered the case where import prices move one-for-one with the exchange rate, so that a 10 percent depreciation of a country's currency leads import prices in that country to increase by 10 percent. Movements in the exchange rate then affect the relative price of goods produced in different countries, a benefit stressed by Friedman (1953). Consider, for instance, a 10 percent depreciation of the dollar vis-à-vis the euro. European consumers see a 10 percent reduction in the price of U.S. goods, with no change in the price they pay for European goods. Similarly, U.S. consumers face a higher dollar price of European goods, with no change in the price of U.S. goods. In both countries the depreciation of the dollar then reduces the price of U.S. goods *relative* to European goods.

In the presence of a connection between the exchange rate and relative good prices, monetary policy should not limit exchange rate fluctuations as they are useful in delivering efficient movements in the terms of trade – the relative price of traded goods produced in different countries – (Obstfeld and Rogoff 2002). Consider a situation where productivity increases in the U.S. If prices are flexible, the higher productivity reduces the price of U.S. goods, which are easier to produce. This affects both the level and the composition of world demand. In terms of the level, the low price of U.S. goods reduces the consumer price index in both the U.S. and Europe, leading to higher real balances and higher demand. In terms of the composition of demand, the fall in the relative price of U.S. goods induces consumers worldwide to shift their demand away from European goods towards U.S. goods. Such a shift is efficient, as U.S. goods are less costly to produce.

In the presence of price rigidities, this adjustment mechanism is not operative. Monetary policy can however generate an efficient response. Specifically, the improvement of U.S. productivity should be accompanied by an expansionary monetary policy in the U.S., leading to a depreciation of the dollar. This policy response affects the composition and level of demand in the same way as price adjustments would have. In terms of the composition, the depreciation of the dollar reduces the relative price of U.S. goods worldwide, leading consumers to shift from European to U.S. goods. In terms of the level of demand, the increase in U.S. nominal balances is transmitted to real balances. This transmission is partial, as the weak dollar raises import prices, hence the U.S. overall price index, and the level of demand in the U.S. increases by less than the monetary expansion. The depreciation of the dollar also affects the level of European consumption, as European consumers now benefit from cheaper imports, leading to a reduction in the European consumer price index, hence an increase in real balances and demand. Overall, the combination of an expansionary monetary policy in the U.S. and a flexible exchange rate brings the economy to *exactly* the same allocation that would prevail with flexibility, which is the best that central banks can aim for.

The above argument hinges on the ability of exchange rate movements to alter import prices. The empirical evidence however finds that the price paid by consumers for imported goods is little affected by exchange rate fluctuations, calling the relevance of the analysis above into question. The exchange rate indeed loses its usefulness when the price paid by consumers for imported goods is not affected by exchange rate movements (Devereux and Engel 2007). While monetary policy still has a role to play, this is now limited to the level of demand. Consider again the case of a productivity gain in the U.S. discussed above. With Europe and the U.S. being of similar size, demand would increase equally in both countries when prices are flexible. With sticky prices, this pattern can be achieved through expansionary monetary policy in both countries, boosting demand through higher nominal and real balances.[7] The best monetary policy can do is then to boost demand equally in the two countries through similar expansions. The policy response does not deliver the flexible price allocation, as it only affects the level of demand, but not its composition across U.S. and European goods. As monetary policy moves in step in both countries, the exchange rate remains unchanged, an aspect that entails no cost, as the exchange rate has no impact on relative prices. To put things succinctly, the prescription may be summarized as "if the exchange rate is powerless, don't use it."

In light of the overwhelming evidence that consumer prices are little affected by exchange rate movements, one could expect the analysis outlined above to have sounded the death-knell of flexible exchange rates. This is however not the case. A first reason is that consumer prices may not be the relevant prices for the allocation of aggregate demand across goods produced in different countries. Consumer prices are only the ultimate stage of a long distribution chain that goes from the foreign producers through domestic importers, and retailers. The evidence shows that exchange rate movements are transmitted to prices at the intermediate stages of this chain much more than to consumer prices, and movements in exchange rate can then alter the composition of demand by inducing intermediaries to substitutes between domestic and imported inputs.

Terms of trade vs. real exchange rate

Another limitation of the analysis above is that it focuses on the terms of trade. This measure compares the relative price of goods produced in different countries that can be shipped across borders, such as manufactured goods. It however abstracts from the price of other goods that cannot be shipped, such as services that can only be consumed where they are produced (a haircut being the standard example). Because services account for the bulk of consumption baskets in many countries, the terms of trade offer only a partial picture. In particular they do not allow for international comparisons of the overall level of consumer prices, including both traded goods and services. Such a comparison relies on another measure of international relative prices, namely the real exchange rate – the ratio between the U.S. consumer price index and the European consumer price index. Thus, a change in the price of services in the U.S. alters the U.S.–Europe real exchange rate, even though the terms of trade are unchanged. As a result, movements in the nominal exchange rate can play a role through the real exchange rate, even when they do not affect the terms of trade (Corsetti 2008; Duarte and Obstfeld 2008).

We illustrate this by considering again a productivity improvement in the U.S. In our discussion so far we assumed that the consumption baskets of U.S. and European consumers are similar, in which case the productivity gain leads to an equal increase in the level of demand in both countries when prices are flexible. In reality, however, the consumption basket in a country is tilted towards domestic goods, through the presence of non-traded goods such as services. U.S. goods then account for the bulk of the U.S. consumption basket, while playing a limited role in the European basket. In this case, a productivity improvement in the U.S. leads to a larger increase in the level of demand in the U.S. than in Europe when prices are flexible, as the now cheaper U.S. goods are most prominent in the U.S. basket.

What happens when prices are sticky? Assume that import prices are insulated from the exchange rate, so that exchange rate movements have no impact on the terms of trade. As discussed above, monetary policy only affects the level of demand, and not its allocation across different goods. Even though monetary policy cannot work through the terms of trade, the optimal policy calls for a larger expansion in the U.S. than in Europe. This policy mix leads to a larger consumption increase in the U.S., as in the case where prices are flexible. The different reaction of monetary policy across the two countries entails a depreciation of the dollar. Therefore, pegging the exchange rate would be suboptimal, even though it has no impact on consumer prices.

The prescription for a flexible exchange rate even when it has no impact on relative prices can appear surprising. However, the optimal policy does not call for moving the exchange rate because it alters import prices. Instead, it indicates that policymakers should not limit their flexibility by stabilizing a variable that is substantially disconnected from real activity. The prescription may be summarized as "if the exchange rate is powerless, don't restrict policy because of it."

Additional extensions

DSGE models also shed light on a range of other questions. First, some currencies occupy a prominent role in international trade and financial markets that goes beyond the size of the country, and Alexander contributed to the analysis of this issue in the context of financial markets (Swoboda 1968, 1969). Recent work using DSGE models shows the asymmetric impact of monetary policy in different countries when one currency is the dominant invoicing vehicle of international trade (Goldberg and Tille 2009). Second, the international spillovers of policy have fed a debate on whether some form of international cooperation between central banks is warranted. The recent literature shows that international spillovers per se do not warrant cooperation. The relevant criterion is instead whether the marginal impact of a country's monetary stance differs between its own residents and foreign consumers. Such a difference does not emerge in general, with notable exceptions such as the case of asymmetric shocks between the traded and non-traded sectors (Canzoneri *et al.* 2005).

The contributions discussed above focus on the ability of the exchange rate to affect the allocation of world demand across goods produced in different countries, the so-called intensive margin of external adjustment. This is however not the only dimension of external linkages, and researchers have stressed the role of the extensive margin (Corsetti *et al.* 2007). Under this alternative channel, a country can boost the value of its exports by extending the range of goods it produces. While increasing sales of existing varieties of goods abroad requires a movement in their relative prices, hence a potential role for the exchange rate, selling new goods does not necessary entail such a reduction in prices.

Although the issue of monetary policy design in an open economy is an ongoing area of work, the recent literature points to the desirability of an inward-looking policy. Specifically, monetary policy is best conducted by aiming at domestic conditions, allowing the exchange rate to freely adjust. This prescription allows for monetary conditions to be in line with the specific conditions of various countries. It may also be understood as a particular application of the general result that monetary policy should focus on stabilizing fluctuations in prices whose adjustment is the most restricted,[8] and let prices that are more flexible, such as the exchange rate, move freely.

3 Exchange rate regimes in practice

While the literature reviewed above has improved our understanding of the appropriate design of monetary policy in open economies, both the earlier and more recent models discussed above face substantial limitations. First, they focus squarely on the short-run stabilization problem faced by a central bank. The analysis is conducted assuming that the central bank is perfectly credible and faces no constraints from fiscal policy or the stability of the financial system. Long-run inflation expectations are well anchored, and the only problem for the central bank is to choose the exact form of the policy rule through which it exerts its influence. Few central banks are as fortunate in the real world.

Furthermore, while the theoretical literature provides plenty of insights into the considerations that should go into the choice of exchange rate regime, it is not straightforward to operationalize them, since the structure of the economy and the nature of shocks are in practice not known.[9]

Overall, it is therefore not surprising that many countries operate monetary policy with an exchange rate arrangement that seems difficult to reconcile with economic theory. This suggests that the models discussed above disregard some factors that play an important role when countries choose an exchange rate regime. We review these factors below.

The exchange rate as a nominal anchor

The models discussed in Section 2 are silent on how inflation expectations are anchored. This abstracts from the common use of a fixed exchange rate as a nominal anchor. This role has been especially prominent in many schemes to prevent episodes of high or extreme inflation.[10] With prices being changed daily or weekly, price indices that are reported monthly cease to provide any information about current developments. Instead, many prices are tied informally or formally to the exchange rate which may be observed in real time. Pegging the exchange rate, even temporarily, then becomes an effective way of slowing inflation. While the adoption of a peg thus seems a simple and effective way to bring inflation under control, it does not remove the need to address the fiscal problem that is typically the root cause of high inflation. That said, pegging the exchange rate can improve the government's fiscal position by raising the real value of tax collections and provides some breathing room during which fiscal reforms can be implemented to bring the budget deficit under control.

In addition to having played an important role in ending occasional episodes of extreme inflation, exchange rate pegs have proved useful in disinflation packages in many emerging market and transition countries.[11] Furthermore, fixing the exchange rate to the currency of a low-inflation neighbor has been seen as a tool to achieve and maintain low inflation by a range of central banks, particularly in Europe, with a history of moderate inflation but poor credibility. Thus, many countries adopted fixed exchange rate pegs against the DM or the ECU in order to reduce inflation on a sustained basis (Giavazzi and Giovannini 1989). While this policy was successful in those countries (e.g., Austria and the Netherlands) that were willing to subordinate monetary policy fully to the maintenance of the peg, many other countries experienced repeated episodes of speculative attacks, typically involving large and sustained increases in short-term interest rates to the detriment of economic activity, often ending in a devaluation. One lesson to be drawn from these episodes is that sustaining a fixed exchange rate under capital mobility requires that monetary policy be completely focused on the exchange rate goal.

However, while a peg may serve as a nominal anchor, it has become increasingly recognized in recent years that fixing the nominal exchange rate against a stable currency does not guarantee a low and stable inflation if equilibrium real exchange rates change over time, due to the Balassa-Samuelson effect or because of shocks. An appreciation of the real exchange rate can take place through high domestic inflation, which is a costly process, or a nominal appreciation, which can be changed more easily.

Under a nominal peg, the country is left only with the first option. Gerlach and Gerlach-Kristen (2006) study the behavior of inflation in Hong Kong and Singapore, whose economies are quite similar but who have different monetary policy regimes. They find that inflation is both higher and more volatile in Hong Kong, which has successfully maintained a peg to the U.S. dollar since 1983 through a currency board arrangement, than in Singapore, where the exchange rate is managed. Similarly, a number of East European countries that maintain fixed exchange rates against the euro are also experiencing high inflation for much the same reason. This suggests that idiosyncratic shocks that affect equilibrium real exchange rates are difficult to deal with under a pegged exchange rate and provide a reason for adopting floating exchange rates.

Overall, it seems that while fixed exchange rates can be a useful nominal anchor when attempting to stabilize the economy in cases of rapid and volatile inflation, it appears to be a less effective tool to maintain low and stable inflation. Instead, many central banks have in the past two decades adopted a floating exchange rate, coupled with an explicit numerical objective for inflation, in many cases by introducing inflation targeting.

Financial integration and resilience

Another factor insufficiently emphasized in the theoretical literature reviewed above is the consequence of the large increase in capital mobility in recent years (Shambaugh *et al.* 2004; Lane and Milesi-Ferretti 2007), which has made it almost impossible to sustain inconsistent fiscal and monetary policies. While the theoretical models assume that central banks under fixed exchange rates are willing to devote policy fully to the need to sustain the exchange rate, in practice central banks cannot completely disregard other objectives, in particular for economic activity. As a consequence, speculative pressures against a fixed exchange rate are almost impossible to avoid: all that is needed is a deep recession for market participants to conclude that maintaining the exchange rate may not be such a good policy, despite the authorities' protestations to the contrary.

But even if the central bank is willing to gear monetary policy fully to maintain the demands of the fixed exchange rate, shocks may occur and lead markets to doubt policy-makers' commitment to the peg. In conditions of perfect capital mobility, this may lead to high and volatile interest rates as the central bank seeks to defend the peg. The degree of sophistication and resilience of the financial sector is then a central dimension (Mussa *et al.* 2000). An essential precondition for a fixed exchange rate regime to function well is consequently that the financial system and corporate borrowers are able to endure such episodes of high interest rates. Pegging the exchange rate is thus most likely to be successful in economies with a resilient financial system, but, of course, such countries tend to be in a good position to conduct monetary policy with a floating exchange rate.

By contrast, in many developing countries with a limited involvement in the global financial system, the central bank does not run the risk of being overwhelmed by in- and outflows. Conducting monetary policy with fixed rates is possible in these cases and has many readily apparent attractions. In particular, it is an easy and transparent strategy policy and is not particularly demanding from the perspective of policy formulation.

Overall, the facts that multiple objectives for monetary policy are almost unavoidable and that few financial systems can endure a protracted episode in which the central bank uses interest rates to sustain the peg play an important role in countries' choices of exchange rate regimes in practice.

Institutions

A third factor disregarded in the theoretical models is the "quality" of institutions, which Alesina and Wagner (2005) argue has a critically influence on countries' exchange rate choice.[12] Weak institutions make it difficult to defend an exchange rate peg and often leads to poor and inconsistent macro-economic policies which puts the peg under pressure.

It is easy to see how weak institutions can make a peg difficult to maintain in practice. As already noted, if banks' balance sheets are weak – because of ineffective supervision, uneven risk control, politically influenced lending, or any of a range of other reasons – or if their borrowers' balance sheets are weak, the central bank's ability to raise interest rates to defend the peg may be limited. Indeed, a fixed exchange rate could actually exacerbate such problems by leading to high levels of borrowing in foreign currency under the mistaken assumption that the exchange rate will always be maintained. Weak institutions may also lead to large fiscal deficits and the government's financial position becoming precarious. If so, speculators may similarly come to doubt the central bank's willingness or ability to raise interest rates sufficiently to fend off an attack on the pegged exchange rate.

Furthermore, weak institutions may lead to political interference in monetary policy, either directly through political control of the central bank or through the adoption of multiple policy objectives that may conflict with the fixed exchange rate. The exchange rate peg may therefore lack credibility and can become the target of speculation.[13]

Alesina and Wagner (2005) therefore argue that countries with very weak institutions should not adopt fixed exchange rate regimes but instead let the exchange rate float freely, and they produce econometric work that supports this hypothesis.

However, while floating rates are common among countries with weak institutions that make it difficult for them to maintain an exchange rate peg, conducting monetary policy under floating exchange rates also places stringent demands on a country's institutions. Thus, many central banks operating under floating exchange rates have adopted price stability, frequently using an inflation target, as the overriding objective of monetary policy. For this to function well, the central bank must enjoy instrument independence. In turn, this requires that fiscal policy and therefore fiscal institutions are strong enough so that fiscal dominance over monetary policy can be avoided. The central bank must also have the capacity to analyze and forecast inflation, and must have made considerable progress in establishing its credibility, since otherwise shocks to inflation can have major effects on inflation expectations and complicate the management of monetary policy.[14]

But for many countries that are unable to pursue policy with a floating exchange rate and a commitment to price stability, yet have enough institutional capacity to conduct purposeful monetary policy, a pegged exchange rate offers an effective mechanism to ensure a predictable monetary environment. Thus, as argued by Alesina and Wagner (2005), many countries with an intermediate level of institutional capacity exhibit a preference for fixed exchange rates.

Changing exchange rate regimes

Above we have explored a set of reasons for why countries may not operate with the type of exchange rate regime suggested by theory. Another reason for this is simply that while economic conditions have changed since the country last rethought its exchange rate strategy, the exchange rate regime has not. Any switch in strategy involves a great deal of uncertainty, particularly if it is undertaken in response to market pressures. Since there may be difficult-to-generate political support for a change in regime in good times, and it may be perceived as too risky to do so when economic conditions are weak, policymakers are naturally hesitant to change regimes unless strictly necessary. Consequently, it seems plausible that quite a few countries operate with a policy regime that has outlived its optimality.

This aspect is illustrated by Gerlach (1999) who studied a sample of twenty-two developed economies, seeking to determine what structural features make an economy likely to adopt floating exchange rates and inflation targeting. Initially, he found little pattern to countries' preferences for inflation targeting, but further inspection showed that this finding depends on the inclusion of Iceland and Norway, which both targeted the exchange rate, in the sample. By dropping them, the probit estimates showed that countries with inflation targets tend to export a narrow range of goods, largely commodities, and are thus subject to major shocks to equilibrium real exchange rates. As both Iceland and Norway are examples of such small open economies, one would have expected them to also operate with an inflation target and a flexible exchange rate. Thus, either the model misses some important feature of exchange rate choice or these two countries operate with a suboptimal exchange rate arrangement. We lean towards the second interpretation, as both countries subsequently introduced inflation targeting and dropped the intermediate exchange rate objective.

4 The exchange rate regime in practice: a case study of Hong Kong

Next we discuss the various elements outlined above in the case of Hong Kong, which has been conducting monetary policy under a currency board arrangement since the early 1980s. Given the fact that Hong Kong is a major financial center with a large and sophisticated economy, its choice of a fixed exchange regime may appear unusual.

The introduction of the currency board

To understand the motivations that have led the authorities to maintain the currency board, it is essential to review its recent monetary history. Hong Kong operated under a silver standard from 1845 to 1935 when it adopted a sterling peg supported by a currency board arrangement. After having let the exchange rate float in the early 1970s, Hong Kong reintroduced a fixed exchange rate in October 1983, when the Hong Kong dollar (HK$) was pegged to the U.S. dollar (US$) at 7.8 HK$/US$.[15] One reason for the introduction of the linked exchange rate system was the 20 percent depreciation of the currency between June 1982 and June 1983. However, the exchange rate continued to depreciate sharply and in October the then two note-issuing banks, the Hongkong and Shanghai Banking Corporation (HSBC) and the Standard Chartered Bank, were required to back the note issue by depositing an equivalent amount in U.S. dollars at the conversion rate of 7.8 HK$/US$ with the government's Exchange Fund. This reintroduced the currency board which is still in force with an unchanged rate of 7.8 HK$/US$.

Two factors led to the change in regime, most obviously the exchange rate collapse in the summer of 1983, which resulted from China's announcement that it intended to regain sovereignty over Hong Kong in 1997. From a macro-economic perspective, it is difficult to see why this announcement would lead to a large depreciation of the currency unless one believed that monetary policy would turn massively inflationary a decade and a half later. A more plausible interpretation is that the depreciation reflected increased risk perceptions. Gerlach and Smets (2000) demonstrate that central banks should stabilize the exchange rate in response to such exchange rate shocks if they leave the equilibrium real exchange rate unaffected.

The second factor underlying the regime change was Hong Kong's poor inflationary experiences following the abandonment of the sterling peg in 1972, which more importantly had entailed the abandonment of currency board principles.[16] Instead, a US$ dollar peg was introduced, which lasted until November 1974 when the HK$ was free to float. Without a central bank, Hong Kong was left without effective monetary control. While HSBC determined the level of HK$ liquidity in the interbank market (since banks settled over its books), it could not function as a fully fledged central bank since it could not take the financial risk associated with trading against the rest of the market. Moreover, any foreign exchange intervention by the Exchange Fund would be sterilized as the HSBC recycled the funds into the market. In terms of the Poole analysis, Hong Kong experienced large fluctuations in the LM curve.

Overall, with a combination of large credibility shocks which were likely to gain in importance as the handover approached, and LM shocks, economic theory suggests that fixing the exchange rate was appropriate. Moreover, a change to a managed float was not possible due to institutional factors; that is, the absence of a central bank that could conduct monetary policy. While the first-best policy might suggest that a central bank should have been established, Latter (2004) argues that given the tradition of a small government, it would have been difficult to muster the necessary political support to establish one. Overall, it is not difficult to understand why the currency board was re-established in 1983.

Options for the future

Twenty-five years later, the currency board remains intact. This is an extraordinary achievement in light of the many large shocks experienced, in particular the Asian financial crisis. However, the factors that led to the reintroduction of the currency board in 1983 have arguably largely disappeared: the handover passed smoothly, Hong Kong's economic regime remains unchanged, China has not been a source of shocks, and the size of capital flows that may be brought to bear on the peg has increased massively. Furthermore, the institutional environment has been transformed with the creation of the Hong Kong Monetary Authority (HKMA) in 1993 and a number of subsequent reforms which would enable the HKMA to manage interbank liquidity and which have enhanced the financial infrastructure, strengthened the banking system, and increased the HKMA's capacity to analyze economic developments.[17] As noted by Latter (2004), the HKMA is now in a position to implement other monetary policy strategies if so decided by the government, which is responsible for the choice of exchange rate arrangement.

So why does the currency board remain? Three factors would appear to play a role. First, it is widely seen as having worked well and enjoys broad support. The political authorities presumably see no need to change it when economic conditions are good, and the risks associated with doing so may loom large when conditions are less benign. Second, while the HKMA enjoys instrument independence, a change in monetary strategy would require further buttressing of the independence of the HKMA and other institutional changes. In an economy in which keeping government small is a widely shared objective, mustering political support for such a change is not easy. Third, the Basic Law governing Hong Kong states that the HK$ shall remain legal tender during a fifty-year transition period after which the renminbi will presumably be sole legal tender. Long before then, market forces may have led to widespread use of the renminbi in Hong Kong. Given this outlook, there is understandably little point in going through the practical complexity of establishing a new policy regime that would necessarily be temporary.

5 Conclusions

In this chapter we have considered the design of monetary policy in an open economy, focusing on the uses and limitations of flexible exchange rates. We first reviewed how the theoretical literature has developed over the past thirty years, with the initial emphasis on the nature of shocks followed by an emphasis on the (in)ability of the exchange rate to assist monetary authorities in moving the economy in line with an efficient allocation.

We next considered several dimensions that, while highly relevant in practice, were substantially set aside in the literature. These include the use of an exchange rate peg as a nominal anchor when the central bank enjoys a limited credibility, the role of financial integration, institutions, and the fact that policymakers appear hesitant to change regimes even if they are no longer optimal. We illustrated these aspects through a small case study of Hong Kong.

Overall we draw two broad conclusions from our analysis. First, when central banks have established their inflation-fighting credentials, the optimal policy regime is targeted at domestic conditions, allowing the exchange rate to adjust. The main benefit of such a strategy is to allow central banks to fine-tune their reaction to asymmetric conditions in different countries. While keeping an eye on exchange rate development is warranted, as the exchange rate adjusts promptly to changing economic conditions and thus conveys useful information to policymakers, conditioning monetary policy narrowly on the exchange rate imposes too much of a strait-jacket.

Second, the usefulness of a peg when central banks have yet to establish credibility should not be overstated. A central, and in our view debatable, assumption underlying the peg-as-a-nominal-anchor view is that while the central bank is unable to commit to price stability on its own, it can commit to maintaining a peg. In practice, maintaining a peg can impose a substantial cost either in the form of foreign exchange reserve losses, or a tightening of policy that is unacceptably high from the point of view of domestic conditions. The turbulences of the European Monetary System in 1992, and the collapse of the Argentina currency board in 2001 are just two of many examples of the exchange rate peg proving too costly.

The several instances of fixed exchange rates breaking down highlight that a peg is not a cure-all policy recipe, and at most buys a country some time in implementing reforms to address limitations in the fiscal or financial environment. Whether to peg or to float is a relatively secondary policy choice, compared to putting fiscal policy on a sustainable path, or establishing a sound financial system, as stressed by Calvo and Mishkin (2003).

Notes

1 Thus, the UK and Ireland left the snake in June 1972 and Italy in February 1973. France left in January 1974, rejoined in July 1975, and left again in March 1976. By the end of 1977, only Germany, Belgium, the Netherlands, Luxembourg, and Denmark remained within the mechanism.
2 The Poole analysis received a new lease of life in the literature on "monetary conditions indices"; e.g., Alexander (1997) or Gerlach and Smets (2000).
3 A similar analysis can be conducted for the case of external shocks which, in the interest of brevity, we omit here.
4 Modern DSGE models nonetheless retain some ad hoc aspects, mostly for tractability reasons. For instance, they consider time-dependent pricing rules for price setters, while state-dependent rules have more appealing features.
5 While policies aimed at raising the structural growth rate of productivity are clearly desirable, they are distinct from monetary policy.
6 Corsetti and Pesenti (2008) present a highly tractable description of these points.
7 As consumer prices are fixed for both domestic and imported goods, nominal and real balances move in step.
8 The ability of monetary policy to bring the economy to the flexible price allocation in some settings may be understood as removing the need for a costly adjustment in prices. If monetary conditions are such that price setters would choose not to adjust their price, if they could change it, then price rigidities cease to be an effective constraint.
9 Moreover, since the literature has evolved over time and may continue to do so, policy-makers may have hesitated to rely on it in choosing exchange rate regime.
10 Dornbusch (1985) discusses the key role in preventing episodes of extreme inflation, focusing on the German hyperinflation in 1923.
11 Mussa *et al.* (2000, Appendix III) review the lesions from a number of exchange rate-based stabilization programs in the 1980s and 1990s.
12 The central role of institutions is also stressed by Calvo and Mishkin (2003). See also the discussion in Genberg and Swoboda (2005).
13 See Obstfeld and Rogoff (1996, section 9.5.4) for an analysis.
14 Interestingly, this framework does not necessarily permit the central bank to disregard the exchange rate in conducting policy. For instance, if liquidity in the foreign exchange market is thin because the economy is small or dominated by a few institutions, the central bank may be required to remain an activity participant.
15 See Jao (1990) for a discussion of the events that led to the adoption of the currency board.

16 See Latter (2004) for a discussion of the adoption of the currency board in 1983.

17 Of course, this reform has also strengthened the ability of the currency board to withstand speculative pressures.

References

Alesina, Alberto and Alexander F. Wagner (2005) "Choosing (and reneging on) exchange rate regimes," Harvard University.

Alexander, Lewis (1997) "Notes on the Poole Model and MCIs," unpublished memo.

Boyer, Russell S. (1978) "Optimal Foreign Exchange Market Intervention," *Journal of Political Economy* 86, 1045–1055.

Calvo, Guillermo and Frederick Mishkin (2003) "The Mirage of Exchange Rate Regimes for Emerging Markets Countries," *Journal of Economic Perspectives* 17(4), 99–118.

Canzoneri, Matthew, Robert Cumby, and Behzad Diba (2005) "The Need for International Policy Coordination: What's Old, What's New, What's Yet to Come," *Journal of International Economics* 66(2), 363–384.

Conference Board (2005) "Do Exchange Rates Matter? A Global Survey of CEOs and CFOs on Exchange Rates," written in cooperation with the Group of Thirty. The Conference Board Research Report R-1349–04-RR.

Corsetti, Giancarlo (2008) "A Modern Reconsideration of the Theory of Optimum Currency Areas," CEPR Discussion Paper 6712.

Corsetti, Giancarlo and Paolo Pesenti (2005) "The Simple Geometry of Transmission and Stabilization in Closed and Open Economies," in Richard Clarida and Francesco Giavazzi (eds.), NBER International Macroeconomic Annual 2007, Chicago, IL: University of Chicago Press, 65–116.

Corsetti, Giancarlo, Paolo Pesenti, and Philippe Martin (2007) "Productivity, Terms of Trade and the 'Home Market Effect'," *Journal of International Economics* 73, 99–127.

Devereux, Michael and Charles Engel (2007) "Expenditure Switching vs. Real Exchange Rate Stabilization: Competing Objectives for Exchange Rate Policy," *Journal of Monetary Economics* 54, 2346–2374.

Dornbusch, Rudiger (1985) "Stopping Hyperinflation: Lessons for the German Inflation Experience of the 1920s," NBER Working Paper series No. 1675.

Duarte, Margarida and Maurice Obstfeld (2008) "Monetary Policy in the Open Economy Revisited: The Case for Exchange-Rate Flexibility Restored," *Journal of International Money and Finance* 27(6), 949–957.

Friedman, Milton (1953) "The Case for Flexible Exchange Rates." Reprinted in *Essays in Positive Economics*. Chicago, IL: University of Chicago Press, 157–203.

Genberg, Hans and Alexander Swoboda (2005) "Exchange-rate Regimes: Does What Countries Say Matter," *IMF Staff Papers* 52, 129–141.

Gerlach, Stefan (1995) "Adjustable Pegs vs. Single Currencies: How Valuable is the Option to Realign?," *European Economic Review* 39, 1155–1170.

Gerlach, Stefan (1999) "Who Targets Inflation Explicitly?" *European Economic Review* 43, 1257–1277.

Gerlach, Stefan and Petra Gerlach-Kristen (2006) "Monetary Policy Regimes and Macroeconomic Outcomes: Hong Kong and Singapore." In *Monetary Policy in Asia: Approaches and Implementation*. BIS Papers No. 31.

Gerlach, Stefan and Frank Smets (2000) "MCIs and Monetary Policy," *European Economic Review* 44, 1677–1700.

Giavazzi, Francesco and Alberto Giovannini (1989) *Limiting Exchange Rate Flexibility: The European Monetary System*. Cambridge, MA: MIT Press.

Goldberg, Linda and Cédric Tille (2009) "Macroeconomic Interdependence and the International Role of the Dollar," *Journal of Monetary Economics* 56, 990–1003.

Jao, Y. C. (1990) "From Sterling Exchange Standard to Dollar Exchange Standard: The Evolution of Hong Kong's Contemporary Monetary System 1967–1989." In Y. C. Jao and Frank H. H. King, *Money in Hong Kong: Historical Perspective and Contemporary Analysis*. Centre for Asian Studies, University of Hong Kong.

Lane, Philip and Gian Maria Milesi-Ferretti (2007) "A Global Perspective on External Positions." In R. Clarida (ed.), *G7 Current Account Imbalances: Sustainability and Adjustment*. Chicago, IL: University of Chicago Press.

Latter, Tony (2004) "Hong Kong's Exchange Rate Regimes in the Twentieth Century: The Story of Three Regime Changes," HKIMR Working Paper No. 17/2004.

Mundell, Robert (1968) *International Economics* New York: Macmillan.

Mussa, Michael, Paul Masson, Alexander Swoboda, Esteban Jadresic, Paulo Mauro, and Andy Berg (2000) "Exchange-rate Regimes in an Increasingly Integrated World Economy," IMF Occasional Paper No. 193.

Obstfeld, Maurice and Kenneth Rogoff (1996) *Foundations of International Macroeconomics*. Princeton, NJ: Princeton University Press.

Obstfeld, Maurice and Kenneth Rogoff (2002) "Global Implications of Self-oriented National Monetary Rules," *The Quarterly Journal of Economics* 117, 503–535.

Poole, William (1970) "Optimal Choice of Monetary Policy Instruments in a Simple Stochastic Macro Model," *Quarterly Journal of Economics* 84, 197–216.

Shambaugh, Jay, Maurice Obstfeld, and Alan Taylor (2004) "The Trilemma in History: Tradeoffs among Exchange Rates, Monetary Policies, and Capital Mobility," *Review of Economics and Statistics* 87(3), 423–438.

Swoboda, Alexander (1968) "The Euro-dollar Market: An Interpretation." In *Essays in International Finance 64*, International Finance Section, Princeton University.

Swoboda, Alexander (1969) "Vehicle Currencies and the Foreign Exchange Market: The Case of the Dollar." In Robert Z. Aliber (ed.), *The International Market for Foreign Exchange*. Praeger Special Studies in International Economics and Development, New York: Frederick A. Praeger Publishers.

9 Central banks' function to maintain financial stability

An uncompleted task

Charles A.E. Goodhart

1 Financial regulation: a lack of instruments

The events of the past year have reminded us all that a central bank does not just have one responsibility, that of achieving price stability. This latter is, indeed, its main focus, its first core purpose (CP1); but as the sole institution that can create cash, and hence bank reserve balances, it also has a responsibility for acting as Lender of Last Resort (LOLR)[1] and maintaining financial stability. This is its second core purpose (CP2).[2]

One of the major problems of central banking is that the pursuit of these two core purposes (CPs) can often conflict, not least because the central bank (CB) currently appears to have only one single main instrument: its command over the short-term interest rate. Indeed, a central purpose of the first two great books on central banking, Henry Thornton's (1802), *An Inquiry into the Nature and Effects of the Paper Credit of Great Britain*, and Walter Bagehot's (1873) *Lombard Street*, was to outline ways to resolve such a conflict, especially when an (external) drain of currency threatened maintenance of the Gold Standard at the same time as an internal drain led to a liquidity panic and contagious bank failures.

Under such circumstances, however, with rising risk aversion, the CB would find that it had *two* instruments: its ability to expand its own balance sheet, e.g., by LoLR lending, at the same time as keeping interest rates high (to deter gold outflows and unnecessary (speculative) borrowing). The greater problem, then and now, was how to avoid excessive commercial bank expansion during good times. With widespread confidence, the commercial banks do not want, or need, to borrow from the CB. A potential restraint is via shrinking the CB's own balance sheet, open market sales, thereby raising interest rates. But increasing interest rates during good times (gold reserves rising and high; inflation targets met), i.e., "leaning into the wind," is then against the "rules of the game," and such minor adjustments to interest rates as may be consistent with such underlying rules are unlikely to have much effect in dampening down the upswing of a powerful asset price boom-and-bust cycle.

Although the terminology has altered, this basic problem has not really changed since the start of central banking in the nineteenth century. An additional analytical twist was given by Hy Minsky who realized that the better the CB succeeded with CP1, the more it was likely to imperil CP2. The reason is that the greater stability engendered by a successful CP1 record is likely to reduce risk premia, and thereby asset price volatility, and so support additional leverage and asset price expansion. The three main examples of financial instability that have occurred in industrialized countries in the last century (USA 1929–1933, Japan 1999–2005, subprime 2007/2009) have all taken place following periods of stellar CP1 performance.

We still have not resolved this conundrum. It shows up in several guises. For example, there is a tension between trying to get banks to behave cautiously and conservatively in the upswing of a financial cycle, and being prepared as a CB to lend against whatever the banks have to offer as collateral during a crisis. Again, the more a CB manages to constrain bank expansion during euphoric upswings (e.g., by various forms of capital and liquidity requirements), the greater the disintermediation to less controlled channels. How far does such disintermediation matter, and what parts of the financial system should a CB be trying to protect; in other words which intermediaries are "systemic"; do we have any clear, ex ante, definition of "systemic," or do we decide, ex post, on a case-by-case basis?

Perhaps these problems are insoluble; certainly they have not been solved. Indeed, recent developments, notably the adoption of more risk-sensitive Basel II capital adequacy ratios and the move towards "fair value" or "mark-to-market" accounting, have arguably tilted the regulatory system towards even greater procyclicality. A possible reason for this could be that the regulators have focused unduly on trying to enhance the risk management of the *individual* bank and insufficiently on the risk management of the financial *system* as a whole. The two issues, individual and systemic risk performance, are sometimes consistent, but often not so. For example, following some financial crisis, the safest line for an individual bank will be to cut lending and to hoard liquidity, but if all banks try to do so, especially simultaneously, the result could be devastating.

The bottom line is that central banks have failed to make much, if any, progress with CP2, just at the time when their success with CP1 has been lauded. This is witnessed not only by the events of 2007/2009, but also by the whole string of financial crises (a sequence of "turmoils") in recent decades. Now there are even suggestions that central banks should have greater (even statutory) responsibility for achieving financial stability (e.g., the Paulson report). But where are the (regulatory) instruments that would enable central banks to constrain excess leverage and "irrational euphoria" in the upswing? Public warnings (e.g., in financial stability reviews) are feeble, bendy reeds. All that central banks have to offer are mechanisms for picking up the pieces after the crash, and the more comprehensively they do so (the Greenspan/Bernanke put), the more the commercial banks will enthusiastically join in the next upswing.

Besides such public warnings, which the industry typically notices and then ignores, the only counter-cyclical instruments recently employed have been the Spanish pre-provisioning measures, and the use of time-varying loan to value (LTV) ratios in a few small countries (e.g., Estonia and Hong Kong). But the

Spanish measures have subsequently been prevented by the latest accounting requirements, the IFRS of the IASB; and the recent fluctuations in actual LTVs have been strongly pro-cyclical, with 100+ LTVs in the housing bubble being rapidly withdrawn in the housing bust.

Indeed, any attempt to introduce counter-cyclical variations in LTVs, or in capital/liquidity requirements will always run into a number of generic criticisms:

- It will disturb the level playing field, and thereby cause disintermediation to less regulated entities (in other segments of the industry, or in other countries). It will thus both be unfair and ineffective.
- It will increase the cost of intermediation during the boom, and thereby reduce desirable economic expansion (and financial innovation).
- It will increase complexity and add to the informational burden.

These criticisms have force. Indeed, there are empirical studies which suggest that countries which allow a less regulated, and more innovative and dynamic, financial system grow faster than their more controlled brethren, despite being more prone to financial (boom/bust) crisis. Nevertheless it should be possible to construct a more counter-cyclical, time-varying, regulatory system in such a way as to mitigate these problems, so long as the regulations *are* relaxed in the downturn after having been built up in the boom.

But those same generic criticisms will also mean that regulators/supervisors will be roundly condemned for tightening regulatory conditions in asset prime booms by the combined forces of lenders, borrowers, and politicians, the latter tending to regard cyclical bubbles as beneficent trend improvements due to their own improved policies. Regulators/supervisors will need some combination of courage, reliance on quantitative triggers, and independence from government if they are to have the strength of mind and purpose to use potential macro-prudential instruments to dampen financial booms.

So the main deficiency, with regard to the achievement of CP2, is that there are no (regulatory) instruments to constrain euphoric expansions (and never have been). Since such instruments have not been found for the last two centuries, this may indicate that their side-effects would be so bad that they represent a chimera. Nevertheless, the CBs have no one but themselves to blame for the absence of effective counter-cyclical instruments. For obvious reasons CBs have been the dominant actors in the promulgation of financial regulations. The international penetration of cross-border banking requires effective financial regulation to be done internationally also; this has been undertaken under the aegis of the Basel Committee on Banking Supervision, a standing committee of the G-10 Central Bank Governors. As that status indicates, the BCBS has been dominated by central banks, although separate bank supervisory agencies have played an (increasing) role in the BCBS since its inception.

2 Financial supervision: what is the best structure?

This brings me to the vexed question of what role CBs should play in supervision. As argued above, CBs must, and do, play a major role in financial regulation (and the regulatory framework is prior and even more crucial than the operation of supervision). They do *not* have to play a lead role in banking supervision, as is evidenced by the historical record. Following the financial turmoil and multiple bank failures in the 1930s, many countries, notably in Europe, established separate, specialized banking supervisory agencies, with more or less connection with their own central bank, whereas other countries, notably the UK and some but not all (e.g., Canada) of the Commonwealth countries, delegated such supervision as was undertaken to the central bank.

For several decades after the 1930s, however, bank supervision became a sinecure. Memories of the Great Depression induced caution and conservatism; interest rates remained low and stable; World War II and socialist ideology led to direct credit controls, which diverted bank funding to the State and to large manufacturing companies. These same direct controls, on bank lending and exchange controls on international flows, constrained innovation and efficiency. Commercial banks became akin to public utilities. Banking became a dull, stagnant industry, but it was, at least, safe. As Bordo, *et al.* (2001) have documented, there were no serious banking crises between the end of the 1930s and the start of the 1970s.

The combination of the restoration of a more liberal economic order, together with innovations in information technology, led to a removal of restrictions on bank operations and a growing internationalization of more competitive financial business, starting with the euro–dollar market. Then, as subsequently, liberalization and innovation led to bank failures and financial crisis. Since most of the Central Banks already had some involvement in bank supervision, and had established a camaraderie, under the aegis of the Bank for International Settlements (BIS) at Basel with monthly meetings of the G-10 Central Bank Governors, the regulatory/supervisory response fell mainly to them.

Nevertheless, the organizational structure of bank supervision (with its patchwork pattern of some countries relying on central banks, others on specialized supervisory agencies, and a bewildering combination of mixtures of the two) remained largely unchanged through into the 1990s. At that point a trend developed to shift bank supervision from CBs to a single financial supervisor with responsibility for supervision over the whole financial system, including securities dealers (investment banks) and insurance companies as well as banks. Scandinavian countries led this move, but it was taken up in many other larger countries including the UK, Germany, Japan, and Korea.

The main reason for this was that greater economic liberalism had led to a blurring of the former sectoral distinctions between the businesses of banks, investment houses and insurance companies. If their businesses overlapped and they competed, the level playing field and efficiency arguments implied that they be supervised by a single body. Moreover there were further arguments that the CB should *not* also take on the role of this single universal Financial Services

Authority (FSA). By this time many CBs had been given operational independence to achieve price stability (CP1). To give them simultaneously a larger supervisory role seemed a step too far.[3] These arguments included:

1 conflicts of interest;
2 reputational risks;
3 an extension of the safety net;
4 excessive power to an unelected institution;
5 going outside CBs' traditional areas of expertise.

There were counter-arguments. In particular, the separation of function between an FSA (supervision) and the CB (LoLR) meant that any financial crisis had to be handled by a committee, rather than a single focus of power/decision. Meanwhile the removal of supervision from CBs tended to diminish their access to relevant information willy-nilly, even if the FSA was happy to share information freely. Moreover, the basic ethos of the FSA (and of securities regulator/supervisors) was almost bound to become focused on conduct of business issues, and driven forward by lawyers and accountants. This contrasts with the greater expertise on market relationships, and economic concern with macro-prudential issues, which is the forte of a CB. Since contagious financial crises, which, though much rarer, have a far more damaging impact than the more mundane conduct of business matters, it is arguable that CBs should be given the lead in handling such macro-prudential issues.

This latter has been argued over the years by the Federal Reserve Board, which has fought to maintain some supervisory oversight of the most important banks in the U.S. system. Moreover, these arguments have been given greater resonance by the shortcomings of the FSA in the UK, of BaFin in Germany, and of the SEC in the U.S., during the recent financial crisis.

These doubts about the worth of the FSA/CB model have led to some resurrection (e.g., in the Paulson Report) of an earlier structural design, known as the "twin-peaks" approach (e.g., Taylor 1995). This involves dividing the function of supervision into two parts: a micro-prudential role focusing mainly on conduct of business issues, and a macro-prudential role focusing on systemic issues (externalities caused by bank failures and dramatic shifts in risk aversion). Only a few countries have adopted the twin-peaks approach, the Netherlands and, to some extent, Australia. The Paulson Report suggested that it be applied in the U.S., but the Report is already coming under fierce criticism, not least by supervisory institutions like the SEC and CFTC who might lose treasured parts of their turf. In any case this Report came too late in the Congressional/Presidential electoral cycle to form the basis for a Bill in the current Congress.

3 Conclusion

From the early 1990s until 2007 central banks had enjoyed a triumphant progress. They appeared to have resolved prior difficulties with the achievement of CP1. They had been (increasingly) granted operational independence to adjust interest rates to achieve inflation targets (price stability), and they had succeeded. But their very success with CP1 helped to exaggerate the financial eurphoria that led to the crisis of 2007/2009. What was then revealed was the inability of CBs to achieve CP2 satisfactorily.

The CBs were able to inject liquidity into the system through a series of increasingly innovative (desperate) measures, but they had had virtually no instruments to contain the prior unsustainable expansion of leverage. The regulatory measures that had previously been introduced, namely Basel II and fair value accounting, tended, if anything, to amplify rather than restrain the financial boom–bust cycle.

Meanwhile the common view was that the organizational structure of banking supervision (the FSA model) that had been put in place in many countries in the previous decades had not performed well in several countries during this crisis. There were calls for a rethink, perhaps to move to a "twin-peaks" model.

So the overall conclusion is that, unlike the settled state of CP1, CBs, indeed all of us, are still searching for an answer with CP2.

Notes

1 My colleague, Willem Buiter, would transfer the function of LOLR to an extended financial services (supervisory) authority by granting the FSA an (unlimited) power to borrow from the central bank for on-lending to private sector financial intermediaries in need. In my view that would effectively make the FSA into the (real) central bank, while the MPC would become an independent arm of the Treasury.

2 There is a third core purpose of any central bank, which is to improve and to foster the efficiency of its own financial system. While the enhancement of financial efficiency is primarily a private sector function, there are often beneficial actions that a central bank, especially in a developing country, can take. I shall not, however, discuss this further here.

3 By the same token, however, national central banks which had ceded their CP1 powers to the (Governing Council of the) ECB became the more determined to hang on to their existing CP2 powers.

References

Bagehot, W. (1873) *Lombard Street: A Description of the Money Market*, London: Henry S. King & Co.

Bordo, M., B. Eichengreen, D. Klingebiel, and M.S. Martinez-Peria (2001) "Is the Crisis Problem Growing More Severe?," *Economic Policy* 32, 51–82.

Paulson, H.M., Jr. (Report) (2008) "The Department of the Treasury Blueprint for a Modernized Financial Regulatory Structure," The Department of the Treasury, USA, March.

Taylor, M. (1995) "'Twin Peaks': A Regulatory Structure for the New Century," CSFI (Committee for the Study of Financial Innovation), London (pamphlet) (December).

Thornton, H. [1802] (1978) *An Inquiry into the Nature and Effects of the Paper Credit of Great Britain*. Fairfield, NJ: Augustus M. Kelley.

10 Is inflation targeting passé?[1]

Ulrich Kohli

1 Evolution, not revolution

The title of Part III, "Central banking, a revolution under way?," sounds rather provocative, since one does not normally think of central bankers as being revolutionaries. The public actually tends to view central bankers as outright conservative, if not just plain boring, although, in all fairness, they should really be described as evolutionists.

Admittedly, many changes have taken place in the theory and the practice of central banking during Alexander's long and distinguished career. I need only mention here the breakdown of the Bretton Woods system and the move from fixed to flexible exchange rates as far as the world's major currencies are concerned; the trend towards full convertibility and the almost perfect international capital mobility; the birth of the euro; the greater independence of central banks with the emphasis on governance, transparency, and accountability; the accent on credibility and communication; the growing recognition of the responsibility of central banks in the area of financial stability; the understanding of the paramount importance of price stability and the rejection of a long-run unemployment–inflation tradeoff; the appreciation of the importance of expectations and of the implications of the rational expectations hypothesis; and, last, but not least, the adoption of inflation targeting (or flexible inflation targeting) as the favored monetary policy framework in many countries.

However, most of these changes took place gradually, so it is more appropriate to talk about evolution rather than revolution. In this chapter, I will focus on just one of these changes, namely the emergence of inflation targeting as the dominant monetary policy recipe, and, in order to nonetheless retain some of the provocative flavour that Charles Wyplosz intended for this session, I will be posing the question: Is inflation targeting passé?

2 The ambiguity of inflation targeting

Nowadays, (flexible) inflation targeting is often understood to designate best practice when it comes to monetary policy. Many central banks throughout the world proudly describe themselves as inflation targeters, while many others, most of them from developing or emerging market economies, make it known that their ambition is to one day become inflation targeters too.

Evolution is certainly a better term than revolution to describe the emergence of inflation targeting. Thus, Rick Mishkin recently wrote in answer to the question whether inflation targeting was true progress or just the repackaging of an old idea:

> Inflation targeting is indeed something new and can be regarded as true progress given its many advantages over earlier monetary policy strategies. It is not revolutionary, however: rather it is a refinement of what has gone before. In fact, inflation targeting continues to evolve as we speak and will continue to be improved in the future.
>
> (Mishkin 2007, pp. 599–600)

Interestingly enough, none of the central banks responsible for the world's three most important currencies – the U.S. dollar, the euro, and the Japanese yen – views itself as an inflation targeter. Neither does the Swiss National Bank (SNB). The SNB usually goes out of its way to explain why it is not an inflation targeter. Its monetary policy framework is much closer to that of the European Central Bank (ECB), for instance, than to that of the Reserve Bank of New Zealand (RBNZ), which arguably invented the concept of inflation targeting.

Ultimately, it is all a matter of definition, however. Inflation targeting means different things to different people. If inflation targeting means that the central bank is trying to achieve a low rate of inflation (i.e., price stability), then we are *all* inflation targeters. In fact, in that sense, the SNB has *always* been an inflation targeter, almost since its inception over a hundred years ago.[2]

One ambiguity with inflation targeting is that the term says explicitly what one tries to achieve (let us hope it is not inflation, though…), but not how one plans to do it. Yet inflation targeting, in the minds of most economists, now has quite a precise meaning when it comes to central bank operations. It is generally understood to imply that the central bank produces an inflation forecast and uses it as a guide to set its (nominal) policy interest rate. That is, the general description of the objective of monetary policy comes loaded with an operational concept. One could certainly argue that the central bank's objective and its operating procedure are two separate issues, and that there is no need – neither is it helpful – to bundle them together.

3 The Swiss way

In many instances of inflation targeting, the central bank is given a target by the government or Parliament. The target might be a yearly one, or it might extend over several years. In any case, it can be adjusted from time to time. The central bank must then set policy in order to achieve the assigned target, and it must answer to the higher authority if it fails to deliver.

Things are quite different in Switzerland.[3] The SNB is required by law to achieve price stability, and it is the SNB itself which defines the meaning of price stability. Its definition turns out to be exactly the same as the ECB's, namely a rate of inflation of less than 2 percent over the medium term.[4] For all practical purposes, this is to be understood as a rate of inflation between zero and 2 percent. This range can be rationalized by noting that, because of measuring errors (due to the substitution bias and quality changes), a measured rate of inflation of 1 percent probably comes close to a constant cost of living. Given that monetary policy is not an exact science, it is reasonable to allow for an error margin. Thus, the target may be understood to be 1 percent, plus or minus one, although the SNB does not seek to attain any particular point within the target range.

Price stability is defined over the medium term. Switzerland, as a small and very open economy, is exposed to a wide range of foreign shocks. Temporary deviations beyond the 0 to 2 percent range are thus to be expected and tolerated. Indeed, it would be counterproductive to overreact to any small divergence, all the more so since, by law, the SNB must also consider the current economic situation when setting its policy.

The SNB then formulates policy as it sees fit in order to achieve price stability. In principle, it could use any monetary policy framework it pleased. Of course, the SNB is required to explain its policy to the public and to the authorities, and it must report to Parliament once a year and account for its actions. It would be inconceivable, however, that the target be modified every now and again just to suit the circumstances, i.e., that the SNB alters its definition of price stability without sound economic justification. Its credibility would be gravely damaged. Price stability cannot mean one thing one day and something else the next.

As already mentioned, the SNB has almost always been aiming for price stability, even under the Gold Standard and at times of monetary targeting, so there is nothing much new under the sun here. What is new, since the introduction of its new monetary policy concept in 2000, is the explicit definition of price stability and the approach that the SNB follows to achieve its objective. It now publishes an inflation forecast four times a year, and uses this as a guide to set an operative target range for the three-month LIBOR. The ultimate goal remains the same; although the route, or rather the signposts, are different. In principle, price stability can be achieved in many different ways: through exchange rate control (including the Gold Standard), through monetary control, perhaps even through fiscal policy, or, undoubtedly, through (nominal or real) interest rate control.

All these can describe procedures used to achieve a desired rate of inflation, and thus they could all be labeled inflation targeting. Inflation targeting, in the commonly accepted sense of the word, however, suggests nominal interest rate control (as opposed to monetary control, for instance). Consider a simple, closed economy, deterministic, neoclassical model. Using the approach pioneered by Poole (1970), it can easily be shown that interest rate control is analytically identical to monetary control. In a stochastic world, however, depending on the nature of the shocks that affect the economy, it will be the case that one policy or the other will be superior in the sense that it leads to smaller fluctuations in the target variable. Interest rate control may thus well be superior to monetary control in some circumstances, but this question is independent of the choice of price stability as the ultimate objective of monetary policy.

It was long believed that central banks needed an intermediate target – a waypoint, so to speak – owing to the long and variable lags with which monetary policy operates.[5] A good intermediate target had to be highly correlated with the ultimate objective of monetary policy. It also had to be observable and controllable. Examples of intermediate targets that come to mind are a broad monetary aggregate such as M3 or a market rate of interest. By setting its instrument (e.g., the monetary base or a policy rate of interest) and aiming at the intermediate target, the central bank had a good chance of reaching its final objective.

Over the past few decades, the thinking has changed in this respect. There seems to be a consensus today that there is no need for an intermediate target and that the central bank can aim at its ultimate objective directly. This change of thinking may be due to the realization that the relationship between the intermediate target and the final objective – both endogenous variables – is not stable: it depends on the nature of the exogenous shocks that affect the system. It may also be that economists have become more confident about their ability to forecast inflation. A note of caution may be in order, though, for as price stability has been maintained for extended periods of time, it is becoming more difficult for econometric models to foresee turning points. Put in other words, would our models recognize inflation if they saw it?

4 Beyond inflation targeting

Setting a sequence of inflation targets certainly makes sense when the initial conditions include a high rate of inflation (as was the case in New Zealand at the time of the adoption of its new monetary policy concept), and one wants to aim at price stability, or at least at a low rate of inflation. It is sensible then to map the way from here to there, both in order to hold policymakers accountable and to shape expectations. But inflation targeting should describe a transitional phase. Once price stability has been attained and the central bank has graduated from the inflation-targeting class, it should be business as usual and the name of the game should be *maintaining* price stability.[6] Of course, an accident could always happen, and then the process would start all over again. Nonetheless, in the normal state of the world, it would make little sense to be given a string of inflation targets.

Inflation targeting almost suggests that there is a moving target, or at least a target that gets shifted periodically. There is a vast literature on the question of rules vs. discretion in monetary economics. It has come to the fairly uncontroversial conclusion that central banks are better off following rules, rather than setting policy discretely, as discretion leads to an inflation bias. What is true for central banks ought to be true for governments and parliaments as well. If the finance minister keeps changing the target as he or she sees fit, we are back in a world of discretion and fine-tuning, which can be difficult to reconcile with central bank independence. Could it be that flexible inflation targeting has made fine-tuning respectable once again?[7] Ultimately, we also have to ask ourselves about what is more damaging to credibility: is it to miss the target, or is it to move the goal posts as one pleases?

By the way, if the name of the game has become the maintenance of price stability, as I suggest it has, then central bankers should rename their periodic reports "price stability reports" or "monetary policy reports" rather than "inflation reports." "Inflation report" is a language inherited from the 1970s and the 1980s. It is somewhat defeatist and apologetic: it is passé.

5 The evolution will go on

Even though there has been considerable convergence in the theory and practice of monetary policy, there are still many unsettled issues, and thus it is a fair bet to say that the evolution will continue. These issues are not specific to targeters or non-targeters. Thus, how should inflation be measured? Should the central bank look at headline inflation or at core inflation, e.g., a measure that excludes volatile food and energy prices? I do not think that there is a generally accepted answer to this question. I personally believe, though, that the main emphasis should be on headline inflation, for at least two reasons. First, if the prime objective of monetary policy is to safeguard the purchasing power of money, then it must be all-inclusive. One must look at the price of the entire basket of goods and services, not just at part of it. If the core inflation rate is measured by excluding some goods from the basket, such as energy and food, then one is no longer considering the general price level, but merely a subcomponent of it. The second reason has to do with communication. At a time of rapidly increasing energy and food prices, how can central banks convince the public that they are successful in achieving price stability if they focus on what some people call the "cold and hungry" index? Energy and food prices are among the most visible ones for the population, and leaving them out is simply not credible.

Should the central bank publish an interest rate path? The SNB does not. In fact, its inflation forecast (it might be more appropriate to call it an inflation projection) is conditional on an unchanged level of the three-month LIBOR over the entire forecasting period. Its inflation forecast, or projection, thus indicates the direction of inflation for the next three years, given the current policy stance. Depending on the direction that is being taken, a change of course might be called for, just as in sailing a lighthouse is a useful landmark: the fact that a boat is heading towards the lighthouse does not mean that the skipper intends to hit it. Admittedly, this approach is open to the Lucas critique. However, it has proven useful as a communication tool.

Alternatively, one could publish an inflation forecast conditional on market expectations regarding the future path of interest rates. Extracting market interest rate expectations from available market data is not straightforward, however. Moreover, it may be that the central bank views these market expectations as unrealistic. It would therefore be problematic for the central bank to base its predictions on hypotheses that it views as far-fetched. A third possibility would be to rely on an estimated reaction function, such as a Taylor rule. The difficulty here is that when several models are being used, the projected interest rate path is not unique. One could take some average of these, but there is no guarantee that such an average interest rate path would also be consistent with the consensus inflation forecast that is being published. Moreover, the projected interest rate path may not be consistent with the current asset prices that enter the various models, if it does not match market expectations.[8] Communication could also be tricky, and indeed credibility could be challenged, if later policy actions do not match earlier forecasts.

Yet another possibility would be simply to use the policy-makers' own projections, as the outcome of an intertemporal optimization problem. This only seems feasible, though, if there is a single decision-maker rather than a monetary policy committee. Furthermore, this also assumes that there is a single model, which, moreover, gives an accurate description of reality, and that the decision-maker's own preferences have indeed been properly formalized. I am rather skeptical of such an ambitious agenda, although I must admit that much progress has been achieved in this direction, and that more advances will undoubtedly be made in the future.

What about asset prices? Should the central bank target asset prices? Should monetary policy react if there is a commodity price bubble in the making? Like many central bankers, I would argue against such a policy course. How can one be sure that the asset price increase is due to a speculative bubble, rather than to legitimate economic forces? Are central bankers better placed than market participants to call a bubble? When Alan Greenspan, then Chairman of the U.S. Federal Reserve Board, gave his famous "irrational exuberance" warning in December 1996, the Dow Jones was trading at around 7,500. It then went on increasing to peak at over 11,700 in January 2000, before falling back to around 7,300 in October 2002. By the end of 2003, the Dow had returned to the 10,000 level, and it broke the 13,000 mark in January 2007. While there is no arguing in hindsight that a stock market bubble did indeed develop, it is certainly debatable whether it was called at the right time.

Furthermore, there is always the risk that a policy intervention would be counterproductive, due to unforeseen side-effects, unknown lags, and so on. And if one were to target asset prices, which price should one focus on? Equity prices, real estate prices, bond prices, foreign exchange rates, or perhaps the price of gold? In the late nineteenth century, policy was successful in fixing the price of gold, but at the cost of large swings in the cost of living. Luckily, no one seriously proposes to turn the clock back and to return to the Gold Standard. In my view, given the multitude of existing assets and the fact that the central bank ultimately only has one independent instrument at its disposal, it should concentrate on maintaining constant the price of the one asset that it is closest to, namely money, and thus focus on keeping the *real* price of money steady. While the *nominal* price of money is unity, the *real* price of money is one divided by the price level. Thus, seeking to keep the real price of money steady is exactly the same as maintaining price stability, which is what central banks should be doing all along.

Yet another intriguing question is whether bygones should be left as bygones. If inflation has been too high for a while, should the central bank try to compensate for this by a lower rate of inflation for some time? In other words, should the central bank target the rate of inflation or the price level?[9] Surely, two wrongs do not make a right, but, on the other hand, a commitment to a price level target (which need not be constant) could be helpful in anchoring expectations. It would also contribute to reducing menu costs over the medium term. This is an interesting issue that the Bank of Canada in particular is actively investigating at the moment.[10]

How about the exchange rate? I do not want to discuss the question of the exchange rate regime, since this is the topic of another session. I take it for granted here that the central bank operates under a flexible exchange rate regime, i.e., that the exchange rate is determined by the market. This is not to say that the exchange rate is irrelevant for monetary policy, and that the central bank should not observe it very closely. However, it must do so with its objective of price stability in mind. That is, it must assess exchange rate movements not per se, but in terms of what they imply for price stability. A depreciation of the home currency, for instance, has several effects on the domestic price level. First, in a small open economy it leads to an increase in the price of imported products, and thus it tends to impact on the price level directly. Second, it might discourage imports and favor exports, thereby stimulating activity and inflationary pressures. Finally, since a depreciating currency might be interpreted as a sign of a lax monetary policy, it can affect inflation expectations and thus reinforce the upward movement in prices.

As already mentioned, the SNB targets the three-month LIBOR. To steer it, it conducts daily repo operations, usually in the one-week segment. As risk and term premia have generally increased since August 2007 in the wake of the turmoil on international financial markets, the SNB has been induced to reduce its repo rate quite substantially. This contrasts with the ECB, which defines its operating target in terms of the repo rate and has thus allowed the euro LIBOR to drift upwards. Comparing the two policies, one can certainly argue that the ECB has become relatively more restrictive or that the SNB has become relatively more expansionary, even though neither has changed its policy stance between September 2007 and July 2008. While the difference between the two concepts seemed pretty trivial until recently, as risk and term premia were fairly steady, it has become quite significant due to recent events. Which procedure is to be preferred? This question needs to be examined carefully in the future, but at this stage I would certainly point out that the Swiss concept presents the great advantage that, since the three-month LIBOR is much more relevant than the one-week repo rate for economic decisions by households and firms, it contains an *automatic monetary stabilizer* that has insulated the non-financial sector from much of the turmoil.[11]

Monetary economists attach much importance to concepts such as potential GDP and the output gap. In a globalized world, where production is fragmented internationally and trade in middle products becomes an essential element of production, we must ask ourselves whether real GDP is indeed the appropriate measure of real value added. Changes in the terms of trade are similar to a technological progress and they can have a marked impact on the level of real income. Commodity and energy exporting countries, such as Australia and Canada, that have enjoyed substantial terms of trade gains in recent years, have seen their real gross domestic income (GDI) increase much more rapidly than their real GDP. This begs the question as to which of these two variables is more relevant for monetary policy. More research would certainly be useful in this area as well.

6 The fundamental instability of nominal interest rate control

While there is currently hardly any debate as to whether or not central banks should use an interest rate as their instruments, we should bear in mind the fact that a nominal interest rate control per se makes for an essentially unstable dynamic process. As shown in Figure 10.1,[12] if the nominal interest rate is kept too low, given the initial conditions, the economy will tend to overheat and inflation will be fueled. Inflation expectations will increase sooner or later, which will lower the real rate of interest and reinforce the process. The end result will be hyper-inflation. If the interest rate is maintained too high, on the other hand, the economy will slow down and inflation will fall. Lower inflation expectations

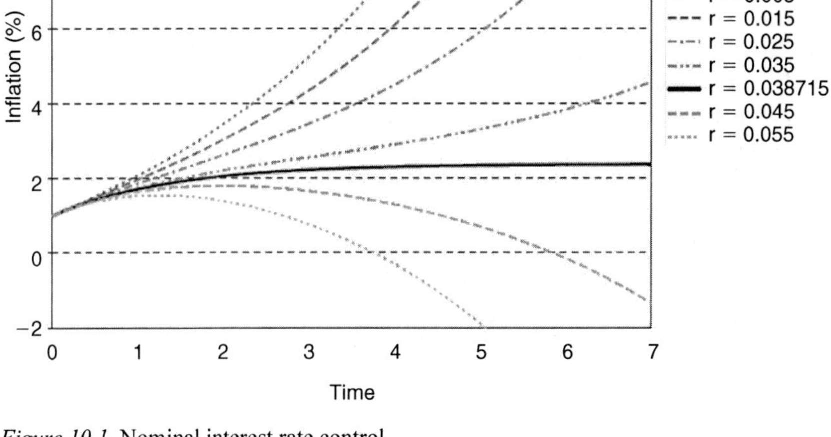

Figure 10.1 Nominal interest rate control.

lead to an increase in the real rate of interest, which slows down the economy even further, throwing the system into a deflationary spiral. To avoid either outcome, it is necessary for policy-makers to be constantly ready to adjust nominal rates one way or the other in order to maintain the economy on the knife-edge path of stability. Even if, by a miracle, the nominal rate were set at exactly the right level (3.8715 percent in the case of Figure 10.1), any shock would throw the economy off its stable path.

As an analogy, we can take a flying wing. A flying wing is a very efficient aircraft design, but one that is fundamentally unstable because its center of gravity is positioned behind its aerodynamic centre. Flying wings were little more than a curiosity – or a death trap – until computers came into play. Fly by wire now makes it possible to keep flying wings in the air through continuous adjustments to the elevators. Without such optimal control, the flying wing would stall or crash in no time.

One remedy to the problem of instability is to add to the model a reaction function (e.g., a Taylor rule). What is essentially needed is a nominal anchor, which can be the commitment to price stability. This would normally be sufficient to restore stability to the system, although if the reaction function is badly calibrated it may lead to undue fluctuations in the price level and in activity. Moreover, there is always the danger that policymakers will become complacent and place more trust in their own intuition than in the model's reaction function.

7 A revolution after all?

The 1960s and 1970s were a very challenging period for central bankers, to say the least, with inflation gradually getting out of control. Much has been learned since, however. Although the distinction between nominal and real interest rates was familiar to many economists back then (the Fisher relation goes back to the 1920s, after all), it appears to have been largely ignored by policy-makers. The role of inflation expectations was probably not well understood either, and mainstream macro-economic thinking was still dominated by the simple Phillips curve model. Fortunately, all this has changed. Real interest rates are now part of the daily jargon, inflation expectations formation mechanisms have been extensively researched, and it is generally well understood that there can be no lasting tradeoff between inflation and unemployment.

As long as the policy-makers bear in mind both the inherent instability of nominal interest control and the endogeneity of inflation expectations, there is nothing much to worry about. History will not repeat itself. If, however, policy-makers are overconfident that inflation expectations are firmly anchored and focus excessively on nominal interest rates and activity, we could experience a relapse and a recurrence of the problems encountered in the 1960s and 1970s. Let us not forget, indeed, that *revolution* can also mean going round in circles....

Appendix: mathematical illustration

A simple example may be used to illustrate the instability of nominal interest rate control. Consider the following simple macro-economic model:

$$\frac{dy(t)}{dt} = \gamma_1[\rho_n - \rho(t)] + \gamma_2[y_p - y(t)] \tag{1}$$

$$\rho(t) = r(t) - \pi^e(t) \tag{2}$$

$$\frac{d\pi^e(t)}{dt} = \lambda[\pi(t) - \pi^e(t)] \tag{3}$$

$$\pi(t) = \pi^e(t) + \alpha[y(t) - y_p]. \tag{4}$$

The variables are defined as follows: y is the logarithm of real GDP, r is the nominal interest rate, ρ is the real interest rate, π is the rate of inflation, π^e is the expected rate of inflation, and t is time. The mode is specified in continuous time. The parameters α, γ_1, γ_2, and λ are all assumed to be strictly positive; ρ_n is the natural rate of interest and y_p is potential real GDP (both of these last two variables are assumed to be constant).

Expression (1) is the equation of the IS curve. Activity is a decreasing function of the real rate of interest. The second term on the right-hand side introduces some inertia to activity. Equation (2) is the Fisher relation. Expression (3) assumes an adaptive expectations formation mechanism. Expression (4), finally, is the augmented Phillips curve. For the purpose of the model, I have assumed the following values to the parameters: $\alpha = 0.8$, $\gamma_1 = 0.5$, $\gamma_2 = 0.4$ and $\lambda = 0.6$.

Assume that the nominal interest rate is set by the central bank, and thus it is exogenous. Expressions (1) to (4) make up a system of four equations in four unknowns (y, ρ, π, and π^e). This system can be solved for the rate of inflation as a function of the nominal rate of interest. Expressions (1) and (3) are differential equations. The solution will therefore not give us a unique value for the rate of inflation, but rather the path of that variable.

After having eliminated y, ρ, and π^e through substitution, we obtain the following second-order differential equation:[13]

$$\frac{d^2\pi(t)}{dt^2} + \gamma_2\frac{d\pi(t)}{dt} - \alpha\lambda\gamma_1\pi(t) = \alpha\lambda\gamma_1\rho_n - \alpha\lambda\gamma_1 r. \tag{5}$$

This equation characterizes the trajectory of the rate of inflation through time. The solution of this equation has the following form:

$$\pi(t) = r - \rho_n + A_1 e^{\xi_1 t} + A_2 e^{\xi_2 t} \tag{6}$$

where A_1 and A_2 are the constants of integration (they depend on the initial conditions), whereas ξ_1 and ξ_2 are the characteristic roots:

$$\xi_{1,2} = \frac{-\gamma_2 \pm \sqrt{\gamma_2^2 + 4\alpha\lambda\gamma_1}}{2}. \tag{7}$$

Given the parameter values assumed earlier, this yields $\xi_1 = -0.72915$ and $\xi_1 = 0.32915$. The initial conditions may be taken to be the rate of inflation and its derivative at time $t = 0$, i.e., π_0 and π'_0 (for the purpose of the figure, I have assumed $\pi_0 = \pi'_0 = 0.01$). This yields the following values for the two constants:

$$A_1 = \frac{\pi'_0 + \xi_2(r - \rho_n - \pi_0)}{\xi_1 - \xi_2} \tag{8}$$

$$A_2 = \frac{\pi'_0 + \xi_1(r - \rho_n - \pi_0)}{\xi_2 - \xi_1} \tag{9}$$

Since α, λ, and γ_1 are all strictly positive, both characteristic roots are real and of opposite signs. Thus, there is only one stable path, and an infinite number of unstable paths as shown in the above model (for the purpose of the model, I have assumed $\rho_n = 0.015$). Apart from the most unlikely event of a stroke of pure luck, the control of the nominal interest rate will thus lead to an explosive path, with the rate of inflation tending towards plus or minus infinity. The only viable option therefore is to repeatedly adjust the nominal rate of interest in order to maintain the inflation rate in an acceptable range. The model presented here is admittedly very simple and could be improved in many ways. Its only purpose, though, is to show that even a simple model can yield a second- (or higher-) order differential equation for the rate of inflation, in which case instability becomes a pressing issue, and it would be wrong to think that there is some equilibrium or natural nominal rate of interest.

Notes

1 I am grateful to Andreas Fischer and Michel Peytrignet for their comments and suggestions, but they are obviously not responsible for any errors or omissions.
2 For a good account of the SNB's first century, see Bordo and James (2007), Bernholz (2007), and Baltensperger (2007).
3 See Jordan and Peytrignet (2007) for an account of the development of the SNB's current monetary policy concept, and Baltensperger *et al.* (2007) for the recent experience.
4 While the ECB and the SNB share literally the same quantitative *definition* of price stability, the ECB, contrary to the SNB, has made it known that it *aims* at a rate of inflation close to the upper bound of the definition over the medium term.
5 See Friedman (1975), for instance.
6 The Bank of Canada draws a distinction between what it calls "inflation-reducing targeting," which corresponds to the transitional phase, and "inflation-control targeting," which is reached when inflation lies within the desired range; see Freedman (1995), for instance.
7 It is noteworthy that the RBNZ's famous list of escape clauses has generally not been replicated in other targeting regimes.
8 Of course, the SNB concept is open to this criticism as well.
9 See Svensson (1999), for instance.
10 Some of the research currently undertaken in Canada on this topic may be found on the following internet site: www.inflationtargeting.ca.
11 Taylor (2008) recently argued that the central bank should lower its risk-free interest rate below what the Taylor rule suggests in order to offset the increase in the risk

premium, and he singled out the SNB as having done just that. Using a New Keynesian model, Cùrdia and Woodford (2008) also find that a 100 percent "spread-adjusted Taylor rule" comes close to the optimal policy in the event of a shock to the financial system.
12 See the Appendix for a description of the model underlying Figure 10.1.
13 See Kohli (1999), pp. 355–357.

References

Baltensperger, Ernst (2007) "The National Bank's Monetary Policy: Evolution of Policy Framework and Policy Performance." In Swiss National Bank (ed.), *The Swiss National Bank, 1907–2007*. Zurich: Neue Zürcher Zeitung Publishing.

Baltensperger, Ernst, Philipp M. Hildebrand, and Thomas J. Jordan (2007) "The Swiss National Bank's Monetary Policy Concept – An Example of a 'Principle-based' Policy Framework," *SNB Economic Studies* 3.

Bernholz, Peter (2007) "From 1945 to 1982: The Transition from Inward Exchange Controls to Money Supply Management under Floating Exchange Rates." In Swiss National Bank (ed.), *The Swiss National Bank, 1907–2007*. Zurich: Neue Zürcher Zeitung Publishing.

Bordo, Michael and Harold James (2007) "From 1907 to 1946: A Happy Childhood or a Troubled Adolescence?" In Swiss National Bank (ed.), *The Swiss National Bank, 1907–2007*. Zurich: Neue Zürcher Zeitung Publishing.

Cùrdia, Vasco and Michael Woodford (2008) "Credit Frictions and Optimal Monetary Policy," presented at the 7th BIS Annual Conference, Lucerne, Switzerland, June 26–27.

Freedman, Charles (1995) "The Canadian Experience with Targets for Reducing and Controlling Inflation." In Leonardo Leiderman and Lars E.O. Svensson (eds), *Inflation Targets*. London: Centre for Economic Policy Research.

Friedman, Benjamin M. (1975) "Targets, Instruments, and Indicators of Monetary Policy," *Journal of Monetary Economics* 1, 443–473.

Jordan, Thomas and Michel Peytrignet (2007) "The Path to Interest Rate Management and Inflation Forecasts." In Swiss National Bank (ed.), *The Swiss National Bank, 1907–2007*. Zurich: Neue Zürcher Zeitung Publishing.

Kohli, Ulrich (1999) *Analyse macroéconomique*. Paris and Brussels: De Boeck.

Mishkin, Frederic S. (2007) "Inflation Targeting: True Progress or Repackaging of an Old Idea?" In Swiss National Bank (ed.), *The Swiss National Bank, 1907–2007*. Zurich: Neue Zürcher Zeitung Publishing.

Poole, William (1970) "Optimal Choice of Monetary Policy Instruments in a Simple Stochastic Macro Model," *Quarterly Journal of Economics* 84, 197–216.

Svensson, Lars E.O. (1999) "Price-level Targeting vs. Inflation Targeting: A Free Lunch?" *Journal of Money, Credit and Banking* 31, 277–295.

Taylor, John (2008) "Monetary Policy and the State of the Economy," Testimony before the Committee of Financial Services. U.S. House of Representatives, February 26.

11 It's what they do, not what they say

How to infer the stabilization objectives of a central bank

Michael K. Salemi

I first visited the Graduate Institute of International Studies in 1982. Alexander Swoboda and Hans Genberg had been awarded a Swiss National Science Foundation grant to study the effect on Switzerland of foreign economic shocks. Alexander and Hans planned to undertake a statistical analysis using Vector Autoregressions and needed a project overseer. They had originally recruited Richard Meese but, late in the Spring, Meese discovered that he could not come.

It thus happened that I received a "cold call" one April evening asking me to join the research team. My immediate reaction was that it was too late to ask for a leave. Teaching assignments had been set and the market for visitors concluded. But, as I told Hans, the opportunity was too good for me to assume that a leave could not be arranged. And so, expecting the worst, I made an appointment to see my department chair.

Sometimes the gods smile. My department chair agreed that the opportunity was too good to pass up. And so, family in tow, I arrived in Geneva the following August to begin a personal and academic adventure that has provided rich opportunities and a lot of fun from then until today.

The project went well. Alexander, Hans, and I were able to publish its findings (Genberg, Salemi and Swoboda, 1983 and 1987). Good things led to others and within a couple of years we began to study Swiss monetary policy. In particular, we were interested in whether a formal analysis would confirm conventional wisdom that the Swiss National Bank (SNB) was an "inflation hawk." The claim was not obviously true since estimates of the SNB reaction function showed that it responded to many different variables including the exchange rate. The SNB project was my first attempt to use inverse control and began a research program that I have been working on ever since. It is that program, which owes its beginning to Alexander, Hans, and HEI, that is the subject of this chapter. Ironically, as I will explain later, the program has cycled back to once again consider Swiss monetary policy.

I first offer a non-technical explanation of inverse control. I describe decisions that a researcher must make to undertake an inverse control analysis. I explain how several coauthors and I have used inverse control to study central bank policy in a variety of settings. Finally, I connect inverse control to some of Alexander's published ideas.

1 What is inverse control?

In the standard control problem, a researcher begins with hypotheses about the economic environment and an agent's objectives and derives a rule for the agent's behavior – the mapping from the environment to the agent's choice variable that provides the highest value of the agent's objective function. Inverse control is inferring the parameters of the agent's objective function from the agent's actions. Both techniques depend crucially on the assumption that the agent behaves optimally.

In a monetary policy application of inverse control, the decision-maker is the central bank and the objective function describes central bank preferences. The central bank may be assumed to minimize a loss function or maximize utility of a representative agent. The rule of the central bank is a reaction function that explains how the bank adjusts its policy instrument to changes in the economic environment. The environment is represented by a model that explains the evolution of the endogenous variables that the bank is trying to stabilize or that affect the utility of the representative agent.

Given an estimated structural model and a characterization of central bank stabilization objectives, the control theory exercise is to find the optimal coefficients of the reaction function. The inverse control theory exercise is to infer the values of the central bank objective function from estimates of the parameters of the economic model and the bank reaction function.

A simple example

The following model, while too simple, provides a useful illustration of inverse control. Let y and p be percentage departures of output and inflation from target values. Let u and v be serially uncorrelated random shocks to aggregate demand and supply and let r be the short-term interest rate used by the bank as its policy instrument. Suppose that y, p, and r evolve according to:

$$y_t = ay_{t-1} - br_t + u_t$$

$$p_t = \alpha p_{t-1} + \beta r_t + v_t$$

$$r_t = \theta_1 u_t + \theta_2 v_t$$

The first equation is a stylized IS schedule in which output is inversely related to the short-term interest rate and u is a demand shock. The second equation is a stylized Phillips schedule in which inflation is also affected by r, possibly because changes in r proxy for changes in aggregate demand. The Phillips curve is specified simply so that it is easy to derive the optimal values for the reaction function coefficients. The third equation is a reaction function that allows the central bank to react to demand and supply shocks. Let $Var(x)$ be the unconditional variance of x and suppose that the central bank minimizes

$$L = Var(p_t) + \lambda Var(y_t)$$

where λ measures the relative importance to the central bank of stabilizing output. The reduced form equations for y and p are:

$$y_t = ay_{t-1} + (1 + b\theta_1)u_t - b\theta_2 v_t$$

$$p_t = \alpha p_{t-1} + \beta\theta_1 u_t + (1 + \beta\theta_2)v_t$$

Assume for simplicity that $\sigma_{uv} = 0$. Straightforward manipulation of the partial derivatives of L with respect to θ_1 and θ_2 shows that the loss-minimizing coefficients of the reaction function are:

$$\theta_1^* = \frac{1}{b}\frac{b^2\lambda(1-\alpha^2)}{(1-\alpha^2)\beta^2 + \lambda b^2(1-\alpha^2)}$$

$$\theta_2^* = \frac{-(1-\alpha^2)\beta}{(1-\alpha^2)\beta^2 + \lambda b^2(1-\alpha^2)} \qquad (1)$$

Even for this very simple model, the optimal settings of the reaction function coefficients are non-linear functions of all the model parameters.

Only in special cases will the mapping simplify in an intuitive way. If for example $\lambda = 0$, the optimal values of θ_1 and θ_2 are zero and $-\frac{1}{\beta}$. When the central bank cares only about stabilizing the inflation rate, it will completely offset the Phillips curve shock and not respond to the demand shock. As $\lambda \rightarrow \infty$, optimal θ_2 converges to zero and optimal θ_1 converges to $\frac{1}{b}$ because when the bank cares only about stabilizing output, it will completely offset the demand shock and not respond to the Phillips curve shock. In general, the central bank will respond to both demand and supply shocks in a way that allows the researcher to infer λ, the relative importance to the bank of stabilizing output.

How would inverse control work in the context of this simple model? The six parameters of the three-equation system for y, p, and r are exactly identified without the auxiliary restriction that the central bank minimizes L. The optimal policy restriction introduces one new parameter, λ, and imposes two new restrictions across the six parameters implying overidentification. Using inverse control amounts to estimating the five free parameters of the model (a, α, b, β, and λ while constraining θ_1 and θ_2 to equal θ_1^* and θ_2^*. A test of the joint hypothesis that the model and loss function are correctly specified and that the central bank minimizes loss is based on the likelihood ratio that compares the fit of the restricted model with the fit of the model when a, α, b, β, θ_1, and θ_2 are treated as free parameters. Estimating the model subject to the optimal policy restrictions provides an estimate of λ and a test of the optimality hypothesis.

Literature

Friedlaender (1973) makes the point that one may not infer the objectives of policy-makers by casual inspection of their policy rules because reaction function coefficients are combinations of preference function and model parameters.

Chow (1975, 1981) provides an early introduction to control and inverse control. Hansen and Sargent (1980) and Sargent (1987) show how to apply control theory to a variety of economic problems. Taylor (1979) provides an early application of control theory to monetary policy.

Others have used an inverse control approach to study monetary policy. Dennis (2005) argues that the reason for the apparent disconnect between optimal and historical policies is that counterfactual policy analysis is often carried out using a parameterized loss function that is inconsistent with outcomes observed in U.S. data. Favero and Rovelli (2003), Ozlale (2003), and Dennis (2005) estimate backward-looking models of aggregate demand and supply subject to an auxiliary condition that the policy rule minimizes a quadratic loss function. Salemi (2006) and Dennis (2004) demonstrate how to expand the inverse control analysis of policy to forward-looking models embodying rational expectations. Dennis and colleagues (2006) use robust control techniques to study the effects of model uncertainty on U.K. monetary policy.

2 Implementing inverse control

Undertaking an inverse control analysis of central bank policy involves several decisions. The first is how to model state transition. One possibility is a VAR although the Lucas critique argues against using the estimated model to predict the implications of alternative policies. Another possibility is a system of expectational difference equations, like that used by Walsh (1998) as a New Keynesian framework for monetary analysis. In this case, the researcher estimates the coefficients of the equation system together with the parameters of the bank objective function. Under the maintained hypothesis that the equation system is invariant to changes in policy, the researcher may use the estimated system to study policy alternatives. A third possibility is to set out a dynamic general equilibrium model in which all the parameters have natural structural interpretations.

The second decision is how to model central bank objectives. One can assume along with Poole (1970) that the central bank minimizes a loss function the elements of which are expected squared departures of economic variables from their target values weighted by parameters that measures the relative importance of each objective. Or one can assume, along with Rotemberg and Woodford (1997), that the central bank maximizes the utility of a representative agent. With the Rotemberg and Woodford approach, the weights on squared departures of p and y in the quadratic approximation are not "free parameters" but fixed and known functions of the parameters of the representative agent model. With the loss function approach, the weights are free parameters up to a normalization.

Both specifications are reasonable and interesting. Given a representative agent model, it is natural to assume that the central bank maximizes social welfare. On the other hand, a researcher might believe, for example, that the central bank places more weight on stabilizing output than is consistent with maximizing representative–agent utility, because the bank believes that the social costs of unemployment fall more heavily on low-income households. In any case, the test that the central bank behaves optimally is separate from the test that it maximizes social welfare. The first test requires the researcher to fit the model with the optimal-policy restrictions imposed and the objective function weights free. The second test requires the researcher to refit the model with the optimal-policy restrictions imposed and the loss function weights set to the values consistent with social welfare maximization.

The researcher must next choose a strategy for imposing the optimal-policy restrictions. To fix ideas, I will explain the alternatives given that the class of admissible policies is the class of simple, fixed-parameter policy rules. In particular, I assume that the central bank policy rule takes the form

$$r_t = \theta' X_{t-1} + w_t \tag{2}$$

where r_t is the short-term interest rate controlled by the central bank, X_{t-1} is a vector of state variables determined at time $t - 1$, θ is a conforming vector of policy-rule coefficients and w_t is a serially uncorrelated error that captures the idiosyncratic part of policy and is sometimes termed a "policy shock." Kydland and Prescott (1977) make the case for policy rules. Levin and colleagues (1999) argue that simple policy rules like (2) perform well across a variety of macroeconomic models featuring rational expectations. McCallum (1999) favors simple rules because they show how a variable the central bank can actually control should vary with information that the bank can readily observe at the beginning of period t.

If the model is very simple it may be possible to derive analytic expressions for the coefficients of the policy rule like (1). In that case, the researcher simply uses these expressions in the course of estimating the model. If the model involves rational expectations of future variables, it is generally not possible to derive analytic expressions for the optimal settings of the policy-rule coefficients and the researcher must resort to numerical methods.

One possibility is a "brute force approach." Suppose that the researcher decides to estimate the model by Full Information Maximum Likelihood (FIML). Let ρ be the vector of structural parameters and θ the vector of policy-rule coefficients. FIML estimation requires a program that computes the likelihood of any ρ and θ. The brute force approach uses an optimization sub-program that finds, for a given ρ, the θ that maximizes the policy objective. Brute force estimation involves computing optimal values of θ a great many times as the FIML hill-climber seeks the value of ρ that maximizes the likelihood function.

Givens and Salemi (2008) provide a second possibility by showing how to write the first order necessary conditions for policy optimality as linear combinations of the elements of the covariance matrix of the model's reduced form errors. Using the sample counterparts of the covariance terms allows the researcher to write the first order conditions as moment conditions and estimate the restricted model by generalized method of moments (GMM) as introduced by Hansen (1982).

3 It's what they do, not what they say

In this section, I explain how coauthors and I have used inverse control to answer a number of questions about monetary policy. Camen, Genberg and Salemi (1990) study Swiss monetary policy under fixed exchange rates (1964–1971) and floating (1973–1981). The paper takes a two-step approach. In the first step, a VAR is estimated using monthly data for the Swiss money base, the Swiss short-term interest rate, Swiss and German wholesale price indexes, and the three-month U.S. Treasury Bill rate plus the Swiss franc dollar exchange rate for the floating rate period. Genberg, Salemi and Swoboda (1987) explain why these variables ought to be used to study Swiss monetary policy and document that Swiss industrial production is remarkably independent of movements in Swiss and foreign macro-variables so that it makes sense to exclude it from the analysis. The VAR equation for base money is treated as a policy rule.

In the second step, the VAR coefficients are held fixed and the parameters of the SNB loss function are estimated. The loss function implies that the SNB has three stabilization objectives: the rate of interest, the inflation rate, and the money base itself. The weight on the money base is normalized to one and the weights on the other two objectives are estimated. The estimation criterion is the sum of squared differences between coefficients of the optimal and estimated reaction functions so that the second step amounts to finding objective function weights that reconcile optimal with observed monetary policy.

The paper reports several interesting findings. The Swiss money base is highly endogenous responding to shocks in all the system variables (including the exchange rate during the floating rate period). The best reconciliation of observed and optimal policy occurs for a loss function with much greater weight placed on inflation stabilization than on either of the other objectives. This finding characterizes both the fixed rate and flexible rate periods and is robust to many features of the specification. The paper concludes that the SNB reacted to changes in the exchange rate not because it sought to stabilize it but because the exchange rate carried information about the future course of inflation. The hypothesis that SNB policy was optimal fails although the two-step approach may mean that the test is biased against the null.

Camen and colleagues (1991) use inverse control to study convergence of central bank policy during the EMS period. The paper estimates VARs for both the French and German economies over the entire floating rate period (1974–1987) and over the EMS sub-period (1979–1987). It characterizes Banque de France and Bundesbank policy by finding loss function weights that reconcile the observed reaction functions with loss-minimizing policy rules.

The analysis reveals that the most important objective of Bundesbank policy was inflation stabilization over the entire period and over the EMS sub-period.

The preferences of the Banque de France were different. During the floating rate period, the best reconciliation of observed and optimal policy occurs for a loss function where the Banque de France places little weight on stabilizing inflation and more weight on stabilizing output and exchange rates (although the restricted reaction function does not fit well for the entire period). During the EMS sub-period, the most important stabilization objective of the Banque de France was clearly stabilization of the inflation rate and there is a much better match between the observed reaction function and a loss-minimizing one. Overall, the analysis provides evidence that the monetary policies of the Bundesbank and Banque de France became far more harmonious during the EMS period.

While the previous papers take a two-step approach to policy analysis, the next three combine the two steps into one. Salemi (1995) asks whether Federal Reserve policy is consistent with loss function minimization and estimates the arguments and weights of the Federal Reserve loss function. It uses monthly data from 1947 through 1992 on industrial production, the producer price index, M1, the S&P composite stock index, the unemployment rate, and several measures of the short-term interest rate and considers three policy regimes: 1947–1969, 1970–1979:9, and 1979:10–1992:10. The state transition equation is a VAR that includes equations for money growth and the interest rate so that both can be considered as candidates for the Fed's policy instrument.

The paper reaches three conclusions. First, for all the regimes, the hypothesis that the Federal Reserve minimized a loss function is not rejected by the data. Second, the optimal-policy restrictions are in better agreement with the data if money growth is the Fed policy instrument until 1982 and if the federal funds rate is the policy instrument after 1982. Third, the Fed pursued different objectives in each policy regime. Between 1947 and 1969, the Fed appeared most interested in stabilizing interest rates and inflation rates. After the Treasury Accord, it placed less weight on stabilizing inflation and more on stabilizing output. In the 1970's, the Fed placed greatest weight on stabilizing output, some weight on stabilizing inflation, and little or no weight on stabilizing interest rates. With the onset of the monetarist experiment in 1979, the Fed placed much greater weight on stabilizing inflation. After 1982, the Fed substantially lowered the weight placed on stabilization of money growth and output so that stabilization of inflation and the interest rate were the chief objectives of monetary policy.

Salemi (2006) again studies U.S. monetary policy using inverse control but uses a state transition equation derived from the following set of forward-looking expectational difference equations:

$$y_t = \lambda E_t y_{t+1} + a_1 y_{t-1} + a_2 y_{t-2} - b(r_t - E_t p_{t+1}) + u_t$$

$$p_t = \beta y_t + \alpha_1 E_t p_{t+1} + \alpha_2 p_{t-1} + v_t$$

$$r_t = \theta_1 y_{t-1} + \theta_2 p_{t-1} + \theta_3 r_{t-1} + \theta_4 y_{t-2} + w_t \qquad (3)$$

The first equation is an IS schedule which can be obtained by combining the linearized Euler equation that characterizes a household's optimal choice of consumption with a market clearing condition. The presence of expected future output results from the desire to smooth consumption and the lags in output result from habit persistence and delays between decision-making and implementation. An increase in the real rate of interest lowers desired consumption and output by making saving more attractive.

The second equation is a Phillips curve where the presence of expected future inflation is due to a Calvo mechanism and the presence of lagged inflation is due to indexation to the economywide inflation rate by firms that are unable to re-optimize their price. An increase in output raises inflation by raising the marginal cost faced by the representative intermediate goods firm. The third equation is the policy rule of the Federal Reserve which is permitted to respond to each variable in the state vector dated $t - 1$ and earlier. The Fed is assumed to choose values for the coefficients of the policy rule that minimize

$$L = E_t \sum_{j=1}^{\infty} \delta^j X'_{t+j} W X_{t+j} \tag{4}$$

where X is the state vector, W is a conformable matrix with Fed stabilization objective weights down the diagonal and δ is the Fed's time rate of discount.

Salemi (2006) reaches several conclusions. First, given quarterly data for 1965 to 2001, there is evidence of a policy regime shift beginning in 1980:I but there is no evidence of a break in the structural equations at that date. Second, estimating the model subject to the optimal policy restrictions sharpens estimates of several structural parameters. In particular, the estimate of α_1 is larger and more significant when the optimal policy restrictions are imposed than when they are not. There is intuition for this result. During the period, short-term interest rates are highly persistent with estimates for θ_3 equal to about 0:90 in the first regime and 0:85 in the second. To reconcile interest rate persistence with optimal behavior requires a model in which private agents are forward-looking. Third, stabilization of inflation was a more important Fed objective than stabilization of other variables before and after 1980. Finally, there is evidence that the Fed's policy rule was not optimal during the 1965–1980 regime because it did not respond strongly enough to inflation shocks.

Salemi (2006) estimates model and loss function parameters by quasi maximum likelihood which requires computation of optimal policy-rule coefficients each time sample likelihood is computed. Givens and Salemi (2007) develop a new GMM algorithm for estimating structural parameters subject to optimal policy restrictions. The algorithm combines the least-squares normal equations with the first order necessary conditions that characterize the policy-maker's optimal choice of policy. The algorithm is computationally more efficient than the brute force approach because it searches freely over values of the structural parameters, the loss function weights, and the policy-rule coefficients for those that satisfy a collection of moment conditions, a subset of which correspond to the first order conditions of the policymaker's control problem. Intuitively, the algorithm "creeps up" on parameter values that both fit the data and satisfy optimality. The algorithm is still an example of inverse control because it estimates monetary policy objectives by observing the actions embodied in the policy rule.

Givens and Salemi report a battery of Monte Carlo simulations that show how the algorithm performs when used to estimate ever more complicated models. When the hypothesis of policy optimality is true, the simulations show that the algorithm returns unbiased estimates of all structural parameters including the relative weights of the central bank's objective function. The benefits from imposing true optimal-policy restrictions emerge in the form of reduced uncertainty about many of the structural parameters. One shortcoming is that for over-identified models application of the standard chi-squared test rejects the optimality restrictions too often, particularly in small samples.

The most interesting finding concerns what happens when false optimality restrictions are imposed in the course of estimation. The simulations indicate that GMM delivers unbiased and precise estimates of the policy-rule coefficients but biased estimates of some of the structural parameters. However, the standard chi-squared test rejects false optimality restrictions with very high frequency even in small samples.

Givens and Salemi also take their models and GMM procedure to data describing U.S. monetary policy between 1979 and 2001. When the model is given by (3), their findings are similar to those reported by Salemi (2006). When they use a representative agent model, they find that imposing optimal-policy restrictions has a very large impact on estimates of the structural parameters. When the policy-rule coefficients are unrestricted, the estimate of the degree of habit formation is close to the values reported in the literature. In the restricted case, the estimate is much larger. The coefficient of relative risk aversion is 4.43 when the optimality restrictions are not imposed and near zero when they are. Imposing the restrictions also affects estimates of supply-side parameters – lowering the degree of price stickiness and raising the degree of inflation indexation by firms unable to re-optimize their price.

In 2005, Rouben Atoian, then a PhD student at UNC, used inverse control theory to analyze Swiss monetary policy. Atoian (2005) builds an open economy, representative agent model in which imported goods are inputs to the production process, contracts explain wage stickiness, and households derive utility from consuming a composite good and using the services of money. The exchange rate is determined by the interest parity condition implied by the Euler equation describing optimal household holdings of domestic and foreign bonds. Atoian assumes that the central bank minimizes a loss function like (4) with the weight on inflation stabilization normalized to one and the weights on output and interest rate stabilization treated as unknown parameters. The reaction function explains how the SNB adjusts the short-term rate of interest in response to changes in output, the real exchange rate, inflation, and the lagged interest rate.

Atoian considers two policy regimes: 1973–1987 and 1988–2003. He finds that the SNB placed relatively little weight on stabilizing output (0.14 in the first regime and 0.06 in the second, neither weight significant). He also finds that the SNB placed small but significant weight on stabilizing interest rates in both regimes.

Atoian's work underscores the theme that it is not possible to infer central bank objectives by a casual inspection of a reaction function. He finds that the reaction function coefficient on lagged inflation is negative in both regimes but that the SNB cared most about stabilizing inflation. The reason for this apparent anomaly is that the other variables in the reaction function also carry information about the future course of inflation. Atoian finds that the most important shocks hitting the Swiss economy were output and risk premium shocks. When he computes the impulse responses implied by the model, he finds that output shocks tend to raise inflation while risk premium shocks tend to lower it. He also finds that the SNB countered the inflation effects of both shocks by raising the interest rate in response to output shocks and lowering it in response to risk premium shocks.

4 Conclusions

What is the connection between the ideas I have presented and those of Alexander? There are several. Swoboda (1973) argues that under fixed exchange rates there is a tradeoff between using monetary policy to pursue, in the short run, internal and external balance and thus points explicitly to the linkage between policy objective functions and policy. Swoboda (1991) discusses policy coordination by central banks and again emphasizes that coordination must be based on short-term policy objectives. The conclusion to Alexander's 1991 paper reads like a recommendation for the approach to policy harmonization set out in Camen *et al.* (1991). Finally, Genberg and Swoboda (2005), in the context of exchange rate regimes, point out that a researcher should pay attention both to what central banks say about their objectives and what they do. What they call a "de facto" classification is very close to what this paper calls inverse control.

Acknowledgments

This paper was prepared for the Graduate Institute of International and Development Studies Conference on the International Monetary System in Honor of Alexander Swoboda. The author is Bowman and Gordon Gray Professor of Economics at the University of North Carolina–Chapel Hill. He thanks Hans Genberg, seminar participants at the Hong Kong Institute for Monetary Research, and his colleagues at UNC for helpful comments.

References

Atoian, Rouben V. (2005) "The Swiss National Bank Case." Chapter 5 in "Econometric Investigation of Policy Preference Evolution: The Case of Small Open Economies," PhD Dissertation, University of North Carolina at Chapel Hill, pp. 64–92.

Camen, Ulrich, Hans Genberg, and Michael Salemi (1990) "Optimal Monetary Policy and the Revealed Preference Function of the Swiss National Bank." In P. Artus and Y. Barroux (eds), *Monetary Policy: A Theoretical and Econometric Approach*, Advanced

Studies in Theoretical and Applied Econometrics, 19. Dordrecht, NL: Kluwer Academic Publishers, 3–14.

Camen, Ulrich, Hans Genberg, and Michael Salemi (1991) "Asymmetric Monetary Policies? The Case of Germany and France," *Open Economies Review* 2, 219–236.

Chow, Gregory (1975) *Analysis and Control of Dynamic Economic Systems*. New York: John Wiley & Sons.

Chow, Gregory (1981) *Econometric Analysis by Control Methods*. New York: John Wiley & Sons.

Dennis, Richard (2004) "Inferring Policy Objectives from Economics Outcomes," *Oxford Bulletin of Economics and Statistics* 66, 735–764.

Dennis, Richard (2005) "The Policy Preferences of the US Federal Reserve," *Journal of Applied Econometrics* 21, 55–77.

Dennis, Richard, Kai Leitemo, and Ulf Soderstrom (2006) "Monetary Policy in a Small Open Economy with a Preference for Robustness," Federal Reserve Bank of San Francisco, Working Paper 2007–14.

Favero, Carlo A. and Ricardo Rovelli (2003) "Macroeconomic Stability and the Preferences of the Fed: A Formal Analysis, 1961–96," *Journal of Money, Credit, and Banking*, 35, 545–556.

Friedlaender, Ann F. (1973) "Macro Policy Goals and Revealed Preference," *Quarterly Journal of Economics* 87, 25–43.

Genberg, Hans and Alexander K. Swoboda (2005) "Exchange Rate Regimes: Does What Countries Say Matter?," *IMF Staff Papers* 52, 129–141.

Genberg, Hans, Michael Salemi, and Alexander Swoboda (1983) "Price Dynamics and Exchange Rate Behavior in Switzerland" (with H. Genberg and A. Swoboda). In *Konjunkturpolitik und Wechselkursentwicklung, Schweizerischere Nationalfonds zur Forderung der Wissenschaftlichen Forschung*, pp. 101–122.

Genberg, Hans, Michael Salemi, and Alexander Swoboda (1987) "The Relative Importance of Foreign and Domestic Disturbances for Aggregate Fluctuations in the Open Economy: Switzerland, 1964–1981," *Journal of Monetary Economics* 19, 45–67.

Givens, Gregory and Michael Salemi (2008) "Generalized Method of Moments and Inverse Control," *Journal of Economic Dynamics and Control* 32(10), 3113–3147.

Hansen, Lars P. (1982) "Large Sample Properties of Generalized Method of Moments Estimators," *Econometrica* 50, 1029–1054.

Hansen, Lars P. and Thomas J. Sargent (1980) "Formulating and Estimating Dynamic Linear Rational Expectations Models," *Journal of Economic Dynamics and Control* 2, 7–46.

Kydland, Finn E. and Edward C. Prescott (1977) "Rules Rather than Discretion: The Inconsistency of Optimal Plans," *Journal of Political Economy* 85, 473–491.

Levin, Andrew T., Volcker Wieland, and John C. Williams (1999) "Robustness of Simple Monetary Policy Rules under Model Uncertainty." In John B. Taylor (ed.), *Monetary Policy Rules*. Chicago and London: University of Chicago Press, pp. 263–299.

McCallum, Bennett T. (1999) "Issues in the Design of Monetary Policy Rules." In John B. Taylor and Michael Woodford (eds), *Handbook of Macroeconomics*. Amsterdam: Elsevier, Volume 1, Part 3, pp. 1483–1530.

Ozlale, Umit (2003) "Price Stability vs. Output Stability: Tales of Federal Reserve Administrations," *Journal of Economic Dynamics and Control* 27, 1595–1610.

Poole, William (1970) "Optimal Choice of Monetary Policy Instruments in a Simple Stochastic Macro Model," *Quarterly Journal of Economics* 84,197–216.

Rotemberg, Julio J. and Michael Woodford (1997) "An Optimization-based Econometric

Framework for the Evaluation of Monetary Policy." In Ben S. Bernanke and Julio J. Rotemberg (eds), *NBER Macroeconomics Annual 1997* Cambridge, MA: MIT Press, pp. 297–346.

Salemi, Michael (1995) "Revealed Preference of the Federal Reserve: Using Inverse Control Theory to Interpret the Policy Equation of a Vector Autoregression," *Journal of Business and Economic Statistics* 13, 419–433.

Salemi, Michael K. (2006) "Econometric Policy Evaluation and Inverse Control," *Journal of Money, Credit, and Banking* 38, 1737–1736.

Sargent, Thomas J. (1987) *Dynamic Macroeconomic Theory.* Cambridge, MA: Harvard University Press.

Swoboda, Alexander K. (1973) "Monetary Policy under Fixed Exchange Rates: Effectiveness, the Speed of Adjustment and Proper Use," *Economica* 40, 136–154.

Swoboda, Alexander K. (1991) "The Changing Role of Central Banks in International Policy Coordination." In Rudiger Dornbusch and Steven Marcus (eds), *International Money and Debt: Challenges for the World Economy.* San Francisco, CA: International Center for Economic Growth.

Taylor, John B. (1979) "Estimation and Control of a Macroeconomic Model with Rational Expectations," *Econometrica* 47, 1267–1286.

Walsh, Carl E. (1998) *Monetary Theory and Policy, First Edition.* Cambridge, MA: MIT Press.

Finale

12 For the celebration of Alexander Swoboda upon his retirement

Paul Volcker

After listening to several of the presentations this morning, I was reminded that in my graduate economic studies at Harvard in the early 1950s I escaped any course in econometrics or mathematical economics – the last year that was possible for a PhD candidate. Times have changed. Today every central bank has a retinue of mathematically trained economists.

When I became President of the Federal Reserve Bank of New York and then Fed Chairman, I had to worry about administrative budgets. Every few years there were requests for bigger, faster, and more expensive computers. A big part of the rationale was the demands of the economic staff for time to run more and more regressions. Today, computing power is much, much cheaper and faster, but I wonder how much the added regressions have contributed to a better monetary policy.

In my view, there is a lot more to making monetary policy than economic theorizing and econometric equations. I think it is still true that the models all show a quicker and bigger response to any tightening of policy by the real economy than by any, even muted, response of prices. Taken at face value that rather restrains enthusiasm for restrictive policies of policy-makers, even though the longer term inflationary consequences are unfortunate.

The fact is that basic economic understanding is important for central bankers, but so are other qualities – judgment, understanding of market (and political) moods and psychology, the ability to communicate and perhaps more important, to convey a sense of credibility.

When Ben Bernanke was appointed Chairman of the Federal Reserve, there was much commentary on his long study and writings about the Great Depression, all relevant. I was even more impressed by the fact that he had been chairman of his local school board – always a difficult and often contentious position; good training for the Federal Reserve.

My old friend, Henry Wallich, was perhaps the best (and certainly best-known) economic scholar on the Fed Board when I was Chairman. Reflecting his personal and family experience in Germany in the 1920s, he, to put it mildly, was inflation-averse, and took every opportunity to cast his vote for tighter money through his fourteen years on the Board. He confided in me more than once that he felt the most important single qualification for a central bank was a sense of conviction and – to use his own slang word – "guts," defined as a willingness to tighten money, when the technical and economic analysis was ambiguous.

Of course, central bankers, whether as highly trained as an economist as Henry was, or not, need to understand the basic lessons: the importance of money, the lags between action and reaction, the role of expectations, and much else. These days, there are ample opportunities to bring on to the central banking staff highly educated and talented economists to keep the policymakers informed.

But not all economists are well equipped to understand and deal with the practicalities of markets and judgments about what is possible and what is not, and the learning process certainly works both ways. I happened to be present to hear newly installed Chairman Bernanke deliver a thoughtful "inaugural lecture" on what economics has contributed to central banking thinking, and the reverse, over the decades that the Federal Reserve has existed. That is precisely the subject matter of this panel. Not surprisingly, he pointed out some crucial lessons of economic analysis, but he also emphasized specifically how much the economics profession learned (or relearned) during the 1970s and 1980s about the importance of price stability as the *sine qua non* of successful monetary policy and a prerequisite for sustained growth.

The man we are celebrating today, Alexander Swoboda, epitomizes the important school of economists that well understands the contributions – and the limitations – of economic analysis in approaching practical problems of financial and economic policy. That is why his writings, and for me his more informal reflections, have been so challenging and important. We were able to talk the same language, to evaluate what was going on amid all the turbulence of the real world, and to consider the pros and cons of what to do amid the inevitable uncertainties.

In his leadership of the Graduate Institute of International and Development Studies here in Geneva he consistently and effectively helped bridge the gap between scholars and practitioners to the benefit of both. I am delighted to join in the celebration of those achievements today. I do so in the expectation that mere retirement from this place will by no means mark the end of either his intellectual contributions or his friendship with us all.

I cannot fail to recognize the role that Manijeh – with her enthusiasm, her energy and good spirit – has played in Alexander's life over the course of their long and loving marriage. We have had the benefit of sharing in the glow of that special relationship – long may it shine.

Index

Page numbers in *italic* refer to tables, numbers in **bold** refer to figures.